Eighteenth-Century Authorship and the Play of Fiction

Routledge Studies in Eighteenth-Century Literature

Eighteenth-Century Authorship and the Play of Fiction

Novels and the Theater, Haywood to Austen

Emily Hodgson Anderson

Routledge
Taylor & Francis Group
New York   London

First published 2009
by Routledge
270 Madison Ave, New York, NY 10016

Simultaneously published in the UK
by Routledge
2 Park Square, Milton Park, Abingdon, Oxon OX14 4RN

Routledge is an imprint of the Taylor & Francis Group, an informa business

© 2009 Taylor & Francis

Typeset in Sabon by IBT Global.
Printed and bound in the United States of America on acid-free paper by IBT Global.

Library of Congress Cataloging in Publication Data
Anderson, Emily Hodgson, 1977-
   Eighteenth-century authorship and the play of fiction : novels and the theater, Haywood to Austen / by Emily Hodgson Anderson.
      p. cm.—(Routledge studies in eighteenth-century literature ; 7)
   Includes bibliographical references and index.
      1. English literature—Women authors—History and criticism.   2. English drama—18th century—History and criticism.   3. English fiction—18th century—History and criticism.   4. Theater—Great Britain—History—18th century.   5. Authorship—History—18th century.   6. Expression in literature.   7. Emotions in literature.   8. Self in literature.   9. Women in the theater.   I. Title.
   PR448.W65A63 2009
   820.9'9287—dc22
   2008048060

ISBN10: 0-415-99905-7 (hbk)
ISBN10: 0-203-87797-7 (ebk)

ISBN13: 978-0-415-99905-2 (hbk)
ISBN13: 978-0-203-87797-5 (ebk)

For my dad,
John Alfred Hodgson

"And then my heart with pleasure fills,

And dances with the daffodils."

—Wordsworth, "I Wandered Lonely as a Cloud"

Contents

Tables

Acknowledgments

I've always maintained that you can learn a lot about a scholar's personality from the book he or she writes, and I hope the same holds true of this one. From the beginning, my wish was that this book's argument be both made and embodied—that in writing it I would be able to preserve the objective detachment necessary to honor the subjects and strategies I described. And, like the women I discuss, I felt that such strategies allowed me to be true to my intellectual ideals, my authorial personality. While this book makes no claims to be "self-expressive" in the conventional sense of the term, I certainly see myself in the pages that follow.

But at last I'm writing that section in which the author is allowed, as Maria Edgeworth would put it, "to peep out from behind the scenes," and I do so now to celebrate how collaborative a process this has been. Many people have shaped this book, just as they have shaped its author; many friends and colleagues should also see themselves in the subsequent pages. It gives me great happiness to be able, finally, to thank them in print.

Working backwards in time and space: Roy Ritchie and the staff at the Huntington Library have been essential to my scholarly pursuits and have made me realize how lucky I am, as an eighteenth-century scholar, to live in Los Angeles. I'm grateful to the Huntington for awarding me two summer grants, a Mellon Match Fellowship and a British Academy Fellowship, which allowed me to continue archival research at home and abroad. I'm also *very* grateful to Roy for permitting my office occupancy to extend beyond the tenure of my fellowships. The various long-term fellows at the Huntington formed an inspirational community; Lisa Freeman deserves particular thanks.

My eighteenth-century colleagues at UCLA have been tirelessly helpful. Felicity Nussbaum, Helen Deutsch, and Sarah Kareem all read drafts of material that appears here, often on tight timelines, and provided encouragement and professional advice. Thanks, too, to Felicity for coordinating the Southern California eighteenth-century reading group and for inviting me early on to participate. I've gotten to know many scholars at this group, Susan Carlisle among them, who have provided friendship and expertise.

I've also found a wonderful set of colleagues and resources at my home institution of USC. Peter Mancall and the Early Modern Studies Institute have both been generous supporters of my work, and the EMSI Faculty Fellowship I received in the Fall of 2005 enabled the first and most difficult revisions of this book. In the Fall of 2007, an "Advancing Scholarship in the Humanities and Social Sciences" grant from the Provost's office provided the combination of reduced teaching and research funds that allowed me to put the finishing touches on the manuscript.

Within my own department I've had many forms of assistance: my various chairs, Joseph Boone, Bruce Smith, and Meg Russett, have been especially attentive and welcoming to a new junior colleague. David Román has been a great resource on all matters theatrical, and, as the Director of Faculty Development, invited me to present my work in various locales—both at UCLA, through an exchange program that he coordinated, and at USC, through a series of junior faculty talks that he convened. My colleagues Meg Russett, Hilary Schor, Rebecca Lemon, Heather James, and Paul Alkon have read reams of material without complaint—and have been some of the most careful, generous readers I've had the privilege to know. I also found incisive readers in my friend Brad Pasanek, then at Pomona, and my graduate student Bonnie Nadzam. A big thank you to Brad, too, for starting the reading group, fondly nicknamed the "HBRG," of which Bonnie, Meg, and myself were members.

Thanks are due to a few scholars outside of Los Angeles who interacted generously with my work without knowing me at all: Toni Bowers, for inviting me to give a talk to the eighteenth-century group at UPenn, Kristina Straub, for reading an earlier draft of the manuscript, and Toril Moi for responding to a completely unsolicited email query, for reading much of my work (often in an embarrassingly unpolished state), and for coming out to USC to give a talk at exactly the right time.

This project had its origins at Yale University, under the auspices of two of the best advisors and role models a graduate student could have. Joseph Roach has been an unflagging source of scholarly and professional wisdom. His commitment to the profession, and the people in it, is something I will forever admire and try to emulate; his stylistic panache, while something to which I aspire, is probably beyond duplication. Jill Campbell remains my model of intellectual integrity and one of the best teachers I've ever had: the lessons she taught me are simply too numerous to list.

Then, there are those who interacted with this project on an even more personal level. Thanks to the graduate school classmates who have gone on to become colleagues and lasting friends: to Jean Otsuki, for introducing me to yoga. To Jessica Leiman, for rooming with me at conferences and sharing her wit, insight (and magazines). To Jason Shaffer, for timely feedback and support. And to Emily Setina and Ayesha Ramachandran, intellectual and emotional anchors, readers extraordinaire. You both have given so much of yourselves to this book—and to me.

Finally, to those who have lived with this project most intimately and longest: my husband Dave, who often understands my work, just as he understands me, better than I do myself. Thank you for your perspective, patience, and unfailing confidence, for being able to read or reassure at a moment's notice. And to my parents, John and Susan Hodgson, who have embraced this project especially in the last few years, but who have been living with my compulsive writing process for much longer. To my mom—thanks for being "on call" for non-medical subjects and for visiting even when I was cranky. And to my dad—for whom expressions of gratitude must fail completely. You first taught me to find joy in books. I hope you find joy in this one; it is dedicated to you.

٭   ٭   ٭

Erica Wetter at Routledge has been an invaluable resource throughout the publication process, from her initial interest in the project to her choice of readers. A special note of thanks is due to these three anonymous scholars, as I was both touched and challenged by their engagement with my work. If I have not been able to answer all their questions, I hope I have at least made those questions more accessible for future debate.

Portions of Chapter 2 have appeared as "Performing the Passions in Eliza Haywood's *Fantomina* and *Miss Betsy Thoughtless*," *The Eighteenth Century: Theory and Interpretation* 46.1 (Spring 2005): 1–15. Portions of Chapter 3 have appeared as "Staging Insensibility in Burney's *Cecilia, Camilla,* and *The Wanderer*: How A Playwright Writes Novels," *Eighteenth-Century Fiction* 14.4 (July 2005): 629–648. Portions of Chapter 4 have appeared as "Revising Theatrical Conventions in *A Simple Story*: Elizabeth Inchbald's Ambiguous Performance," *Journal for Early Modern Cultural Studies* 6.1 (Spring / Summer 2006): 5–30. I thank all journals for permission to reproduce that material here.

1 Introduction
Playing at Authorship

Consider the prologue to a 1730 production of William Hatchett's play *The Rival Father*. The author Hatchett, "who ne'er before . . . [the] buskin wore," is applauded for assuming the part of Achilles, our "Favour" solicited for this, "his first Attempt." But if Hatchett's "hard Task" is made harder by his inexperience both on the stage and the battlefield (we are told the "Warrior's Truncheon" is as unfamiliar to his hand as the "buskin" to his foot), his leading lady promises by contrast a special treat: "To play Briseis while Eliza deigns, / All will be Real, that she only feigns."[1] Eliza here is novelist and playwright Eliza Haywood, and as long as she is willing to act the part, we are told, acting will be more than just acting.

By 1730, Haywood was already infamous for the erotic novellas she wrote and the provocative life she lived; in fact, she and Hatchett were supposedly live-in-lovers, perhaps even the parents of at least one illegitimate child.[2] Cast in the part of Achilles's abandoned, lascivious mistress—and playing opposite to the man whose mistress she was rumored to be—Haywood capitalizes on her own scandalous reputation, recently perpetuated by Alexander Pope's caustic portrayal of her in *The Dunciad* (1728). The actor and the theatrical role are played off each other to advertise the negative assumptions about female behavior that swirl around both Haywood and the character she depicts. Yet the process also illustrates how Haywood turns these negative assumptions to her advantage, as her performance at once exposes and overturns the criticisms that were meant to silence her and end her professional career. Her achievement depends upon a "play" within the play: the oscillation between the "real" Haywood and the "feigned" Briseis, the fact that her performance functions as a space for self-expression, even as audiences are conditioned to recognize what transpires in this forum as feigned.

This anecdote effectively illustrates the central thesis of this book, what it will claim as a potential explored with particular frequency on the eighteenth-century stage, and with particular frequency by the eighteenth-century women working on and around it. As opposed to dichotomizing artifice and reality, theatrical frames often enable the articulation of truths and passions that may, under alternate conditions, be otherwise inexpressible. Frequently, it is precisely *because* the audience assumes actors don't speak for themselves that the stage may become a space in which to do or say something personal, something un-feigned, something that it is perhaps socially unacceptable to say or do in any other way. In the eighteenth century, dramatists and actors manipulated these conventions, with the result that the playhouse, in addition to offering actors fictional roles, also "provided, at least for the leading players, manifold opportunities for self-expression."[3] This ability quickly infiltrates eighteenth-century literature and society more generally: the eighteenth-century fanaticism for masquerade, in which costumes allowed for a "dialectical fluidity between opposites" and enabled a frenzied, at times dangerous "perfect freedom" of expression, provides one noted example of its workings.[4] While such freedoms could be enjoyed by men and women alike, this book contends that gender-specific constraints on expression—and types of authorship—made the eighteenth-century woman particularly likely to gravitate toward such frames, particularly attuned to issues of self-expression within her life and work.

The subsequent chapters trace four exemplary authors, Eliza Haywood, Frances Burney, Elizabeth Inchbald, and Maria Edgeworth, who consciously explore this strategy on two levels: both, in a process similar to that examined recently by Wendy Doniger, through their descriptions of heroines who disguise themselves to express themselves,[5] and also through their own authorial choices to work between two specific eighteenth-century genres, novels and plays. The writers in this study were especially devoted to both literary forms, and they often repositioned elements—characters, plots—from one genre into another: they often recast characters from their plays into their novels, rewrite their plays as novels, or (in the case of Inchbald) rewrite their novels as plays. Moreover, they use these re-written scenes and characters to investigate the paradoxical, self-expressive potential of theatrical performance. These investigations take on a necessary level of self-consciousness as they reflect on the authors' own struggles to succeed, as playwrights or actors, on the stage. These investigations also reflect self-consciously on the fictional status of the novel itself. For the novel, like the playhouse or the masquerade, could offer its authors yet another theatrical frame; the fictional text, which announces a discrepancy between its author and the sentiments it conveys, could function as an act of disguise; and authorship could become an act of performance.

This book thus bridges two fissures in current eighteenth-century scholarship. First, it addresses the practical divisions that exist between studies of the novel and drama. In the words of G. Gabrielle Starr, "no model of generic displacement is sufficient" to account for the rise of the novel, and yet theater historians tend to neglect the novel, while critics of the novel tend to leave the theater behind.[6] Even the critic David Marshall, writing on *The Figure of Theater*, presents a brilliant analysis of theatrical formulations in fictional narratives, philosophical dialogues, and eighteenth-century social criticism without referring back to the way these formulations did or did not function in actual theatrical performances of the time.[7] These divisions in criticism are curious, given the widespread destablization of generic categories during the seventeenth and eighteenth centuries, and the perception of the eighteenth century as "a discursive field," in which a "multiplicity of books, broadsides, pamphlets and periodicals jostl[e] against each other in booksellers' stalls."[8] Playbooks and play manuscripts often outnumbered the novels in these stalls, while play-going was an integral part of eighteenth-century life and entertainment, for all classes. As a result many eighteenth-century readers and writers were concurrently spectators, performers, and playwrights.

In light of this fact, the contemporary divisions among our critical ranks—between scholars of the novel, and scholars of the drama—resonate as more than just a function of overspecialization. They reflect an ingrained sense that theatrical performance and fiction are entirely different practices: the one public, the other private, the one embodied, the other imagined, the one bound in time, the other in text. Yet eighteenth-century writers and audiences saw more connections than divergences between theater and the novel, and by traversing freely between the stage and the page, this book takes up the invitation offered by numerous eighteenth-century writers themselves, namely to consider the mechanisms for creative expression afforded by working not merely *in* two genres, but by working *through* them at the same time. Significantly, the authors to engage most frequently in this kind of cross-genre experimentation were women. While eighteenth-century men did experiment simultaneously with these same generic forms (Henry Fielding and Oliver Goldsmith are the obvious examples), and many other well-known male novelists (such as Defoe and Richardson) were heavily influenced by the theater, eighteenth-century women writers worked in multiple genres, and especially the novel and drama, far more frequently than their male counterparts.[9]

The second aim of this book is therefore to challenge, even as it takes seriously, the conceptual divisions that remain between literary and biographical study. Instead of relying on the formalist tendency to privilege genre—that is, the tendency to situate texts within a broad narrative on the rise of the novel and the collapse of the theater[10]—or the historicist tendency to privilege the broader cultural and material contexts of a work, this book returns us to the author and to the specific historical circumstances of authorial experience. It acknowledges that there has in fact been a "conscious volitio[n] to make an art-work of such and such a sort," and that writers respond to social circumstances in an attempt to shape texts, and the practice of authorship, to their own purposes.[11] "I am sure that nobody could please me so entirely as yourself on the *art* of novel writing—the *art* of dramatic composition," writes Mary Hoare to her friend Elizabeth Inchbald, in soliciting her to contribute an essay to the literary critical publication, *The Artist*. "Or," she goes on to add, "(if it may be called an *art*) that of propriety of female conduct."[12] The quotation is a testament to the fact that Inchbald worked persistently, and successfully, in both genres. But it also associates this literary experimentation, one woman's decision to write both plays and novels, with the "propriety of female conduct," and Inchbald's oscillation between genres seems to be summoned as evidence of her compliance with these codes. In the eighteenth century, modes of authorship and assumptions about personal conduct were tightly connected. To engage more fully the evolutions in these genres, we must consider the professional and biographical circumstances that impelled eighteenth-century women to experiment with these specific literary forms.

When we do, we see that this overlooked fact in genre studies—that eighteenth-century novelists were frequently also playwrights, and that the authors to engage most frequently in this generic experimentation were women—reveals a similarly overlooked potential in the development of the novel. Novel studies have long traced a consistent pattern in this genre's rise: by the middle of the eighteenth century, novels no longer began with the assertions of factuality that marked earlier, though no less fictional narratives.[13] In other words, novelists became more interested in establishing their novels as a place of fiction, rather than needing to gain reader interest or textual legitimacy with the allurement of fact. While critics have summoned various explanations for this shift—the development of copyright laws that privileged originality, or the institution of taxes that required readers to make a distinction between journalism and fiction[14]—eighteenth-century theatrical practices endow this pattern with a new source and significance. The fictional frame of the novel, which is highlighted with increasing insistence as the century progresses, comes to duplicate the frame of the playhouse: it signals that everything contained therein is artifice. Yet the allegedly artificial frame may itself be deceptive, and the frame of the stage proved alluring precisely because of its deceptive potential. Because it was a place of supposed "artifice," eighteenth-century actors often used the stage to articulate personal grievances; once acknowledged as fictional, the eighteenth-century novel had the potential to become a similarly covert, self-expressive space.

Situating this trend in the context of my larger claim, that women writers consciously explored the self-expressive capabilities of artifice, establishes a new way to read their choices to move between novels and plays, and, more generally, a new way to read the relationship of authors to the texts they produce. Specifically, there remains a critical tendency to read the work of early modern women writers as a form of autobiography, to conflate author and heroine or narrator, and thereby to lose the dimensionality created by an author's choice to write fiction. At the same time, when we resist this assumption, we do so in part because the choice to write a novel or to play a role seems to indicate a clear authorial decision not to speak openly or exclusively about oneself. In fact, these two expressive possibilities may coexist and influence each other. Indeed, this study shows that we must acknowledge these possibilities simultaneously, since both an over-reliance on and an over-suspicion of an individual's capacity for self-expression limits our ability to recognize what to eighteenth-century audiences was patently clear: that sincerity and feigning, reality and fiction, cannot be safely compartmentalized but exist together, in a dynamic relationship.

THEATRICAL WOMEN

Women who wanted to be playwrights in the eighteenth century faced two related sets of obstacles: gender-specific assumptions about what constituted proper female conduct, and professional prohibitions to working on the stage that emerge from these same assumptions.[15] The association between actress and whore begins almost as soon as women start acting, and by the time Eliza Haywood takes up her pen in 1719, women playwrights were also reviled as sexually promiscuous—attacked for their assumed private, personal conduct—because of the offensively public nature of their chosen career.[16] While certain women transcended this criticism (usually, like Hannah More, through deference to a male patron and a careful public presentation), we see aspiring dramatists Frances Burney and Maria Edgeworth suffering from similar criticisms and insecurities over a hundred years after the woman playwright started writing for the stage. This continuity in criticism is striking: in 1707, the playwright Susannah Centlivre would write that if an anonymous play is identified as being "fatherless . . . immediately it flags in the Opinion of those that extolled it before, and the Bookseller falls in his Price, with this Reason, *It's a Woman's*." In 1800, Joanna Baillie's *Plays on the Passions* met the same fate: "no sooner, however, did an unknown girl own the work, than the value so fell, her booksellers complained they could not get themselves paid for what they did, nor did their merits ever again swell the throat of public applause."[17]

The reasons for women writers to move from plays to novels thus seem more evident than their reasons for returning to plays, or for writing plays in the first place. Yet the persistent efforts of Frances Burney and Maria Edgeworth to write and produce plays, regardless of their solid establishment as novel writers and the financial earnings they could expect from that career, or Elizabeth Inchbald's decision to recast themes and characters from a successful novel into a comedy, show a common attraction to playwriting, despite the additional obstacles faced by the woman dramatist. The attraction could be financial, and Inchbald would lament the time spent writing a novel by observing, "I have frequently obtained more pecuniary advantage by ten days' labour in the dramatic way than by the labour of this ten months."[18] Though novels could at times be quite lucrative (in 1796 Burney earned 2,000 pounds for *Camilla*), earnings were usually more modest, and the income was offset by the added time it took to complete such a work. Plays, on the other hand, could be produced more quickly, and in greater numbers.

But these women also contrast plays and novels in a manner that suggests their choice of genre to be a personal, artistic one. Maria Edgeworth wrote plays specifically to practice "the art of condensing character and sentiment by a few strokes of the pencil"; Burney writes that a good theatrical performance "brings forth on the very instant, all the effect which, to the closet reader, an author can hope to produce from reflection"; Inchbald's critical preface to *The Winter's Tale* states that some scenes are simply "far more grand in exhibition than the reader [can] possibly behold in idea."[19] These comments reveal the authors' awareness that visual spectacle, publicity— all that is implied by "exhibition"—can influence the audience differently than the printed page and show a desire on the part of these authors to exert this type of influence.

And yet the very factors that made the theater a "golden drea[m]" for women made it challenging for them in gender-specific ways.[20] As a place of public display and artifice, the theater stood for everything a woman should not be and do, and the link between theater and women is forged ironically by their detractors. "Women have long been portrayed," state Tracy Davis and Thomas Postlewait, "as duplicitous, deceptive, costumed, showy, and thus as a sex inherently theatrical."[21] Antitheatrical and anti-feminist criticism of this period share a broad vocabulary;[22] Mary Hoare's reference to the *art* "of propriety of female conduct" inevitably associates female behavior with artifice, even as it underlines very different expectations for female decorum that playwriting threatened to violate. A woman was expected to be private, self-effacing, and reserved, so much so that in a letter to her sister, Frances Burney would explain that you should bite off a piece of your cheek before you should sneeze in public, and that if a hairpin pierced your scalp, you should let the blood run into your eyes before you would wipe it away.[23]

No wonder Burney found the theater attractive—and daunting. Plays were a public genre, both in the moment of performance and in the required social networking that led up to performance. A successfully produced play depended on many people in addition to the playwright (the theater managers, the Lord Chamberlain's office, the actors, the audience), and the complex relationships required of the playwright proved much more difficult to negotiate for the eighteenth-century woman writer than for her male counterpart. Often, as we will see with Frances Burney and Maria Edgeworth, these professional frustrations would force women writers to transpose ideas or characters from a rejected play into a novel. Sometimes, as we will see with Elizabeth Inchbald, the generic and professional opportunities of theater would encourage a writer to transpose ideas and characters from a novel into a play.

Either way, the literary productions of these women, when read as responses to professional and social factors, revise recent scholarship that has modified assumptions about female decorum in the eighteenth century and the implication of any type of gender-specific constraint.[24] While this book, along with such scholarship, illustrates that women were actively involved in political and literary public forums, how women became involved still bears analysis. In "playing at authorship," women writers played on and played up the derogatory assumptions about authorship that they transcended. For example, *Nobody's Story*, Catherine Gallagher's study of eighteenth-century women writers in the marketplace, shows that even as these authors engaged in public careers that violated conduct book rules of decorum, they were invested in obscuring the fact of their authorship; they crafted illusions in response to the very codes of propriety they were transgressing.[25] Such a formulation does not efface the "constraints" on female expression so much as present them in a more affirmative way: complications become advantages, become methods. We see this process in the way that difficulties in the theater encouraged women to turn their creative energies to the novel. But we also see it in the methods of expression they explore within these texts themselves.

The negative associations of hypocrisy that accompany the theater, and women as "theatrical" in this hypocritical sense, make theatrical performance a particularly efficacious forum for expression, and make women a group particularly attuned and suited to explore it.[26] The authors in this book do so with insistent regularity, even as they exemplify those writers who would experiment most persistently with genre. In their novels and their plays, they depict characters who perform their feelings. Haywood's Fantomina and Miss Betsy, Burney's Camilla and Elinor Joddrel, Inchbald's Miss Milner, Edgeworth's Lady Delacour—while these heroines to varying degrees anticipate how and when they will express certain emotions, this premeditation does not invalidate the authenticity of the emotion once it is expressed. These heroines illustrate that feelings could be both staged and sincere, at once personal and performed. In so doing, they ask us to revisit a critical discourse on subjectivity in the eighteenth century that has heretofore associated theatricality with a superficial, protean idea of the "self."

PERFORMING THE PASSIONS, PERFORMING THE SELF

These heroines also ask us to revisit a more contemporary critical discourse that questions whether we can in fact own, or "express," our feelings at all.[27] Using the term "expression" potentially leads me back through a series of fallacies that critics such as Rei Terada have tried to dispel: "*because* the history of thought about emotion has invested in theories of expression . . . emotions appear to be exemplary inner content."[28] Terada's challenge to the interior status of emotion stems in part from identifying modes of expression as "theatrical" and then defining theatricality as a productive, not an expressive, practice. "There is no reason to guard mental life against theatricality, to guard emotion against representation . . . its only cost is that we do not like to think of our personal feelings as of the second order," states

Terada. Drawing upon Derrida and Rousseau, she showcases critics who see theater as drawing emotions *from* us, as "importing the very emotions that we call our own to express."[29]

Yet the ownership and origin of emotion was in fact a crucial debate on the eighteenth-century stage. While eighteenth-century science and physiognomy reasoned that the human body reacts to emotion in consistent ways, eighteenth-century actors remained divided between two main theories of emotional experience: Aaron Hill's, which maintained that the vivid imagining of a passion would result in its characteristic impressions to appear on the face, and Gotthold Lessing's, which held that moving the body in appropriate ways could on its own excite emotion.[30] For Lessing, the process worked from the outside, in; for Hill, from the inside, out. Lessing's actor produces emotion, while Hill's actor, in the most literal sense of the term, expresses it.

Diderot, on the other hand, was not convinced that an actor even had to experience the emotion he conveyed, a conclusion that formed the crux of his seminal work on acting theory in the eighteenth century, the *Paradox*.[31] The physiological debates of Hill and Lessing circle a more ideological question: is it even acting, if you play what you feel? Not according to Partridge, the bumbling sidekick in *Tom Jones*. Convinced that David Garrick's Hamlet really feels the way he acts, Partridge decides in favor of the distinctly more artificial King when asked to name the better actor.[32] Partridge reveals a persistent assumption that acting is insincere, and the very concept of hypocrisy, a term that owes its origins to the Greek word for an actor on the stage, illustrates this link.[33] Simultaneously, the obvious naïveté of Partridge's criticism confirms what Lisa Freeman notes, that savvy eighteenth-century audience members knew better than to associate Garrick too closely with his part; in practice, even the actor celebrated for bringing a "naturalistic" style to the stage was himself "more concerned with how well he 'put on' the passion than with whether he actually felt it."[34] Garrick's innovations did little to strip the eighteenth-century stage of its associations with hypocrisy; if anything, they added more layers to the debate.

These same associations enable the authors in this study to use theatrical performance in an antithetical, self-expressive manner—and suggest a link between theatricality and emotional depth. The scientific and artistic desire to see the body as a reliable signifier of internal emotions was coupled with the knowledge that gesture and action could be used to conceal intentions and sentiments, as illustrated in Henry Fielding's "An Essay on the Knowledge of the Characters of Men." Beginning with the assertion that "the passions of men do commonly imprint sufficient marks on the countenance," Fielding nonetheless concludes, "sure no honest undesigning man can ever be too much on his guard against the hypocrite," a statement that points to the problems, and the awareness of the problems, that come with depending on a direct relationship between the body and the feelings.[35] Yet while

Dror Wahrman reads the resulting eighteenth-century adage *fronti nulla fides* (trust not to appearances) as evidence of the malleable, superficial nature of the early eighteenth-century "self," it can also be, more simply, a nod to the contemporary prevalence of literal and metaphorical masking that Fielding's essay exposes, and that introduces a spatial dimension characteristic of a more stable, interior concept of identity. Trust not to appearances, not just because there are so many potential appearances, but because appearances layer over what Wahrman himself elsewhere explicates as some "inner truth behind a misleading façade."[36] Masks create dimensionality; they produce the very inwardness that they obscure.

Still, theater is not typically the place we go, at least in the eighteenth century, in search of depth, selfhood, or authenticity. Especially when contrasted to the rising novel, eighteenth-century theater has traditionally been read as a realm of artifice and surfaces, of superficial characters and characteristics. A space in which identities were exchanged and manipulated, theater represents to many critics the kind of flatness or mutability that distinguished characterization in the better part of the eighteenth century from the later, deeper romantic conceptions of subjectivity, and women in particular were understood in the superficial and protean terms of the stage.[37]

But while scholars such as Freeman have identified eighteenth-century theater as concerned primarily with the superficial dimensions of character,[38] the stage nonetheless disseminated a model of identity that assumed the possibility of a gap between part and actor, between external appearance and internal essence. As Diderot would delineate, the actor's art is a creative process that relies on an "inner model," and the performing women studied here seem invested in the interior status of their emotions.[39] Their descriptions of their heroines—and themselves—often make author and character seem like time bombs, filled with repressed feelings that must and will find some external outlet. They present emotions as preexisting their representation, and their frequent emphasis on repression, the flip side of expression, indicates that in their world expression is not an inevitable or necessary result of feeling: emotions can be felt without being represented, so that there is often a separation between what one feels on the inside and what one expresses on the surface. Indeed, as Frances Burney found while at court, the oppressive grip society had on external conduct often forced women to meditate on their internal feelings, so that an interior self also seems formed and shaped by social rules. The idea of an interior self was very much in play in the eighteenth century, as was the fear that this interior self might never be discovered.

Theatrical performance provided one answer to these fears, for while the stage may emphasize the importance of surfaces, it does so without asking us to discard the idea of interiority that gives meaning to the term "expression." The theater's use of costumes and vizards provides a physical source for the metaphorical layering that occurs in theatrical presentation, so that as theatrical presentation provides a surface, it simultaneously suggests an element of depth. And if, as these chapters detail, we shouldn't always look behind a woman's "mask," we are nonetheless encouraged to appreciate the mask as indicative or evocative of the self upon which it is layered. Because the strategic aspect of theatrical self-expression is that it necessarily occurs under the guise of performance, even when the masks these women don are expressive and not obfuscating, this extra layer is essential to maintain. Like the episode in Fielding's *Amelia,* in which his heroine removes her beautiful mask to reveal an equally beautiful face, these masks may ultimately "mar[k] no discontinuity between devious appearance and a world of truth."[40] And yet unmasking for the women in this book is not an option, as their expressions depend on the suggestion of discontinuity, however fictional it might be.

The concept of selfhood understood and described by the authors in this study thus seems at once less buried and more vexed than the one most eighteenth-century critics (especially critics of the novel) describe.[41] As the modes of self-expression in these works depend on the assertion of artifice—and thus on a constant play between actor and role, or self and mask—the concept of selfhood that emerges is neither consistently superficial nor interior, but instead contingent upon a dynamic oscillation.[42] These authors present the impulse to probe beneath a woman's surface representations as a misleading one; at the same time, they posit these multiple, superficial representations as distinct—both from each other and from the woman performing them—and crucial to maintain. These distinctions are what enable the act of expression, preserve a sense of interiority, and yield to some final coherence; such performance strategies create a link, not merely a gap, between self and persona, with a relationship between the two that is not consistently deceptive. Instead of indicating a "splitting of identity" characteristic of the early eighteenth century,[43] these shifts in personae enable the expression of some consistently felt, otherwise inexpressible feeling.

In other words, the authors featured here privilege emotion as the defining, consistent component of identity. This is a variation on early modern theories of humoral passions, believed to travel fluidly between a permeable body and its environment.[44] It is also a development encouraged by the eighteenth-century stage. While theater would seem to challenge the idea of innate characteristics, eighteenth-century actors nonetheless interpreted character in consistent ways. They distilled their roles into sequentialized emotional "points" or postures, and spectators bragged that they could use these poses, each representative of a discrete feeling, to follow the significant action of a play without the benefit of words.[45] Both traditions imply that emotion provides the most obvious link to how a theatrical character, at least, could be known. And while it bemoans the very theatricality that makes character unknowable, Fielding's essay on hypocrisy shares the same bias; he depicts the "inner truth" all-too-often disguised by performance as preexisting and emotional in nature. If "identity" and "self" become synonymous once "identity" is understood as something "personal, interiorized . . . even innate," then the theater's approach to emotional expression provides, not an exception to emerging ideas of selfhood, but an important platform for them.[46]

In considering the concept of "self-expression," this project therefore travels freely between the concepts of emotions and the self, and freely, too, among the various terms that characterized emotion at the time.[47] Just as Adela Pinch uses the terms feeling, passion, and emotion "almost interchangeably" in her study on eighteenth-century epistemologies of emotion to "reflec[t] the fluidity these terms had in the period,"[48] the authors in this study range freely among their terms and the expressions these terms entail. At times, expressions involve a specific emotion: Haywood, for example, often focuses on love, and her characters constantly shift roles to convey their romantic desires. For Burney, the emotion is grief or suffering, and her later heroines in particular vent by taking to the stage. Inchbald, in contrast, treats feelings much more comprehensively: her characters perform to express emotions, and to break free from the static theatrical conventions that depict the emotions in a discrete, sequential manner. Edgeworth takes this model one step further as she associates thinking and feeling, and expression in her work finally signifies the articulation of a rational and emotional process. Taken together, these authors represent the progression toward a more comprehensive treatment of sentiment within literature, and toward the romantic association of emotion with self-knowledge.

But these authors are exploring expression both within their texts and through them, and the professional and personal obstacles they faced in the course of trying to write plays or novels lead to strong emotions that are about the very nature of expression itself. As they discover, certain acts of expression convey specific feelings that exist prior to the moment of expression, but just as frequently, constraints on expression will produce the feelings that impel it. For example, the angry preface to Sophia Lee's play *The Chapter of Accidents* captures a feeling shared by many women who would write for the stage:

> Life opened gradually upon me, and dissipated the illusions of imagination. I learnt that merit merely is a very insufficient recommendation to [theater] managers in general! And as I had neither a prostituted pen or person to offer Mr. Harris, I gave up, without a trial, all thoughts of the Drama. . . . [49]

Lee was one of many women who would go on to write novels instead. Compare her preface with the young Frances Burney's eagerness as she imagines the opening of her first play, "I actually shook from head to foot! I felt myself already at Drury Lane, amidst the hubbub of a first night." Or, note Burney's poignant middle-aged reflection on her persistent desires to be a playwright, "The combinations for another long work did not occur to me. Incidents & effects for a Drama did. I thought the field more than open—inviting to me. The chance held out golden dreams."[50]

The resulting plays and novels thus seem expressive of some authorial sentiment, though not simply in terms of the biographical fallacy—in the sense that we must read Lee's novel as a reflection on her personal experience. Sometimes these women do turn to literary texts as a way to communicate a very personal and otherwise inexpressible feeling, as when an angry Mary Hays responded to a snub from Jacobin philosopher William Godwin by transcribing their epistolary correspondence into a novel, and attributing it to her fictional protagonists.[51] But Lee's and Burney's frustration at not being able to be a playwright underlines a more general desire to express oneself creatively in one's genre of choice. The sense of "self-expression" here broadens from an association with autobiography, meaning a conscious narration of self, to an association with the autobiographical, distinguished as an ability to speak for oneself. After all, these women didn't just want to talk about themselves; they wanted genuine creative freedom. They craved the ability to speak of their own experience, and they craved the ability to speak outside of it, to speak fictionally. In this model, even metatheatrical reflections on the status of authorship, or the role played by an author in her work, become autobiographical in nature. These authors define themselves through the practice of authorship, so that what is expressed by these texts is finally a desire for authorship, a desire for expression itself.

At the outset, this goal was attained through theatrical performance, and like many men and women before them, eighteenth-century women writers often demonstrated a tendency to see life "under the aspect of theater."[52] In particular, they deploy theatrical metaphors to describe their own literary careers. While the professional challenges of the theater might prompt women writers to shift from plays to novels, and prompt them to reposition elements from one genre to another, they also often used their non-dramatic texts to pay tribute to the expressive potential of the stage. Frances Burney's second novel *Cecilia* is in many ways a revision of her suppressed play *The Witlings*, and many key scenes in her final novel *The Wanderer* take place on stages. But even more significantly, her heroine Juliet's experiences as an actress echo (practically verbatim) Burney's own youthful experiences in home theatricals, as described in her early journals. The performing heroines in these novels, who take up roles to achieve expression, gain the potential to embody—not merely their author's experiences—but their author's approach to authorship. As they do so, the sense of performance expands from a theatrical act located within the novel, to the theatrical act of novel-writing, itself.

So when Maria Edgeworth uses a theatrical metaphor to criticize the behaviors of the popular novelist, she illustrates that the authorship of fictional texts becomes an act of performance and, simultaneously, a potential locus for self-expression: "there are few who can . . . bear the *mortification* of staying behind the scenes. They peep out, eager for applause, and destroy all illusion by crying, '*I* said it; *I* wrote it; *I* invented it all! Call me on the stage and crown me directly.'"[53] Edgeworth's statement shows the authorship of a fictional text treated as a version of theatrical performance, such that the author's relationship to her text is akin to the actor's relationship to her role. But for her, the crucial component of this relationship is the maintenance of the theatrical "illusion," the need for the author to remain behind the scenes, and preserve the discrepancy—granted by both fiction and theatrical performance—between the character's "I" and the "I" of the author or actor. Fiction in this model becomes, not a genre, but a behavior: fiction, for Edgeworth, becomes a performance.

FICTION AS PERFORMANCE

In contrast, we today slide comfortably between the terms "fiction" and "novel," a habit that begins, Catherine Gallagher suggests, in the eighteenth century.[54] While the term fiction is acknowledged to be much more capacious in earlier periods of literary study, scholars of our period often perpetuate the contemporary trend; we too conflate the novel, a particular genre, with fiction, more properly a convention of genre. And yet, Samuel Johnson, writing in 1751, presents fiction quite differently:

> The Muses wove in the loom of Pallas, a loose and changeable robe, like that in which Falsehood captivated her admirers; with this they invested Truth, and named her Fiction. She now went out to conquer with more success; for when she demanded entrances of the Passions, they often mistook her for Falsehood, and delivered up their charge; but when she had once taken possession, she was soon disrobed by Reason, and shown out, in her original form, with native effulgence and resistless dignity.[55]

The excerpt is from a fable in which the personified figure of Falsehood has been insinuating herself with an audience of personified Passions. Yet if we read the fable carefully, we realize that Fiction is not the persona of Truth—that's Falsehood—but the process by which Truth performs this persona. Fiction is a practice more than a personification, a form of expression, meant not to be obfuscating, but strategically sincere. Fiction, for Johnson, is a form of theater.

In the context of this anecdote, our critical tendency to label fiction as a genre exposes one of the key problems in novel studies: not just how we can define the novel, but when we can define it, when the myriad examples of narrative prose can justly be said to coalesce and form a genre. Early eighteenth-century "novels" were just that, new examples of prose often packaged under the different headings of histories, memoirs, intrigues, and travel narratives. But toward the middle of the century, "the" novel became attached to certain essential characteristics, one of which was the tendency to acknowledge its fictional nature. As Gallagher puts it, "overt fictions [and by this she means novels], invented narratives about people who never were, became both more strongly marked and more positively valued in the mid-eighteenth century than they had been previously."[56]

Correspondingly, our unmarked shift in terminology—from fiction as a convention of narrative, to fiction as narrative form—signals more than a gesture toward the novel's growing dominance in our historical period. Earlier in the eighteenth century, when we describe genre in terms of fiction, we are implicitly buying into Carolyn Miller's definition of genre as "centered not on the substance or the form of discourse, but on the action it is used to accomplish."[57] We are discussing a genre in terms of what it does, how it acts, which is why our Renaissance colleagues would find nothing innovative in the application of "fiction" to multiple genres. But by the end of the century, when we use the terms "fiction" and "novel" interchangeably, we are also indicating that one particular genre has appropriated the performative actions of another, the drama.

For as the novel embraced its fictional nature, it also advertised its relationship to the theater, and by the nineteenth century, this advertisement often occurred in very explicit terms: note William Makepeace Thackeray's prologue to *Vanity Fair*, titled "Before the Curtain," in which the author becomes the "Manager of the Performance," the characters become puppets, and the first chapter begins as "the curtain rises."[58] With such gestures, the fictional novel was appropriating a time-worn strategy of the stage, the tendency of players and playwrights to "improvise conventions of performance that deliberately acknowledged the fabricated character of the play world."[59] By announcing itself as fictional, the novel announced itself as engaged in a type of performance that could manipulate the same expectations of artifice put forward by the stage. And as shown by Johnson's costumed Truth, this process of manipulation remains consistent for both fiction and theatrical performance: in this model, any potential to express that which is "real" remains contingent on the ability to express that which is feigned. Expression remains a dynamic process that simultaneously links and opposes epistemological and theoretical concepts, a process that consists of a constant oscillation between Truth and Falsehood, the real and the feigned, individual desires and the cultural or textual productions of these desires.

The figure of the author in these novels and plays thus remains a construction of the text or performance. But the dynamic nature of this relationship also acknowledges what we cannot deny: that the author plays a role in constructing the text. As critics, how do we acknowledge this fact without foreclosing interpretative possibilities? Put another way, how can we look for links between social experience and literary texts without reducing texts to a social experience? In the past, this focus has threatened to limit our readings, and women's writing especially has suffered from these constraints. It continues to be probed for autobiographical details, with the common pitfall that critics "mistak[e] psychological and biographical origins for the meaning and direction of [a] work."[60] As Pinch puts it, while "literary critics no longer treat women's literary writings as being fundamentally or exclusively about . . . their lives as women . . . nineteenth- and twentieth-century feminisms have a long tradition of emphasizing women's emotional lives"—and of finding these "emotional lives" in their literary productions.[61] We label the feelings, if not the circumstances, described in women's fiction as autobiographical, though in so doing, we efface the fictional dimensions of the author's text.

Another way to understand this kind of effacement is to think of the analysis of literary style, an approach to literary work (taken up more fully in my epilogue) that traditionally links its form to some type of self-expression. As Jill Campbell notes, there is also a long tradition of understanding the style, of fictional or even critical work, "not as . . . an achievement of de-personalization, but rather, as the opposite."[62] This critical tradition believes that "the distinctive stylistic voice . . . provided for [the] narrator . . . may express deep features of the author himself, ones that he himself would not have been able to name."[63] This approach to literature, often dismissed as overly simplistic or ahistorical, threatens to collapse author and narrator, author and text.

Yet there is a difference between connection and conflation, and even this approach does not claim that author and narrator are the same. Instead, the narrator is recognized as a crucial mouthpiece, and it is because the narrator remains different from the author that he or she is able to channel these "deep features" that an author otherwise "would not have been able to name." As fiction masks authorial voices, it also channels them; it provides the added layer that makes authorial features "deep" and that enables these features to be "expressed." Fiction has the ability, as Campbell puts it, "to activate one person's voice through another's."[64] This ability is distinctly theatrical, and as shown by the Johnson anecdote, fiction in the eighteenth century was embraced in theatrical terms. So if, at times, we look for a self in fiction, we are not collapsing author and character, but recognizing fiction as a potential conduit for other voices; we are reading fiction in theatrical terms and from a specific historical mindset. To recognize fiction as a form of theatrical performance is to recognize that fiction may reflect on its author without becoming autobiography; indeed, it is to recognize that fiction conveys authorial sentiments by maintaining its discrete, fictional nature.

Similarly, theatrical performance, even at its most expressive, never completely collapses the categories of actor and role. To highlight the theater and theatrical performance as a recognized site for self-expressive behavior is to complicate, but not erase, the disjunction between actor and character, and it is the continued separation of these categories that enables the women in this study to use performance in the manner that they do. But the theater is not an exceptional site for this process of mediation. As the century, and this book, progresses, we see perhaps the most fascinating potential for the theater's influence on other genres: the novel, by highlighting its fictionality, evolves into a form of narrative that can access or efface the same dimensions, the same spaces, put forward by the stage. The fictional frame announces a discrepancy between the author of the text and the literary, fictional status of that text. But I'm also suggesting that this discrepancy is efficacious, that the very fictionality of the text creates the potential for it to function simultaneously in an autobiographical manner. "All will be real, that she only feigns": fiction for the author, like theatrical performance for the actor, maintains both these expressive possibilities, or indeed presents self-expression as the potential to oscillate between them. This is what I mean by "the play of fiction."

THE *DRAMATIS PERSONAE*

Given its investment in the figure of the author, this book is, appropriately, organized as a series of case studies. The women in this book represent some of the more recognizable literary figures of the eighteenth century; during their lifetimes they generated much text, and were the subjects of much more, providing ample evidence of their impact in both literary and social realms. These women also had complementary professional relationships to the stage. All of them were fascinated by drama, but Haywood and Inchbald were actively engaged in the theater world as professional actresses and playwrights, whereas Burney and Edgeworth had only limited acting experience in home theatricals and struggled to have their plays produced. This sampling allows me to follow the relationship of gender to professional success, the fluctuating fortunes of the eighteenth-century stage, and the influence of these fluctuations on the evolution of the novel.

The time frame represented by this sampling also challenges current modes of organizing a century that, as represented in recent conferences and scholarship, has become either very long or very short. This study purposefully falls somewhere in between. Not as broad-ranging as those studies of the long, ever expanding eighteenth century (that now threatens to swallow up both the Renaissance and Romanticism), and not as specific as the popular and focused look at a single decade, the time frame of this work can address trajectory, yet examine in more depth—and thus expose as more subtle—movements within an eighty year period that longer historical surveys have often summoned as major and definitive benchmarks of change. These movements will include the reaction to the Theater Licensing Act of 1737 (which put drama under the direct control of the Lord Chamberlain and confined the production of legitimate plays to the two royal theaters: Drury Lane and Covent Garden); the shift to the didactic novel (1740s and

1750s); the fascination with the literature of sensibility (1780s and 1790s); and the emergence of a romantic conception of subjectivity (1790s–1800s).

The surprising consistencies that emerge among my chapters reflect the fact that, despite their somewhat different literary-historical placements, these women all began professional careers once a social response to their type of literary activity had been established. The absence of Aphra Behn and the epilogue on Jane Austen thus carefully outline the historical and conceptual patterns that motivate this study. As recognized "bookends," these canonical poles indicate the polarities of theatrical and novelistic form: on one hand, the author as a "nobody" who is all performance; on the other, the "impersonal" novelistic style that has been enabled by the women writers featured here.[65] Behn and Austen also frame, historically, what Ellen Donkin identifies as "two rather distinct clusters of activity" for women in the theater: one, from 1670–1717, the second, from about 1765–1800, with a gradual reintegration beginning as early as 1750s.[66] Behn entered the field of theater at the very beginning of this first period, and because the woman playwright was so new, there were few cultural inhibitions or prohibitions in place to counter, or shape, the public response.[67] As a result, when Behn uses her non-dramatic prose to meditate on questions of performance, the issues at stake have more to do with the creative possibilities afforded by genre, than they do with the artist's ability to pursue them.[68] Haywood, whose literary career spans 1719–1756, emerges in the maelstrom of negative public opinions that Behn and her contemporaries had elicited. A public response to the woman playwright was established and growing. Haywood's experiences in the theater register the increasingly critical attitude toward the stage and a woman's place on it, an attitude that leads to her mid-century forays in the "reformed" novel and its didactic presentation of sentiment.

Haywood—an author unique for both the duration and generic range of her career—provides an ideal initial test case to search for continuities in early to mid-eighteenth-century literature. Her canon offers an evolution in literary styles, from the erotic fiction of the early eighteenth century to the domestic fiction of the mid-century and beyond. As political and gender-specific restrictions (the Licensing Act; the critical associations of actress and prostitute) hinder her early career in the theater, Haywood repositions elements from her plays into her early novellas and her later didactic novels and periodicals. Within each of these genres, Haywood explores a strategy of what I term self-conscious performance: women acting roles that they have independently conceived to express romantic desires that would, if articulated outside of performance, be met with disastrous results. Haywood's conscious authorial decision to shift from genre to genre, and her complementary decision to shift her professional personae (from playwright, to scandal writer, to reformed, didactic novelist) read as a version of this same strategy—not because these personae signal some romantic desire held by the author herself, but because these conscious shifts highlight a desire for authorial expression and form the means to achieve it. This first chapter sets up the way I talk about the work produced by subsequent authors. Within her texts, Haywood presents performance as self-expressive, even as she presents the practice of authorship as a form of performance. This is the paradigm I apply throughout.

This is not to say that all these authors had the same literary careers—far from it—or that cultural attitudes toward the woman writer remained consistent for these eighty years. As my subsequent chapters detail, "performance" means something different for each author. Haywood and Inchbald, both authors with professional experience as actors and playwrights, use their work and their own public personae to play upon the contemporary paranoia that one's external, public presentation is often feigned and that the "real" essence of a person lurks beneath the surface. Even as their fictional characters adopt roles that express their own emotions, these same characters encourage the audience to recognize these presentations as consciously displayed and as such, encourage the audience's suspicion that what is expressed during the display is most likely "put on."

In contrast, certain Burney heroines engage in forms of voluntary self-display that are designed to disguise their voluntary nature: women willingly begin a physiological process (starving themselves, denying themselves sleep) that they understand will not make them noticeable until it has escaped their control. Theatrical performance in Burney's novels is manifested by a planned moment of unconsciousness, and these insensible heroines simultaneously enact and obscure the desire for display that Burney (a frustrated playwright) recognizes as improper, unfeminine, and in danger of discrediting the emotions it enables her to express. Another frustrated playwright, Edgeworth also has her heroines disguise the constructed nature of their expressive displays, in this case so that the same displays may have a pedagogical effect. In Edgeworth's fiction, characters perform their passions for didactic, not cathartic, ends, and targeted observers learn from these performances when they react to them with their own emotions. To encourage this active emotional response, the pedagogical performer must obscure the staged nature of her feelings.

These groupings illustrate a regular oscillation between the two possible ways of activating artifice: one can either highlight the fact of it (as do Haywood and Inchbald) or one can, in a second act of artifice, try to disguise it (as do Burney and Edgeworth). My chronological progression from author to author thus becomes something of a call and a response. As the theater and overtly theatrical heroines such as Haywood's Fantomina incite criticism, they yield to novels and the more subtle performances of Haywood's Miss Betsy, or of Burney's women. Yet as Burney's heroines, and Burney herself, obscure the staged nature of their emotional displays, they are condemned for publishing sufferings that are too obviously their own. Burney forms a painful case study for her persistent yet relatively unsuccessful attempts to write for the stage, and the critical response to female suffering that characterizes her life and work illustrates the danger in having a performance lose its theatrical nature and align too obviously with personal experience. Inchbald, on the other hand, advertises the performed nature of her characters' displays, and advocates a more mediated form of expression that will come to be characteristic of late eighteenth-century fiction itself.

For if this shifting approach to performance complements these authors' own professional experiences with the stage, their approaches and experiences suggestively mirror some larger trends in eighteenth-century theater and novels. Fiction, as a performance, can also be presented in two main ways. As the French critic Marthe Robert specifies, a fictional narrative may pass off imaginary characters, events, and objects for real ones; it is engaged in a performance that it endeavors (in a second act of performance) to disguise. In the second case, a fictional narrative may acknowledge the very art of masquerade, the acts of feigning or imagining that comprise its narrative.[69] These two trends go in and out of style in this century, with early eighteenth-century novels disguising their fictional nature, and later eighteenth-century novels promoting it.

I situate these developments in light of the 1737 Theater Licensing Act, pointing out that the lull in theatrical activity prompted by this legislation, the brief corresponding lull in antitheatrical sentiment, and the "rise of fictionality" that came to characterize the novel are complementary historical trends.[70] As the theater came under fire for its increasingly satirical or referential nature, novels were embraced for their fictional status; the recognized conventions of these genres trade places in a chiastic shift. Sentimental novels in particular echoed the demand for unpremeditated, less theatrical behavior through their depiction of spontaneous emotional displays, yet such depictions themselves soon came up against the necessary role of conventionality. They exhibited a desired consciousness of emotion that registered in the growing ridicule of the literature of sensibility, and perhaps in Inchbald's decision to rewrite a heroine from her first novel into a play.

Austen's novel *Mansfield Park* also responds to this kind of criticism by turning antitheatricalism (ostensibly) back on the theater. My final chapters contextualize the shift that Austen and my epilogue represent: a stylistic move into free indirect discourse, what D.A. Miller calls an "impersonal" narrator, and, not coincidentally, a move away from the stage.[71] *Mansfield Park* targets the theater and theatrical displays of feeling, yet the way feeling is staged in this novel has changed once again. Performance—as described in the plays and novels of other authors—functions as a self-expressive space when readers or audience members are conditioned to dismiss it instead as a moment of artifice. This type of expressive strategy depends on the preservation of a particular kind of antitheatrical prejudice that opposes the actor to the act, and this is the kind of theatricality characteristic of the early part of the century and deployed by writers such as Behn or Haywood. Yet as the century progresses, and this type of theatricality becomes more consistently deployed by women and women writers in the manner I expose, it becomes correspondingly less efficacious. The trajectory of my argument thus leads to the disastrous theatricals at Mansfield Park, which signify an unmediated understanding of theater that collapses the actor with the act, the play with reality. Austen's "impersonal narrator" becomes, in response, not so much a denial or rejection of theater as itself a new form of mediated theatricality, Austen's novel, a new form of theater.

Throughout the book, I read these women and their texts as representative of larger literary-historical patterns within the time frame of 1719–1800, and I intersperse my more extensive investigations with contemporaneous anecdotes to show that this book presents a model by which other eighteenth-century writers can be read. Yet even as this project offers a form of literary history, it is equally a conceptual work that builds from a concrete set of texts, people, and events. This book insists upon a study of these authors as individuals, in part because it argues for the study of the author as an individual, and the broader theoretical concepts that my study explores emerge from the specific people who exemplify them. As they do, they remind us of how a select example can spark more general thought, how a select individual can start a trend. While drawing upon the value and richness of more historical approaches to literature, this project also asks us to acknowledge the inevitability with which we extrapolate from specific examples, and the epistemological value inherent in probing a specific example, as well as accumulating many. And without dismissing the valuable work that has been done to present the author or the individual as a cultural construction, I would say again that culture and society are comprised of the myriad individuals that they are said to construct, and that the influence does of course go in both directions. I'd like to remind us of our own ability to be individuals, to be idiosyncratic and independent, even as we are products of our time, place, politics, and families. The quirky, passionate women who follow reminded me of this ability; as individuals, they first captured my interest and imagination, and the book is framed around them to reflect that fact.

2   Rehearsing Desire
Eliza Haywood's
Self-Conscious Performance

Great Arbitress of Passion! wond'rous Art!
As the despotick Will the Limbs, thou mov'st
the Heart;
Persuasion waits on all your bright Designs,
And where you point, the varying Soul inclines;
See! Love and Friendship, the fair Theme inspires
We glow with Zeal, we melt in soft Desires! [1]

   —James Sterling, "To Mrs. Eliza Haywood, on Her Writings" (1732)

While "passion" can mean any overpowering feeling or emotion,[2] Sterling's poem celebrates Eliza Haywood as the Arbitress of one particular valence of passion: love, or desire. The tribute is appropriate, for Haywood is still best known for the reams of amatory fiction that characterized her early career. Her racy bestseller, *Love in Excess* (1719), would earn her a place with Aphra Behn and Delariviere Manley in the "fair Triumvirate of Wit,"[3] a group of writers known for their ability to incite desire—and the physiological signs of desire—in their readers. But the "passions" that these women invoke have a personal valence, too. As Haywood's dedication to *The Fatal Secret* (1725) claims, women wrote about love because it was within the realm of their admittedly limited experience. They knew about it:

> But as I am a Woman, and consequently depriv'd of those Advantages of Education which the other Sex enjoy, I cannot so far flatter my Desires, as to imagine it in my Power to soar to any Subject higher than that which Nature is not negligent to teach us. Love . . . requires no Aids of Learning, no general Conversation, no Application . . . this is a Theme, therefore, which . . . frees me from the Imputation of Vain or Self-Sufficient:—None can tax me with having too great an Opinion of my own Genius, when I aim at nothing but what the meanest may perform.[4]

Despite Haywood's carefully deprecating acknowledgment that even the meanest may perform the craft that she professes, this passage indicates that for her it comes naturally. Indeed, love was an acceptable subject for female exploration in part because popular assumptions granted women more natural insight into this subject; Richard Steele comments in the *Tatler* that, for men, "craft in love is an act of invention, and not, as with women, the effect of nature and instinct."[5] Such formulations necessarily project the woman into her writing, for if a woman knows about love intuitively, not empirically, then she too must feel the passion that she describes.

Like Haywood, Manley and Behn played up connections between their subject matter and themselves; they encouraged audiences to find their feelings (those of the audience and the author) in their fictions.[6] Yet unlike her two Triumvirate counterparts, Haywood would outlive the risqué climate of the restoration and early eighteenth century, and she would be censured for the titillating style that once won her praise. As Pope's scathing portrayal of her in *The Dunciad* would evidence, criticism, like praise, got personal: only a lascivious woman could write lascivious tales, so if Haywood manipulates the passions of others, she must be in the grip of violent, corrupting passions herself.[7] By the end of her literary career, in the mid-1750s, she was known for her conduct-oriented periodicals, her didactic novels, and her moral essays, and her professional shift was again read in terms of a personal, emotional progression. She was famously praised by Clara Reeve for the propriety of her later works, and for the personal reformation she must have experienced to write them.[8]

This type of identification between a woman writer and her material is one that Paula Backscheider, in an essay titled "Women Writers and the Chains of Identification," defines as "confin[ing]" to a woman writer's creativity. The way that men and women wrote about women writers in the eighteenth century enforced the idea that "while men might be artists, creators, and thinkers, women were usually merely repeaters of their own or other women's autobiographical stories."[9] In making this claim, Backscheider implies that both repetition and the pressure to be autobiographical undermine a woman's ability to be creative; as her title indicates, these are "chains" of identification. Yet given the contemporary expectations for female expression, a woman's ability to tell her own story is perhaps rightfully read as more of an achievement than a constraint.[10] And in contrast to Backscheider's claim, Haywood's texts illustrate a surprisingly creative strategy by which the eighteenth-century woman repeats other's stories to tell her own.

A prolific actress, playwright, translator, bookseller, editor, and novelist who wrote more than eighty works over the course of fifty-four years, Haywood reflects the major evolutions in eighteenth-century literary style and taste. While a single chapter cannot account for the depth and breadth of her canon, the following discussion takes a representative cross section of works that correspond to facets of her career: *A Wife to be Lett* (1723, a dramatic comedy); *Fantomina* (1725, an amorous novella); and *The History of Miss Betsy Thoughtless* (1751, a didactic novel). These selections demonstrate both Haywood's range and focus, for despite the differences in genre and historical context, these texts repeatedly explore a strategy of what I term "self-conscious performance": they feature women who disguise themselves to express otherwise inexpressible desires. These desires are frequently sexual or romantic in nature; Haywood's heroines adopt roles to articulate feelings of love that, according to convention, must otherwise go unspoken.

But just as "passion" can encompass many valences of emotion, "desire" can refer both to a sense of lust and to a more general longing that is less about love, and more about possession or control. The nature of desire in Haywood's work, while often sexual, actually has several layers: " . . . her design was once more to engage him, to hear him sigh, to see him languish . . . to be sweetly forced to what she wished with equal Ardour was what she wanted and what she had formed a Stratagem to obtain."[11] Fantomina, the subject of the above quotation, wants sex, but she also wants to be forced into sex, even, if we read the syntax carefully, wants to force her lover to force her into sex. Her "stratagem" becomes just as much about her desire for expression, and the control of that expression, as it is about the expression of her desire.

Fantomina thus forms an exception to the eighteenth-century assumption that passions in general, and especially female passions, were irrational and dangerously uncontrollable.[12] Yet unique as this ability may seem, Haywood's work sets up a paradigm that I trace through the chapters that follow. These heroines, who turn to theatrical performance to communicate their love, contradict the eighteenth-century antitheatrical tradition that associates performance with falseness and manipulation.[13] The emotions expressed by Haywood's consciously performing heroines are presented as no less genuine because these heroines form a "stratagem" to convey them; instead, for emotional expression to register with an audience, to be at all effective, the Haywoodian heroine must plan the moment and mode. As heroines like Fantomina will demonstrate, the woman who anticipates how and when she may indulge her passion avoids much of the typical pain and suffering experienced by other sexually indulgent women; such expressions of desire are depicted as both staged and sincere, and with happier consequences than when they are not.[14]

Still, talking about love as staged sounds unrealistic, or at least unromantic. We think of desire as dependent upon spontaneity and novelty—an assumption that Haywood's libertines, constantly in search of the new and different conquest, firmly support.[15] Staging passion means anticipating and analyzing it, rehearsing and repeating it, all acts that would seem to detract from the excitement and variety that comprise our understanding of desire itself. And yet, as Joseph Roach illustrates, "no action or sequence of actions may be performed exactly the same way twice; they must be reinvented or recreated at each appearance."[16] Repetition invokes difference as much as similarity, and theorists regularly locate the expression of a subordinate culture or individual in the difference that is masked (even as it is produced) by the sameness of mimetic behavior.[17]

The repeated behaviors of Haywood's women create a similar space for individual expression, yet these heroines adopt roles that are meant to register with their audience as unique: difference is advertised, whereas the sameness of their strategies is obscured. One goal of this chapter then is to illustrate not the obvious similarities among Haywood's texts or heroines, but the overlooked continuities—to reveal Haywood's carefully hidden repetitions. As the opening tribute from Sterling makes clear, Haywood made a career, and a very successful, long-standing one at that, out of repeating love plots, but analysis reveals Haywood's heroines and plots to be first blatantly, then covertly formulaic. Haywood reinvents herself and her work so successfully that many critics read her as almost two different authors, and she does so in response to changing professional conditions that endorse different forms of authorship: plays, scandal intrigues, didactic novels.

This chapter thus moves between what happens within Haywood's work and her authorial decisions about how to present this work. This movement shows that the strategy Haywood develops for select female characters in her writing duplicates the strategy she applies to her own literary career. But as the preceding pages establish, to read Haywood's work in terms of its author is not merely to make a simplistic association between author and text. The concept of self-expression for Haywood is contingent upon a carefully preserved detachment: as her heroines channel their feelings through roles, every role must yield to another role to sustain expression. According to this formula, Haywood's heroines can become mouthpieces for their author only when they adopt mouthpieces of their own. The figure of the author retreats, persistently, behind the scenes; her fictional texts remain, persistently, theatrical in nature. At stake in this authorial experiment is the desire for expression itself.

THE PLAYWRIGHT AND THE ACTRESS

In 1723, Theophilus Cibber, the twenty-year-old, bandy-legged son of theater-manager Colley Cibber, strode onstage at Drury Lane to utter the opening prologue of Haywood's comedy, *A Wife to be Lett*:

> Criticks! Be dumb to-night—no Skill display;
> A dangerous *Woman-Poet* wrote the Play:
> One, who not fears your fury, tho prevailing,
> More than your Match, in everything, but Railing.
> Give her fair Quarter, and whene'er she tries ye,
> Safe in Superior *Spirit*, she defies ye:
> Measure her Force, by her *known Novels*, writ
> With manly Vigour, and with Woman's Wit.
> Then tremble, and depend, if ye beset her,
> She, who can talk so well, may act yet better.[18]

The prologue highlights three crucial points. First, the play is explicitly the product of a "woman-poet," though the author's gender is highlighted by way of her atypical, unwomanly traits. Dangerous and defiant in her composition for the stage, she is also known for her novels' paradoxical combination of "manly vigour" and "woman's wit." By the time this play was produced, Haywood had already published a number of successful novels, including *The British Recluse* and her bestseller *Love in Excess*, and both comedy and author are introduced in the context of these known publications. Reflections on gender emerge—and this is my second point—from reflections on genre. Lastly, the prologue reinforces what was also announced on the accompanying playbill, that Haywood is engaged with her play on multiple levels. The final line, "she, who can talk so well, may act yet better," constitutes another rather unfeminine threat: if you attack her critically, Haywood will—and can—pay you back in more than full measure. And she can do so because she herself acted the part of Mrs. Graspall, one of the female leads in this play. This link between author and actress prevents us from reading "acting" as automatically synonymous with "dissembling." Instead, the final lines create a link between expression and performance: Haywood's defiant refusal to be silenced ("she, who may talk so well") is extended to and maintained by her prowess on the stage ("may act yet better").[19]

While much of Haywood's life and career remains shrouded in mystery, we know that she began her professional career in the theater, and we know something about the environment and logistics of the early eighteenth-century playhouse.[20] A place that Lawrence Klein has described as a "nodal poin[t] in the network of new urban culture,"[21] the theater welcomed many social classes (even as the seating arrangements demarcated them), and the audience was raucous and interactive, both with each other and with the players onstage.[22] The playhouse was not a place to escape the pressures of society—it was a microcosm of it—and this was an especially volatile society when it came to women dramatists. As women working in the theater would discover, it was often difficult to find an audience, or acknowledgment, for their personal and professional concerns. When Charles Fleetwood fired the actress and playwright Charlotte Charke from Drury Lane, Charke was irate, more so because the expulsion came on the heels of a violent quarrel with her father, Colley Cibber, who did nothing to overturn Fleetwood's decision.[23] And yet, theater could offer a way out of the professional difficulties it posed. Renting out Lincoln's Inn Fields, Charke mounted a production of her father's play *The Careless Husband* and later staged her own play, *The Art of Management*, as a way to air personal grievances and to garner the town's support for her in the family's quarrel.[24] The permeability of the fourth wall in eighteenth-century theater meant that to work on the stage really was, as it were, to hold "the mirror up to nature."[25] Haywood started her professional career in an environment that insistently reflected on her gender and even more insistently blurred the boundaries between public and private, life and art.

A Wife to be Lett (1723) explores these same tensions as the plot hinges on the public exposure of the most private and gendered interactions—courtship and sex. As the title indicates, the depiction of women as a saleable commodity runs throughout the drama. Mr. Graspall, who is most likely impotent, wants to capitalize on Sir Harry Beaumont's lustful interest in his wife, and Mrs. Graspall is under Covert-Baron and so can transact nothing without her husband's leave (46).[26] When she tries to verbalize her dissatisfaction with her husband's pimping plan, Mr. Graspall disregards her protests; he even shows her a letter stating that she agrees to the liaison, which he forged in her name (45–47). The letter in particular exemplifies how a woman's ability to communicate is compromised by marriage: as Mrs. Graspall's possessions are her husband's possessions, so his words and feelings come to stand in for hers. The play ends with a reunion between husband and wife and Mrs. Graspall's renewed pledge of obedience.

The plot summary indicates that women's expression in this play is often and ultimately effaced. Yet while the play ends conventionally, with the roles of authoritative husband and obedient, subservient wife securely in place, Haywood includes within the main plot several examples of women, wronged by men, who stage scenes to vocalize their discontent and assert their virtue. Amadea, Beaumont's abandoned mistress, and Mrs. Graspall, the potentially prostituted wife, both summon other characters to join them in acting out designs they have independently conceived. Amadea and Mrs. Graspall both function as playwrights and actresses in their own mini-dramas.

Amadea, whom we eventually learn has been tracking her fickle lover from London to Salisbury, appears early in the play, dressed in boy's clothes and shadowing Mrs. Graspall. In a very direct manner (Mrs. Graspall calls her "bold Adviser"), she cautions Mrs. Graspall on receiving Beaumont's visits, or even listening to addresses of any man who is not her husband. While Mrs. Graspall agrees that a woman's self-control should encompass not only what she says, but what she hears—"'tis a Crime to Vertue ev'n but to hear what loose Desires suggest" (16)—Amadea, by contrast, displays almost no constraint. The male disguise that endows her with free and easy speech reinforces the gender-specific nature of her warnings, a social commentary made all the more pointed given that an actress herself now played this "breeches part."[27]

Yet in the course of the play, we will witness how Amadea "convers[es] only as a man, [and] is silenced as a woman."[28] The juxtaposition of the frustrated Mrs. Graspall and the unconstrained "male" Amadea highlights the limits currently placed on the expression of Mrs. Graspall and, by extension, the limits that would (and will) be placed on Amadea, were she not in male garb. For unlike Aphra Behn's Hellena, Amadea cannot use this disguise to accost her rover.[29] Since the nature of Beaumont's crimes, and the force of Amadea's accusations, are inseparable from gender, she cannot effectively confront her wayward lover in drag. To articulate her feelings as a wronged woman, she abandons her male disguise and appears *as* a woman, but as a woman playwright: she plans a scene in which Mrs. Graspall is a knowing participant, Sir Harry Beaumont an unknowing one (49).

Amadea's pre-planned drama demonstrates her ability to predict and control the responses of her lover, which in turn enables her to articulate those personal grievances that have previously gone unheard. Amadea encourages Mrs. Graspall to plan the meeting her husband desires, then, from behind the scenes, she watches as Mrs. Graspall catechizes Sir Harry on his previous affections. Sir Harry finally admits to both his former love of Amadea and his broken vows; with Sir Harry's admission, Amadea makes her entrance. Dressed in her own clothes, she reveals the full story of her actions and reassures Sir Harry that he still possesses her love. While her role in this scene is to forgive, not accuse, she has created the conditions that lead Sir Harry to articulate her wrongs. In a clever reversal of Mr. Graspall's verbal appropriations, Amadea makes Sir Harry's words her own: his confession is also hers, lodged within the dialogue she created to prompt it.

The scene also reveals that the relationship between repetition and truth in this play varies with gender. In the sense that Amadea and Mrs. Graspall have rehearsed their parts, what they say has been said (or at least discussed) before, yet the veracity of their confessions gains emphasis from duplication. When Sir Harry tries to use the same rhetorical technique, to claim that "repeated Vows and Imprecations" gain "Force" from their repeated nature, he is interrupted by Mrs. Graspall's decided negative (59). The vows of constancy he makes to Mrs. Graspall are identical to the ones he made to Amadea; his repeated promises are meaningless because they are repeated. Amadea's strategy sets up an approach to expression that associates repetition with honest assertions for women, dishonest protestations for men.

Fittingly then, Amadea's success prompts, from Mrs. Graspall, a repeat performance. Pleased with the conclusion of Amadea's plot, Mrs. Graspall states, "I cannot find in my heart to forgive my Husband's base Design upon me, and have thought of a way to be revenged" (63). While Mrs. Graspall's unforgiving nature and dark talk of revenge may conjure up images of violent physical retribution, her plan is theatrical in nature. She has attempted to chastise her husband before, with no result (46–48). Now she responds to her husband's insensitivity by staging a play for their dinner guests, in which she finally succeeds in exposing him as mercenary and abusive.

Mrs. Graspall assures her husband that she has in fact "receiv'd whatever Favours [Beaumont] cou'd intreat," earned Mr. Graspall the 2,000 pounds he charged Beaumont for the visitation, and now wishes to spend a portion of that sum on a dinner party (75). With this occasion to summon spectators, she gathers a carefully selected group of guests. Then, in the middle of dinner, Beaumont and Amadea (disguised again as a man) enter fighting, with Mrs. Graspall in tow. In front of the guests, Beaumont testifies that he has caught Amadea and Mrs. Graspall in an embrace. To the shock of all, Mrs. Graspall boldly agrees. She then asserts that she will have liaisons with as many men as she wants and that she has broken open her husband's closet and stolen back Beaumont's 2,000 pounds. She justifies these supposed actions with the statement that her husband taught her "to despise all Sense of Shame" when he "let [her] out to Hire, and forc'd [her] trembling Vertue to obey" (76). When the audience reacts with renewed shock, Mr. Graspall with remorse and penitence (though he does seem to regret the loss of his money more than the loss of his wife), Beaumont jumps in to explain that "the seeming gentleman with whom I fought . . . [is] a Woman" and that "this plot was laid on purpose to cure you . . . of that covetous, sordid Disposition . . . and a little also to revenge the Contempt you seem'd to have of so good a Wife" (77).

The best-planned scene masks all signs of planning, and in a strategy later adopted by swooning Burney heroines and Edgeworthian educators alike, Mrs. Graspall carefully designs her confessional moment to obscure her responsibility for it. Much like Amadea, Mrs. Graspall stages her revenge so that ultimately she can forgive and not accuse, yet Beaumont's role as explicator grants him a responsibility that, upon careful reading, the passive voice of his speech does not support. Though Mrs. Graspall merely pronounces her virtue and embraces her husband, the end of Act 4 makes it clear that the design is all her own. Beaumont acts a role and speaks the dialogue she has assigned him.

The spontaneous reactions of Mrs. Graspall's dinner party guests, especially their horrified responses to her supposed lack of virtue, are similarly engineered. Unlike the invited guests, we may observe how Mrs. Graspall's plan to vindicate herself begins curiously with a series of damning, and *un*true, admissions. We know that she has not consummated her bargain with Sir Harry, that the second "man" she claims to have seduced is a woman, and that the only true statement in her script is the accusation levied at her husband. Yet her untruths, damning as they are, purposefully work her audience up to an emotional pitch that subsumes whatever reaction they may have independently had to her main accusation: that her husband tried to sell her body for sex. In what emerges as prototype for Edgeworth's experimental theatrics, Mrs. Graspall couches one potentially inappropriate and honest assertion, the public accusation of her husband, within other invented claims to infidelity. While her declarations are universally shocking, her main accusation is protected, its impact lessened, by being located within a scenario that she will momentarily reveal as feigned.

Taken independently, Mrs. Graspall's stratagem within the play already asks us to see her as a model for the playwright. Coupled with the facts that Haywood chose to play this role in her own production, that Haywood, like her title character, likely experienced difficulties with her marriage, and that the playbills advertised Haywood's identity as both author and lead actress, the connections among author, actress, and character become purposeful and pronounced.[30] Haywood's numerous and overlapping public careers offered theater audiences a complex appeal: she intrigued audiences with the suspected scandalous circumstances of her private life and the scandalous circumstances of the erotic narratives she published while working on stage.[31] In Henry Fielding's *The Historical Register* (1737), Haywood plays Mrs. Screen, a character who refuses to purchase even a grain of modesty. In Hatchett's *The Rival Father* (1730) she is Briseis, the cast-off lover of Achilles. In Fielding's *Eurydice Hiss'd* (1737), she plays the Muse, an explicitly sexual character who speaks of herself as an abandoned mistress. Such characters are reminiscent of her titillating heroines in novellas such as *The Mercenary Lover* (1726) or *The British Recluse* (1722); these acting choices ask her audience to identify the actress with the novelist, the novelist with her all-too-amorous ingénues. Haywood's public presentations show a conscious decision to play these roles off each other, and as her theatrical roles reflect back on her novelistic ones, her professional movements among these roles become theatrical in nature.

Haywood's intertwined professional personae also establish the crucial element of her public appeal. Haywood was outspoken about her dissatisfaction with the theatrical profession—a 1719 letter to the publisher of her first novel claimed that "the Stage not answering my Expectation, and the averseness of my Relations to it, has made me Turn my Genius another Way"[32]—and the 1737 Theater Licensing Act would finally force her, along with many other peripheral playwrights, off the stage for good. Yet she remained actively involved in the theater for thirteen years after her 1719 letter, and her ultimate shift from theater to non-dramatic prose seems to be the result of politics, not personal preference: she acted up until the day that the Little Haymarket was forced to close.[33] Disadvantages and dissatisfaction aside, the theater proved an invaluable place to advertise her fiction in terms of her own authorial personae. It provided a tantalizing model for identity that rendered the author simultaneously mysterious and accessible to her public.

But the profession that offered the most obvious location for what Dror Wahrman calls "identity play" also offered the most resistance to it.[34] What Haywood meant in 1719, when she accused the stage of "not answering her expectations," remains ambiguous. Most likely she refers to finances (though if so, we could question why she continued to devote so much time to a non-lucrative career), but the reference can also encompass her creative expectations. The eighteenth-century playwright was subject to numerous external controls: she had to please the acting company, the theater manager, and the audience to ensure the continued performance of her play. Haywood's decision to take over a leading role in *A Wife to be Lett* can be read as a strategic appeal to an audience already intrigued by her novel *Love in Excess* (1719) or a psychological attempt to articulate personal complaints; it can also signify her desire to maintain a certain amount of control over the presentation, if not the outcome, of her own play.

A Wife to be Lett met with reasonable success, running for three nights so that Haywood garnered a benefit performance, but on the fourth night the performance ended. As a playwright and actress, Haywood found herself as stifled as the character she portrayed—for if Mrs. Graspall saves her reputation, she nonetheless remains bound to a detestable husband, and such an ending does not portray her performances as permanently redemptive. How and when a woman can assert her own desires remains complicated in this play, especially given Mrs. Graspall's claim that "cou'd I with Honour receive Sir Harry's love, how happy were my Lot" (16). Mirroring Lady Fullbank's conflict at the conclusion of Behn's play *The Lucky Chance* (1686), Mrs. Graspall realizes that to assert independence in what she says and does, she must—ironically—suppress how she feels. Amadea's role contains a similar contradiction; the full and honest expression of her status involves the admission of her gender, her feelings, and her relationship to Sir Harry—all admissions that render her silent after they are made.

Unlike her heroines, though, Haywood can overcome these restraints by eluding the constraints placed upon her by genre. The novel allowed Haywood to reposition tropes of performance in a genre not bound by the same temporal constraints or subject to the same sphere of public negotiation as the theater. With the novel, she had a generic form that needed the approval of fewer people in order to circulate and that did not require instantaneous popularity to remain in circulation. Haywood's novels show that if a woman's attitudes toward love and marriage could not be staged, they could nonetheless be performed.

THE COQUETTE AND THE AUTHOR OF INTRIGUE

The idea that a woman could perform attitudes of love was not a new one in the eighteenth century, as the character of the coquette figures prominently in both eighteenth-century fiction and conduct literature. But the typical coquette engages in a form of performance that is necessarily hypocritical, finite, and self-destructive. Henry Fielding, in *Joseph Andrews,* defines her as a manipulative creature whose

> Life is one constant Lye, and the only Rule by which you can form any Judgment of them is, that they are never what they seem. If it was possible for a Coquette to love (as it is not, for if ever it attains this Passion, the Coquette ceases instantly), it would wear the Face of Indifference if not of hatred to the beloved Object . . . [35]

Fielding's definition depends on a discrepancy between feeling and behavior: if and when feigned emotions lead to genuine ones, "the Coquette ceases."

Yet for Haywood, the most dangerous part of coquetry is that such behavior produces the very emotions that undo it. In *The Female Spectator,* her coquette Melissa initially has "no other view in entertaining [the married] Dorimon . . . than the same she had in treating with a like Behavior Numbers before him, merely for the sake of hearing herself praised, and giving Pain, as she imagined, to others of her Admirers":

> But how dangerous a Thing it is to have too great an Intimacy with a Person of a different Sex, many of a greater Share of Discretion than Melissa have experienced.—This unwary Lady, in meditating new Arts, the more to captivate her Lover, became ensnared herself;—in fine, she liked, she loved . . . and Dorimon had as ample a Gratification of his Desires, as his most sanguine Hopes could have presented him an Idea of.[36]

Haywood here suggests that insincere flirtation encourages the very emotions that it initially feigns, those "dangerous . . . Thing[s]" that "ensnare" a Lady.[37]

The coquette's days would then seem to be numbered. Even one with great foresight does not often anticipate the consequences of flirtation or clearly understand how these consequences will affect her ability to perform. For one, a woman's control of rhetoric and innuendo can be overpowered by masculine force; the most calculating maiden may find herself at the mercy of a more powerful suitor who decides simply to take his pleasure. And even consensual sex can be damaging, in a theatrical if not a psychological sense. Aside from the scandal that a loss of virtue can produce, sex exposes a woman, physically and emotionally, in a way that destroys the potential for future dissembling. Melissa's passions are dangerous not in themselves, but because they encourage the "ample Gratification" of male desires that leave no room for modesty, secrets, or answering passions to hide. The self-made coquette quickly becomes a male creation: the seduced maiden. The consequences of such a performance prevent its repetition.[38]

Haywood's Fantomina, the heroine of Haywood's 1725 novella of the same name, is by contrast an "unconventional heroine."[39] Unlike Fielding's coquette, she can love and manipulate the man she loves—without putting on an expression of indifference. Indeed, Melissa-like she indulges her and her lover's desires, but unlike Haywood's Melissa she can do so without becoming "ensnared." Fantomina's singular achievement is her ability to seduce the same man again and again, as she adopts a series of disguises to perpetuate her own seduction.[40] She first dissembles as a prostitute to encourage the addresses of her secret man-of-choice, Beauplaisir. During the course of her adventures, she repeatedly re-inflames his fading desire by masquerading as a servant girl, a widow, and a fair "incognita." The result of her actions is that while Beauplaisir seduces the same body night after night, he is convinced that he has conquered four different women.

Though unconventional as a coquette, Fantomina is not as unconventional for Haywood as critics claim. The methods Fantomina employs and the story's tenuous balance between comedy and tragedy link this text and heroine to Haywood's earlier play. Fantomina, like Amadea and Mrs. Graspall, conceives and carries out various stratagems to communicate her feelings, and like the women in *A Wife to be Lett*, she covertly manipulates her lover's behavior. Play and novella cater to an audience intrigued by intrigues, but while both texts are concerned with female sexuality, and both are composed in a literary moment that was relatively tolerant of risqué themes, *Fantomina* addresses issues of desire much more directly than Haywood's play. In *A Wife to Be Lett*, sex resides offstage, though the play references it through innuendo, reminiscence, and asides. In *Fantomina*, sex is—repeatedly—front and center. The novella features an unmarried woman with a high libido, and the narrative indulges, if not endorses, her sexual freedoms. One easy explanation for these differences is genre: since *Fantomina* is not performed the author may indulge in behaviors that she could never stage.

And yet, of course, the idea of performance is inescapable in *Fantomina*, as the very title signifies not a name but the alias of a "Young Lady of distinguished Birth, Beauty, Wit, and Spirit" (227). The opening scene is set in a playhouse, and, inspired by her setting, Fantomina succeeds in her plans because she is such a talented performer. Progressing from the performance within the playhouse to the performances of the heroine outside of it, *Fantomina* stresses connections between theater and social life that can be read in one of two ways: negatively, as a sign of the inevitable artifice that permeates society—or more positively, as indicative of the theater's ability to be a realistic, even useful model for social interactions. For if Fantomina's repeated performances mark her as a chronic dissembler, her strategy also enables her to express her desire for Beauplaisir while avoiding the typical consequences of such indulgence. Her behavior is more honest, in this sense, than that of the loving heroine who represses signs of her affection, or the typical coquette who dissembles her "love."

Her behavior is more honest, even, than that of the impulsive maiden who spontaneously acts on her desire. While Fantomina is obviously a talented performer, her first foray into the world of feigning is not completely premeditated. Her idea to dress up as a prostitute is "a little Whim" (227), and when Beauplaisir's intentions quickly progress from conversation to sex, Fantomina rather naïvely "f[inds] herself in a Difficulty which had never before entered into her Head" (228). Their first sexual encounter thus reads very much like a rape, as shown by her involuntary post-coital tears and imprecations. Such a breakdown seems to suggest the emergence of sincerity from the façade of dissimulation: she "quite forget[s] the Part she had assumed" (231). And yet these involuntary tears and imprecations are expected and dismissed by both lover and reader. John Richetti describes such post-rape narrative moments, which abound in Haywood's amatory prose, as "a breathless rush of erotic / pathetic clichés that is in a real sense unreadable. Such prose is designed to be scanned hastily, not to be pondered closely or logically as language and thought but to evoke by its conventional formulas familiar and thrilling scenes."[41] If expression is defined as "the purposeful and effective use of the resources of language,"[42] then the seduced maiden is denied self-defining expression just at the moment she ceases to dissemble.

Luckily, our heroine "recollect[s] herself" in time to be other than herself (231), to craft the alias and story of Fantomina. Complete disaster is averted by her ability to dissemble once again, yet her account, while misleading in terms of her name and background, remains true to her motivations: "She told him so much of the Truth, as to what related to the Frolic she had taken of satisfying her curiosity in what Manner Mistresses, of the Sort she appeared to be, were treated by those who addressed them" (231). "Truth" here equals her emotional and intellectual inclinations. Much like Mrs. Graspall's, her untrue stories enable her to talk safely and honestly about her feelings; they allow her to make these admissions without ceasing to perform.

This ability is best demonstrated in her final appearance as the "Incognita," what is at once the heroine's most overtly theatrical and most honest role. Her new insistence on obscuring her face—she wears a mask, has sex in a pitch-black, heavily curtained room, and meets her lover the next morning, masked again—seems at first quite odd. By this point, Beauplaisir has seen her face many times in different disguises with no result; because "she had the Power of putting on almost what Face she pleased" (238), there is no easy link between Fantomina's face and her identity. To unmask would not automatically expose her to ruin or make her "known." The importance of this final mask, then, is not that it hides her face or her identity, but that it reveals the fact of her performance and her ability to maintain it. She advertises her inaccessibility even as she unveils, through her masking, the fact of her continued masquerade.[43] This is also the first time Fantomina becomes threatening to Beauplaisir—not so much because she is more open about her sexual desires, but because after sex she can leave Beauplaisir, quite literally, in the dark.

Still, protean as she is, Fantomina can control her shape-shifting for only so long. She discovers that she is pregnant, the growing fetus a physical threat to her future ability to dissemble. Yet as the narrative distinguishes between the external and internal effects of pregnancy, it illustrates that it is not the body per se, but compulsions that move the body—those "inward Agitations of the Soul" (247)—that betray our heroine. The gradual external changes she is able to monitor and disguise, thanks to "eating little, lacing prodigious strait, and the Advantage of a great Hoop-Petticoat" (246); it is the internal effects of imminent labor that cannot be anticipated or hidden. Fantomina is transformed by "the sudden Rack which all at once invaded her," and her "wildly rolling Eyes, the Distortion of her Features, and the Convulsions which shook her whole Frame, in spite of her" (246) represent extreme versions of previous involuntary responses, the emotional outbursts that follow the loss of her virginity. All such sensations are dangerous because unfamiliar and unanticipated: she has *not* had them before.

If Fantomina's onset of labor pains and her resulting collapse illustrate the danger of impulsive behaviors, her response to this collapse illustrates the redemptive nature of repetition. Impulsive actions cannot be undone, but, if repeated, they retroactively become rehearsals. In Fantomina's case, she triumphs over her involuntary exposé by repeating it on her own terms. At the urging of her mother, she "relates the whole Truth" to her mother and Beauplaisir (248), a narrative that marks a distinct change from the involuntary struggles of labor and the involuntary admissions that these struggles forced her to utter. And instead of exposing her former roles, this final explication reinserts them within the larger performance she has scripted. Her listeners' reactions are a testament to its power: her mother and Beauplaisir remain for some time "in a profound Revery," and Beauplaisir leaves "more confused than ever he had known in his whole Life" (248).

Fantomina's final, summary tale of passion is at once repetitive, autobiographical, and strategic. Repetition in this final scene involves saying more than doing: Fantomina describes her previous exploits as opposed to reenacting them. But as she ends her story by retelling it, we are encouraged to loop back to the beginning of the tale and to recall en route her first foray into both deceptive actions and story-telling, that titular anecdote of the country girl Fantomina. If her first story conveys "so much of the Truth" framed by the inventions of her alias and background, her final narrative conveys "the whole Truth," even as it rearticulates her repeated deceptions (231, 248). Fantomina's staged confession—so similar to Mrs. Graspall's final scene—demonstrates again that for Haywood's women truth is produced as artifice is reproduced. In this case, truth is produced through a narration that reflects self-consciously on the narrative structure of the story we read, ourselves.

It is telling, then, that the closing lines of *Fantomina* point to an achievement that can refer to the heroine's sexual escapades—or to the author's account of them: "thus ended an Intrigue, which, considering the Time it lasted, was as full of Variety as any, perhaps, that many Ages has produced" (248). Exploits and tales are both at an end, and Fantomina has seduced her lover in much the same way Haywood has seduced her reader. This story closes with what can be read as a meditation on authorship, and an exploration of those authorial strategies that can remain remarkably consistent, even as the forms of authorship vary. In this, Fantomina's bedside confession will have ramifications for Haywood's later career; it provides a final example of how "Variety" and desire are simultaneously expressed, not in one-night stands or impulsive admissions, but in Intrigues, both narrative and sexual, that are constantly staged and repeated.

THE DIDACTIC NOVELIST AND THE THOUGHTLESS HEROINE

Yet from the time Haywood published *Fantomina*, in 1725, to the appearance of her novel *The History of Miss Betsy Thoughtless*, in 1751, much had changed—in her career, in British politics, and in popular literature. Just how much is evidenced by Haywood's novelistic reflections on the state of the stage:

> All that troubled Miss Betsy now, was, that her brother happened to come to London at a season of the year, in which he could not receive the least satisfaction . . . there were no plays, no operas, no masquerades, no balls, no public shews, except at the little theatre in the Haymarket, then known by the name of F_____g's scandal shop; because he frequently exhibited there certain drolls, or, more properly, invectives against the ministry: in doing which it appears extremely probable, that he had two views; the one to get money, which he very much wanted, from such as delighted in low humor, and could not distinguish true satire from scurrility; and the other, in the hope of having some post given him by those whom he had abused, in order to silence his dramatic talent.[44]

The heroine of Haywood's final novel, Miss Betsy, laments that her brother arrives during London's "off-season," possibly dating this reference to the summer of 1735. At this time, Charles Fleetwood had closed down Drury Lane, and the Little Haymarket was the one of the few venues available for summer players and summer plays.[45] The Haymarket was also under the management of Henry Fielding, the F_____g of Haywood's "scandal shop," whose "invectives against the ministry" would soon (as Haywood, writing in 1751, well knew) result in the Theater Licensing Act of 1737 and the end of his theatrical career. While Fielding's connection to the Licensing Act was common knowledge, Haywood had an insider's perspective; she had worked closely with Fielding at the Haymarket—indeed, she had acted in two of the "invectives" (*The Historical Register* and *Eurydice Hiss'd*) that resulted in the theater's closure. This rather lengthy attack on her former partner is therefore, according to Beth Fowkes Tobin, "somewhat surprising."[46]

Regardless of the exact motivations behind Haywood's critique, it shows, again, that much has changed: Haywood's attitude toward her colleague, the general attitude toward the theater—and the role of the novel in publicizing these sentiments. The theater, traditionally a place for staging political discontent, had overstepped its boundaries (Peter Lewis dubs *The Historical Register* and *Eurydice Hiss'd* as containing "the most audacious political satire that had ever appeared on the English stage"[47]), and with the Licensing Act, the development of drama in London would be stifled for centuries. But as the very title of Haywood's novel suggests, another genre now encouraged audiences to approach it with the same "willing suspension of disbelief" they once brought to the stage.[48]

The Licensing Act did more than prompt authors such as Haywood and Fielding to turn to novels instead of plays. It prompted these authors to turn to novels *and* to frame those novels as fictional. The lull in theatrical activity that postdates the Licensing Act coincides with a spurt of novel writing;

it also coincides with the novel's tendency to reveal its own fictionality, to "reveal . . . the conventions to which it has decided to submit."[49] The novel's evolution into a overtly fictional genre—a genre that made a virtue of its fictional nature—can be read as a re-direction of theatrical strategies that existed prior to the 1737 Theater Licensing Act and a response to criticism levied at an early eighteenth-century stage that, in becoming overly satirical, had ceased to expose its own fabricated character. These mid-century trends in plays and novels register as complementary historical shifts.

The tendency for readers and authors to embrace novels as fictional thus suggests a revised understanding of what was considered threatening about the theater and its conventions. While earlier antitheatricalists could criticize the stage for its innately deceptive potential, the Licensing Act identified the theater as an overly referential space, dangerous for its connections to current events and political scandal.[50] In the process, the theater also became dangerous for the interpretative discrepancies it could introduce through the staging of these events. The Licensing Act necessarily identified theater not only as a forum for political commentary, but as a venue for the imitative abilities that produced deception, rather than a place of innate deceitfulness manifested through staged and imaginary characters. As the stage became too true to life, it called attention to the discrepancies that imitative behavior inevitably generates, despite the similarity it essays to preserve.

At roughly the same historical moment, the novel was being presented as innately untrue. As Catherine Gallagher has noted, fiction became a valued, positive characteristic of novels at the middle of the century, so that novels of this time were more clearly demarcated as tales of events that never actually happened, people who never actually lived.[51] *The History of Miss Betsy Thoughtless* fits into this trajectory, even as it appropriates a long-standing stage tradition in which an external appellation is representative of internal character traits. The title's assertion that this tale is a "history" is immediately derailed by the stereotypical name that follows; the title announces a character-type, a general individual who is realistic yet has no historical reference.[52] While this borrowed stage convention reflects the fact that novels were becoming more open about, and their readers more comfortable with, the idea of fiction, Haywood's novel concurrently becomes the place, as her attack on Fielding demonstrates, for the real-life "invectives" that formerly held the stage. More overtly fictional (and more overtly didactic) than her early "secret histories," Haywood's later novel functions as a space for personal expression, and the strategies of expression sketched in her earlier works suggest it may do so because its fictionality is more blatant.

In criticizing Fielding, Haywood was getting both personal—he had criticized her, or at least novel writers like her, in *The Author's Farce, Joseph Andrews,* and *Tom Jones*—and professional. Fielding had been and continued to be a competitor as much as a colleague. By the 1750s, he and Samuel Richardson had set a new standard for the popular novel, which was at least superficially in opposition to Haywood's earlier narrative style. Haywood's attempt to disassociate herself from Fielding's "scandal shop" reminds us of Fielding's "scandalous" origins even as it is couched in a novel that is advertised as an attempt to disassociate herself from her own. The novel, once a place for romance, had now become a place for manners, and Miss Betsy is correspondingly more restrained in (or more oblivious to) her sexual desire than the indulgent Fantomina. Yet the space between eroticism and propriety is not as vast or as un-bridgeable as authors such as Richardson would have it; just as *Pamela* remains suspect for its titillating tendencies, Haywood's later works remain indebted to her earlier roots.[53]

Kathryn King wisely cautions "of the dangers of splitting [Haywood's] oeuvre into opposing literary types and its creator into two Haywoods: early and late, scandalous and moralizing, erotic and reformed."[54] While King's warning can be applied more broadly to the way eighteenth-century fiction as a body is perhaps too strictly relegated to "opposing literary types . . . early and late, scandalous and moralizing, erotic and reformed," there are formal and thematic links among Haywood's works that reflect Haywood's own shifting career from playwright to novelist and beyond. *The History of Miss Betsy Thoughtless*, a supposedly very different and didactic novel, recasts explicitly theatrical scenes from *Fantomina*, while Fantomina and Miss Betsy, heroines considered by critics to be diametrically opposed, both come to adopt strategies of self-conscious performance. As Haywood places characters who do not have Fantomina's foresight into situations that bear striking parallels to scenes in *Fantomina*, the unfortunate consequences illustrate that by the 1750s, female sexuality in the novel must be condemned and not indulged. But these scenarios also remind us of how and why Fantomina succeeded where these heroines fail. The happy ending of Haywood's novel therefore celebrates not so much the rewards of virtue as Betsy's mastery of Fantomina's methods. It also models Haywood's approach to her own career, and her decision to recast scenes from her own amatory fiction into her periodicals and later novels.

As in *Fantomina*, the seduction scene (or the near-seduction scene) is repeated throughout Haywood's novel, yet instead of depicting a seduction planned and consummated by the heroine, this novel dwells on Betsy's near-rapes and narrow escapes. And as the title indicates, Betsy's "thoughtlessness" is to blame. Her careless and impulsive nature means she has an inability to reflect on the consequences of actions already committed, or to anticipate consequences before they have occurred; instead, she mindlessly imitates behaviors presented to her by society. While the novel posits this kind of female mimicry as responsible for the resulting threat of rape, the similarities between Betsy's actions and Fantomina's show it is not her behaviors, but the level of self-consciousness that motivates her behaviors, that determines their danger to the heroine.

This comparison is encouraged when Miss Betsy reunites in London with her school friend Miss Forward at a play. In its setting and implications, the scene is reminiscent of the opening of *Fantomina*, down to the seating arrangements—as in *Fantomina*, the house is full when they arrive, so Miss Betsy and her friend must sit up front. Yet while Fantomina purposefully engineers her seating arrangements and the expectations they encourage,[55] Miss Betsy is a much more passive, and trusting, figure. Unaware that her friend is now a kept mistress, she is thus also unaware that the gentlemen who flirt with them assume she, too, is conscious, even desirous, of their sexual expectations (204). Whereas Fantomina goes to the theater precisely to be seen, Betsy goes "to see the play, not to be seen myself" (202). And whereas Fantomina engineers her ensuing conversations, Betsy finds herself accosted unexpectedly by her male companion and violently alarmed. Her terror and objections barely convince her escort that she is not what she appears to be, a tragic potential that suggests she would have been better served by making a spectacle of herself.

Miss Betsy needs a model for premeditated female behavior, but standard coquetry, the most obvious example, will not solve her problems. In this novel, Haywood also revises *Fantomina's* Incognita intrigue to reinforce once more the tragically temporary power of the typical coquette. When Miss Flora, the daughter of Miss Betsy's guardian, finds herself smitten with Miss Betsy's lover (the somewhat controversially termed "Trueworth"), she writes him a letter as "Incognita" in which she proposes a rendezvous.[56] The combination of anonymous letter and disguise permit her to vocalize her desire while protecting her reputation, and both objects frame the meeting as staged. Yet her influence will be short-lived. In a shift that recalls Beauplaisir's reaction to his Incognita—"as much Satisfaction as he found in her Embraces, nothing ever longed for the Approach of Day with more Impatience than he did" (*Fantomina*, 245)—Trueworth's desire to identify subsumes his sexual passion. In this place of sexual intrigue, Haywood tells us that, "the discovery of her face was what [Trueworth] chiefly wanted" (270). Haywood's libertines desire to "know" their women in a sexual and intellectual sense, a conflation that Trueworth, at least, achieves. When he leads his still anonymous lover to a darkened room and begs that she remove her mask, Miss Flora, unlike Fantomina, agrees. "'Well,' cried she, 'you are not to be resisted, and I will venture'" (271).

While her unmasking does not immediately end or even dampen the intrigue, it shifts the power dynamic, making Trueworth the player and Miss Flora the played-upon. As Trueworth falls in love with the virtuous Miss Harriot Loveit, Flora in her turn must at least superficially "fall in with Mr. Trueworth's way of thinking,—seem to be convinced by his reasons, and ready to submit to whatever suited with his interest or convenience" (350). Similarly, Betsy's careless actions allow others to impose their own expectations on her. Her refusal to dissemble puts her under the control of libertines and rakes; more seriously, it finally places her under the control of Mr. Munden, a mercenary, bad-tempered, and unfaithful husband.

Yet it is also Miss Betsy's unhappy marriage that teaches her how to reflect on her feelings and frame them as a performance. Even Betsy's guardian Lady Trusty uses the metaphor when she explains to Betsy that she has "entered into a state, the happiness of which greatly depends on the part you act in the first scenes of it" (436). This lesson, according to Richard Barney, aligns Betsy uncomfortably with the contemporary sense of female hypocrisy; the married Betsy progresses from her initial "aversion to dissimulation" (167) to an ability "to engage in a kind of 'honest' theater, in which she assumes the role of self-reflective and virtuous woman."[57] Barney uses the term "honest" to juxtapose her performance with Miss Flora's more overtly manipulative one, but keeps the term in quotation marks, playing off the antitheatrical assumption that theater and acting inevitably involve some level of dissimulation and deceit. Yet Betsy does gain powers of reflection, and by considering the possible consequences of her speech and action, she becomes capable of planning her actions in a way that will allow her to express—safely, virtuously—her true feelings for Trueworth.

Miss Betsy's practiced self-control ultimately frames a space from within which she can articulate her feelings of desire, exemplified first in the written correspondence she maintains with a widowed Trueworth for the year after her own husband dies. This dialogue allows her to achieve that paradox of passionate indulgence and control, to "maintai[n] that reserve, which she thought the situation demanded, and at the same time indul[ge] the tenderness of her heart for a man" (559). And in their first meeting after the year of separation, Betsy and Trueworth receive full gratification in a passage that runs very much counter to Beth Tobin's statement that in "*Miss Betsy Thoughtless* . . . the explicit delineation of female sexual desire is erased." As Betsy and Trueworth are as yet unmarried, neither does the passage fit into Tobin's later claim that "marriage was the only space (if any) where women could legitimately experience sexual desire":[58]

> Prepared as she was by the expectation of his arrival, all her presence of mind was not sufficient to enable her to stand the sudden rush of joy, which on sight of him burst in upon her heart;—nor was he less overcome,—he sprang into her arms, which of themselves opened to receive him, and while he kissed away the tears that trickled from her eyes, his own bedewed her cheeks.—'Oh have I lived to see you thus!'—cried he,—'thus ravishingly kind!'—'And have I lived,' rejoined she, 'to receive these proofs of affection from the best and most ill used of men.' (564)

The reactions of both parties are impulsive and sexual, but this time the result is one of joy and not disaster. The meeting has been carefully planned; reserve breaks down in a moment that has been staged to create a safe space for spontaneity.

And yet . . . Betsy is not completely responsible for her own bliss. The very convenient deaths of Mr. Munden and Mrs. Harriot Trueworth leave Miss Betsy and Mr. Trueworth free, finally, to marry—an improbable circumstance that "call[s] attention to the artificiality of the plot structure that allows such a reversal of fortune to occur."[59] We are encouraged to recognize the ending of this novel as artificial, unrealistic, contrived. But we are not encouraged to dismiss it. According to Fielding, such departures from verisimilitude could be valuable, since "the great art of poetry is to mix truth with fiction, in order to join the credible with the surprising"; these improbable coincidences are what "ma[ke] it possible to weave the whole narrative into a very neat and entertaining formal structure."[60] The staged nature of Betsy's happy ending reminds us that the novelistic narrative is itself an artistic performance. Haywood's conclusion recalls the techniques of her heroines, who mix truth within fiction, and who invoke theatricality as a frame for truth.

PARROTING ONESELF

Haywood's tendency to recycle material into later, more didactic publications lends a staged quality to all her textual productions. Final, concrete evidence of this tendency appears as Haywood's late career periodical, *The Parrot, with a Compendium of the Times* (1746), repeats the plot of her 1726 tale of intrigue, *The Mercenary Lover*.[61] Haywood's earlier version of the intrigue details Clitander's attempts to gain the fortune of both his wife and his wife's sister, Althea,[62] while Haywood's later collection of moralizing essays includes a parallel, cautionary tale of a young Heiress who becomes the victim of a mercenary and married clerk.[63] The one significant difference is that in the periodical, the omniscient narrator is replaced by a parrot: the recycled nature of the anecdote is emphasized by attributing it to a persona whose expressive powers are dependent on repetition.

Still, this is no ordinary talking bird. While Haywood's speaker does exhibit the parrot-like tendency to "report whatever [he] heard," he also "scorn[s] the mean Subterfuges of Equivocation and Evasion, and, above all Things, detest[s] a Lye" (183). He styles himself, therefore, as

> not a meer Parrot, which without Distinction utters all that he hears, and is the Eccho of every foolish Rumor; but a Thing—a Thing to which I cannot give a Name, but I mean a Thing sent by the Gods, and by them inspired to utter only sacred Truths. (185)

This Poll is not a mindless, garrulous mimic but a sentient being, whose repetitiveness and verbosity account for his ability to disseminate "sacred Truths."

If Haywood's "parrot" is quite a singular example of the species, her "parroting" strategy is quite singular as well. Catherine Ingrassia observes that

Haywood's periodical "'parrot[s]' both the rumors floating around her and the style of other periodicals," making this new persona enact his author's narrative techniques. [64] Yet this is not quite the parodic approach that Ingrassia would claim, of "simultaneously engaging in an attempt to secure a commercial success . . . while disengaging herself . . . through her imitative and repetitive gestures."[65] Through the parrot, Haywood repeats a tale that she has told before, but her new mouthpiece advertises very different benefits to such repetition. As confessional moments in Haywood are repeatedly structured around the reiteration of fictional exploits, the truth of retold stories rests not in the initially factual nature of the tale that is told, but in the veracity of the teller—in telling them again, the teller becomes a truth-teller.[66] As her new persona repeats a story crafted by a previous iteration of his current author, he illustrates a strategy that is not simply one of disengagement: the more roles, the more stories, the more fictions that we have, the greater access we have to the "sacred Truth" of the author who creates them.

Finding the woman in her fiction is thus dependent on finding the fictions in the woman, such that authorial statements are inevitably mediated, even when (especially when) they claim to be least so. What seemingly autobiographical assertions we have from Haywood—for example, her introduction to *The Female Spectator,* in which she claims to "give some Account of what I am"[67]—cannot be read literally without unjustly simplifying Haywood's authorial technique: Haywood's confession here would have resonated with her contemporary audience as a bit of deliberate persona-making.[68] Yet to recognize personae as such is not to admit to the ultimate inaccessibility of identity; instead, it is to revise our understanding of how identity can be known. Haywood's ingonitas cannot unmask without effacing the very identity that unmasking would offer to reveal. Theatrical performance thus becomes privileged as the conduit for self-defining characteristics.

It is finally quite telling that of all the genres Haywood attempted, she never wrote anything explicitly cast as an autobiography.[69] Instead, she quite intentionally made the historian's and critic's job more difficult by placing

> a solemn injunction on a person, who was well acquainted with all the particulars of [her life], not to communicate to any one the least circumstance relating to her; so that probably, unless some very ample account should appear from that quarter itself . . . the world will still be left in the dark with regard to it.[70]

Haywood purposefully frustrates all attempts to unearth the "real" Haywood from beneath the various constructed roles, yet the context of her own work should render this obscurity less trying. Like Beauplaisir when faced with his veiled Incognita, we often forget that masks convey as much as they obscure. In Haywood's own terms, identity is crafted through repeated performances, and such performances, if they are to be perpetuated, require the performer to maintain a level of obscurity about herself.

Haywood, then, had a desire to keep performing, a desire to keep writing. And by her own terms knowing that is enough. She tells us that the true (and truthful) Haywood is in her fictions—not behind them.

GENERIC EVOLUTIONS: HAYWOOD TO BURNEY

If one may find the eighteenth-century woman in her fiction, it is significant that by the 1750s fiction was not hard to find. The advertisement of fiction that marked later eighteenth-century novels also marked the novels of Haywood's later career. Yet this shift for Haywood perpetuates the function of her earlier experiments in ostensibly "non-fictional" prose. Both narrative forms claim to efface personal expression: either, like Haywood's "eye-witness" accounts of intrigue, or even her parrot's stories, the narrative claims to be simply a factual reiteration of others' behaviors, or, in the case of overtly fictional tales, the narrative insists it has no foundation in the real world at all. Both scenarios, in my argument, create the very space for thoughts and feelings that the frame disavows; indeed, both may characterize the prose narratives produced by men or women.[71] But for certain women writers, the tendency to embrace novels as fictional coincides with a growing and articulated anxiety about repetition as a narrative strategy. This anxiety can be seen in Haywood's increasing efforts to distance herself (superficially at least) from her formulaic literary past, and the same anxieties are evident in the career and literary philosophies of the next author in this study, Frances Burney. The question then becomes why repetition, a safe, strategic way by which to disavow personal investment, becomes recognized by these authors as dangerous and unacceptable, and what this may say, more generally, about the shifting conventions of eighteenth-century novels and plays.[72]

"In all the Arts," Burney writes in the preface to *Evelina* (1778), her first published novel,

> the value of copies can only be proportioned to the scarceness of originals: among sculptors and painters, a fine statue, or a beautiful picture, of some great master, may deservedly employ the imitative talents of younger and inferior artists, that their appropriation to one spot, may not wholly prevent the more general expansion of their excellence; but, among authors, the reverse is the case, since the noblest productions of literature, are almost equally attainable with the meanest. In books, therefore, imitation cannot be shunned too sedulously; for the very perfection of a model which is frequently seen, serves but more forcibly to mark the inferiority of a copy. (8)

Repetition, or in Burney's words, imitation, is here disavowed partly on aesthetic grounds; as in the Platonic tradition, the copy is always inferior to the original. But Burney's concern with "copies" in this passage is less about their inherent deficiency and more about the extent to which the discrepancy between original and copy can be perceived. In writing, as opposed to other forms of art, the good originals are accessible and circulated, so that the derivation of the copy is more evident to the audience of readers. The danger in repeating something is that, as Burney's diatribe illustrates, one cannot do so exactly, and the imitation—that pretends to be like, but isn't, quite—will, if perceived, be construed as more artificial in its pretensions than the imagined original, which has no model from which to go astray. This risk highlights the inevitable discrepancies that accompany any act of imitation, discrepancies that make referentiality within art into an act of deception, not a laudable attempt at verisimilitude. Significantly, these were the same risks that the satirical theater of the earlier eighteenth century had exposed: the theater that, in advertising its connections to real life, both produced and obscured its own departures from it.

Elizabeth Inchbald, writing almost thirty years later, would reinforce these connections. While condemning the strictures that the Licensing Act placed upon dramatic composition, Inchbald applauds the creative freedom enjoyed by the novelist: "the novel-writer has the whole world to range, in search of men and topics . . . Nothing is forbidden, nothing is withheld from the imitation of a novelist, except—other novels."[73] What Inchbald makes more evident is that a certain type of imitation is acceptable: novelists (more so than the still-censured playwrights) can imitate events from life; they simply should not imitate each other. And if we read Burney's formulation carefully, we notice that her celebrated "originals" are not necessarily the real world referents, but the first artistic renditions of real world referents: both women specifically condemn the imitative tendencies of the author or artist, not the work itself. But the two issues inevitably conflate, and Clifford Siskin notes how "efforts to reconcile imitation of other novelists with imitation of the real produced almost disabling levels of distinction."[74] Indeed, the novelist who appropriates a hackneyed style for her own, and the referential novel that masquerades as a "slice of life," may be criticized in similar, theatrical terms: as deceitful performers "wholly intent on concealing [their] tricks."[75]

The fear of this particular type of criticism, and its links to propriety, are especially evident in Burney's novels and journals. Provocatively, Burney herself was known to be a talented mimic and was often pestered by friends to entertain them with her impersonations—requests that she insists she could not fulfill. "Though I had run on in Mrs. Holroyd's way, to Mrs. Thrale for half an Hour together," she admits, "it had been *accidentally*, & when some of her *Cackle* just *occurred* to me, not *deliberately*, & by *way* of exhibition."[76] If repetition is scandalous or misleading, it is also, throughout Burney's work, disavowed on the grounds that it exposes a conscious desire for attention that Haywood's work and career make all too apparent. While Haywood's parrot, for instance, insists that he is not responsible for the content of what he circulates, he is quite outspoken about his responsibility for its circulation. In contrast, Burney's journals criticize the conscious decision to imitate (through narration or impersonation) as that which produces inevitable discrepancies that can be labeled as deceptive, and as that which implies a desire for attention she finds particularly problematic. By the time Burney takes up her pen, the originality of an artistic production, its acknowledged lack of referent, characterizes it for her as a once in a lifetime, unanticipated event that is therefore forgivable in its appearance and honest in its representations.

The focus of Burney's novels also responds to these anxieties, and their link to propriety, by shifting away from Haywood's rehearsed displays of feeling and toward depictions of spontaneous emotion. The fainting heroines that litter the pages of her novels—and the novels of her contemporaries— embody the demand for originality, for completely unrehearsed behavior, that the fictional convention of the novel itself reinforced. Of course, as Fielding's cynical readings of Pamela's swoons would make clear, new objections to this response quickly arose. Sentimental behaviors became themselves recognized as convention and susceptible to charges of deliberation.

So if, as Haywood's biographer George Whicher claims, the step from *Miss Betsy Thoughtless* (1751) to Frances Burney's *Evelina* (1778) was a comparatively small one, it was nevertheless a step.[77] Both novels are examples of didactic and sentimental literature, but from the 1750s to the 1770s, the "cult of sensibility" became less about teaching propriety in emotional response (or non-response), and more about encouraging any emotional reaction through the text's exploitations of excessive feeling. As the century progressed, sentimental literature "prided itself more on making its readers weep and in teaching them when and how much to weep."[78] In so doing, such literature responded to the growing assumption that the consciousness of feeling could and should be developed. But the conscious exploitation of feeling subjected emotion to the possibility of manipulation; in practice this belief meant that anyone, at any time they desired, could learn to show evidence that they were "sensible." As a result, expressions of feeling became less reliable or respected, and "from the 1780s onwards, sentimental literature and the principles behind it were bombarded with criticism and ridicule."[79] These displays of feeling were devalued both by their proliferation, and by their increasingly conscious and public nature.

What this literature of the later eighteenth century did, then, was to publicize a concept of emotional expression that writers such as Haywood had deployed in a much more subtle manner. Its perceived goal was to manipulate, and to teach its readers when and how to manipulate, a sign of feeling. The theatrical tendency of novels to duplicate and control emotions—an investment in what Janet Todd calls "a kind of pedagogy of seeing and of the physical reaction that this seeing should produce"[80]—eventually left readers and spectators attuned to, but skeptical of, this approach to feeling and expression. This cult of sentimental display also corresponded to a resurgence in theatrical activity, and as sentimentality was being ridiculed as overly theatrical in novels, it was also, concurrently, finding its way back to the stage (much to Goldsmith's chagrin).[81] The contradictory attitudes of late eighteenth-century culture, which at once wanted to cultivate feeling and preserve its innate character, are encompassed in the tensions between the major genres of the time: the theater, which epitomized the practiced display of emotion, and the novel, which increasingly foregrounded, only to problematize, spontaneous outbursts of sentimentality.

The remainder of this book traces the effect of these tensions, both aesthetic and professional, on late eighteenth-century developments in plays and novels. Again, the focus remains on the woman writer, as the subject for whom these tensions remain most powerful and problematic. By the end of the century, Mary Wollstonecraft's brand of feminism would have conflated with ideas about sentiment to produce an intense antagonism to female artifice; Wollstonecraft in particular sought to combat the hypocritical conduct that sentimental codes required of women and that threatened to make dissimulation into the defining characteristic of the sex.[82] Yet the latter authors in this study all dispute this antagonism by redeeming acts of artifice and dissimulation; such acts become exactly what enable a woman to comply with Wollstonecraft's demands, to reveal that she has "that within that passeth show."[83]

Such redemption extended from a woman's social to her literary conduct. The turn to the novel, and to fiction, countered assumptions about theatricality that haunted both the eighteenth-century woman writer and the playhouse; as Gallagher puts it, "by mid-century, innocence had . . . become a hallmark of women's writing, one intimately connected both with the nonreferential, hence nonscandalous, 'pure' fiction they supposedly produced, and with the nonlibidinous, sexually passive 'nature' they newly claimed."[84] Fiction here is lauded for its nonreferential nature, its resulting links to "purity" or innocence. In this formulation, the woman novelist diffuses the conjoined anxieties about deceitfulness and display that targeted women—and an overly referential, scandalous eighteenth-century stage.

Due to professional complications that reflected insistently on social expectations specific to her sex, Frances Burney would find that her own relationship to genre inevitably invoked her relationship to emotional expression: what literary form it was or was not appropriate for her to employ was directly linked to the question of how she should appropriately convey her feelings. As a woman writer working in the latter part of the century, Burney found herself working within certain established expectations; she was required to communicate, as Gallagher observes, "innocently," through "pure" and "passive" channels. Yet these very restrictions could produce, even be used to manage, the emotional displays that were required to be spontaneous and non-theatrical in nature. As Burney and her heroines would discover, eighteenth-century prohibitions on theatrical expression could be enough to make one faint—albeit in a carefully premeditated way.

3 Forgetting the Self
Frances Burney and Staged Insensibility

The works and career of Frances Burney exemplify a late eighteenth-century conundrum—as authors were called upon to deny the staged elements of expression, in their lives and in their writing, the very act of denial produced the staged qualities it was meant to negate. For Burney's heroines, expression evolves from the very opposite characteristics of silence and repression, as they communicate their feelings through a symbol associated at once with emotional excess and excessive restraint: the swoon. The scenes and vocabulary of unconsciousness that proliferate in Burney's work navigate the late-eighteenth-century ambivalence toward theatricality. They answer contemporary anxieties about conscious display (because one is literally insensible to any resulting spectacle), artifice or deception (because one is genuinely unconscious), and repetition (because in most cases the swoon is either so extreme as to be fatal, or so climactic as to end the book or play). But the recurrence of these moments, and their acknowledged effectiveness throughout Burney's work, hint at a paradoxically conscious deployment of unconsciousness. As Burney explores how prohibitions on feeling lead inevitably to an involuntary emotional breakdown, her work also exposes the fact that this repression, if itself controlled, can be used to coordinate when and how the emotional breakdown occurs.

For Burney's suffering heroines, such spectacular breakdowns are as efficacious as they are damaging, in that they enable her heroines to communicate previously repressed internal torments so that they are acknowledged and responded to by an audience. Yet if the efficacy of spectacle is that it is noticed, the drawback is that it often and obviously wants to be noticed, and a perverse audience will look the other way if this appeal is made too consciously. Samuel Richardson, a forerunner in the engineering of unconsciousness, would experience this reaction firsthand, as Fielding famously mocked both Pamela and her author for the manipulative effect of her repeated swoons. Richardson at least had anticipated this criticism within his own novel; like Fielding, Mrs. Jewkes scoffs at Pamela's fits, assuring Mr. B that women feign insensibility merely to escape the sexual demands of men.[1] In her early novels, Burney tries to remove this suspicion by presenting the moment of insensibility as involuntary and brought on by the heroine's too assiduous compliance with societal dictates of decorum. Evelina and Cecilia are good girls who unintentionally make spectacles of themselves. They collapse without planning to, and when Evelina faints during Mr. Macartney's suicide attempt, she showcases both her emotional turmoil and the accidental effect an unconscious female body has on its observers.[2]

But Burney's later heroines develop an increased regard for how this process may be staged, so that their physical torments, which often result in unconsciousness or death, are also often engineered by the heroine herself.[3] By purposefully adopting behaviors of extreme self-restraint, such as denying themselves food or sleep, these characters voluntarily initiate a physiological process that they understand will at some point escape their control. Examples here include the premeditated death of Albany's fiancée in *Cecilia* (1782), Camilla's death wish and subsequent "deathbed" scene in *Camilla* (1796), and Elinor Joddrel's second suicide attempt and subsequent swoon in *The Wanderer* (1814). These later heroines simultaneously exhibit and excuse the kind of agency over expression that Burney herself found so troubling about theatrical displays of feeling, and a theatrical career.

Studied mainly for her novels and letters, Frances Burney nonetheless exemplifies an eighteenth-century female author with an intense, vexed personal investment in the theater. Indeed, every novel she wrote was preceded, and followed, by an experiment with the stage (table 3.1). This chapter will emulate this pattern, interleaving readings of her novels with commentary on her dramatic compositions and her characterization of these compositions in her journals. The lines of influence between Burney's novels and plays that emerge thus exist on a formal level—in the way she repositions a heroine from her first, suppressed play into her subsequent novel, or in the way characters from this first play appear again in her final comedy, which itself repeats plot devices from her first novel, *Evelina*—and also on a biographical one. For example, her letters show that she was composing her third novel, *Camilla*, as she was revising her tragedy *Edwy and Elgiva*, and her decision to shift from one genre to the other is a clear result of her personal, professional experiences with the stage.

Such patterns do not underline a simplistic, causal claim—that Burney's novels are about her own problems in the theater—so much as they reveal that Burney's interest in the theater represents an interest in a certain type of expression, and that what Burney found attractive about the theater was exactly what she found problematic about it. Burney's own love-hate relationship to spectacle, carefully documented in her journals, reflects the dilemma of her fictional heroines. How could she guarantee herself a fair hearing, working in careers associated so perniciously with display? How could this desire for attention be mitigated, disguised? The idea of staged insensibility seems to be one way out of this dilemma, and Burney characterizes her own writing process in precisely these terms: she describes her literary productions, her novels and her plays, as unconscious creative endeavors, moments

Table 3.1   A Chronology of Frances Burney's Dramatic and Nondramatic Work

1767	Destroys her juvenilia in a bonfire on her fifteenth birthday: "farces and tragedies" among the papers burned.
1778	Publishes novel: *Evelina*.
1779	Completes dramatic comedy *The Witlings*: play suppressed.
1782	Publishes novel: *Cecilia*.
1786–1791	Resides at court as the Keeper of the Robes to Queen Charlotte. While there, composes four tragedies: *Edwy & Elgiva, Hubert de Vere, The Seige of Pevensey*, and *Elberta* (unfinished).
1793	*Hubert de Vere* accepted for production at Drury Lane; Burney later withdraws it in favor of *Edwy and Elgiva*.
1795	*Edwy and Elgiva* produced at Drury Lane for one night.
1796	Publishes novel: *Camilla*.
1797	Returns to *Hubert de Vere* with thoughts to publish it as a closet drama; no publisher approached.
1799	Comedy *Love and Fashion* accepted by Thomas Harris; withdrawn 2 February 1800.
ca.1799	Begins novel: *The Wanderer*.
1800–1802	Works on comedies *The Woman-Hater, A Busy Day* (neither produced).
1814	Publishes novel: *The Wanderer* (28 March).
	Resumes work on *Elberta* after her father's death (12 April).
1832	Publishes *The Memoirs of Doctor Burney*.
1836	Times readings of *Hubert de Vere* and *The Siege of Pevensey*.

of uncalled for artistic inspiration that render her oblivious to herself and her surroundings. But, like her heroines, she also seems remarkably adept at attaining, even engineering, this unconscious state.

STAGE FRIGHT, UNCONSCIOUS SPECTACLE, AND *EVELINA*

Burney's was a childhood full of theater. The family numbered David Garrick and George Colman the Elder among their close friends, and in addition to witnessing many visits and impromptu performances from Garrick himself, Burney was attending the theater before she was eight years old.[4] The stage would serve as a crucial creative and intellectual influence, for the woman who would become a compulsive writer could not read or write until sometime after her eighth birthday. What literature she knew before this time was gained by listening to and memorizing her sisters' lessons[5]— and by going to plays. Her father mentions how, after having seen a play in Mrs. Garrick's box, Frances would "take the actors off, and compose speeches for their characters; for she could not read them."[6] Not surprisingly then, while *Evelina* is Burney's first published work, it was preceded by several "Farces and Tragedies" that she famously destroyed in a bonfire on her fifteenth birthday, and her first novel's epistolary format echoes the dramatic assignment of dialogue she often employed in her juvenilia and early journals.

Burney, gifted with an incredible memory and imitative skill, would have been quite the actress herself, had she not suffered so severely from stage fright. Her niece Charlotte Barrett describes in her aunt "an under-current . . . of deep-feeling" that was "concealed by shyness, except when her own individuality was forgotten in the zest with which she would enact other personages. . . . But in company, or before strangers, she was silent, backward, and timid, even to sheepishness."[7] Barrett sketches a conflicted figure who enjoys performance for the expression of "deep-feelings" that are otherwise repressed, yet who can perform only when she forgets herself and never consciously before strangers. In this insecurity, Burney will resemble her early novelistic heroines, as her fear of display supposedly stands in the way of any intentional act of performance. Yet Barrett's observation also describes in Burney a suppressed affinity for theatrical behavior and a recognition that performance can be a medium for self-expression.

This paradoxical coexistence of stage fright and a desire to perform would extend beyond Burney's childhood years. About seven months prior to the publication of *Evelina*, Burney recalls her participation in an elaborate home theatrical sequence: Arthur Murphy's *The Way to Keep Him* followed by Henry Fielding's *Tom Thumb*. Burney agreed to play the parts of Mrs. Lovemore and Huncamunca, though at the actual performance she realized that she knew only two people in the audience and desired to give up the parts.[8] She testifies that she was "quite sick . . . I seemed seized with an Ague fit . . . I know not whether I spoke or not."[9] Her fear persisted for the entire first performance, and she declared herself "totally, wholly, & entirely—dissatisfied with myself . . . not once could I command my voice to any steadiness."[10] Yet fortunately for Burney, "[her] part & [her] spirits . . . had great simpathy [sic]" in these scenes.[11] The audience reads her misery as the feigned pathos and melancholy feelings of the character she portrays: "circumstances were so happily miserable for me, that I believe some of my auditors thought me a much better and more *artificial* actress than I really was & I had the satisfaction of hearing some few *buzzes* of approbation."[12] Far from inviting criticism, Burney's shaky performance draws praise for her acting ability—praise that, despite her stage fright, she seems singularly pleased to receive.

Still, her achievement threatens to be short-lived, since the comic Huncamunca precludes the sympathetic identification between terrified actor and tragic role that aided Burney before. Yet again a sympathetic identification emerges. Four-year-old Anna Maria Burney ("little Nancy") was cast in the

second piece as Tom Thumb, and Burney says that "seeing the first act, &
my being so much interested about Nance, made me quite forget my *self,*
&, to my great satisfaction, I found myself forsaken by the Horrors."[13] Burney is first paralyzed by the knowledge that she is unwillingly on display,
then relieved when she becomes absorbed in the performance before her,
"forgetting herself" and consequently captivating the audience.[14] Much like
Diderot's rejected actor of sensibility, who "forgets himself . . . forgets that
he is on a stage" and simply "is the very character he plays,"[15] Burney forgets both her position and individuality. In the process, she paradoxically
frees herself, as Barrett puts it, to give vent to that "under-current . . . of
deep-feeling" always and uniquely hers.[16]

Burney's first novelistic heroine, Evelina, relies on a similar process of
self-forgetting to bring catharsis. Evelina is always the unwilling center of
attention (with a certain tension between "always" and "unwilling"), and
her persistent discomfort with this position leads, in one particular occur-
rence, to near insensibility. After a fireworks display in Marylebone Gar-
dens, a shower of sparks causes Evelina to flee self-protectively, and she
finds herself separated unintentionally from her friends, alone and in need
of assistance. She fends off a strange man who "with great violence . . .
seize[s] [her] hand" and turns to two women for help (260). Yet she has
"sought protection from insult, of those who were themselves most likely to
offer it!" (261)—the women are prostitutes, who subject her to both physical and mental indignities. They laugh at and taunt her, and they also, like
the strange man, try to "h[o]ld [her] fast" (261). The sense of force increases
as the episode progresses. When Evelina finds her companions, the prostitutes declare they will join the party, and one "very boldly t[akes] hold of
[her] arm." Evelina again wishes to separate herself, but her arm "was held
so tight, I could not move it" (262).

The episode establishes a link between physical and emotional pressure.
While Evelina does not cry out, her friend Mr. Brown, similarly grasped
by the other prostitute, protests that "there's no need to squeeze one's arm
so!" and "Ladies, you hurt me like any thing!" (263, 264). Evelina's mute
suffering, by contrast, traps her in a vicious cycle; while her quiet stoicism
conforms to the codes of female decorum, Evelina ironically makes herself
even more noticeable by refusing to make a scene. As Ruth Yeazell claims,
Evelina persistently draws the public eye "because of her attempts to efface
herself,"[17] and specifically because such attempts produce the kind of spectacular breakdown they are meant to avoid. Burney depicts the repression
of emotions as producing additional emotions, so that the body becomes a
veritable time bomb, waiting to explode with pent-up feeling. In this case,
Evelina's toleration of the prostitutes' treatment leads to her being marched
before the gaze of her lover, Lord Orville, which in turn provokes new
emotions in Evelina that she cannot vocalize to Orville or, even later, to
Villars. She experiences "shame, vexation, and a thousand other feelings,
for which I have no expressions" (263). But though she cannot put feelings

into words, her body speaks to her inner turmoil: "so great was my emotion . . . I thought I should have fainted" (263).

This time, instead of fainting, Evelina finds herself endowed with almost masculine strength. Her emotional crisis enables her to "absolutely t[ea]r [her]self from the woman's arm" (263) and at least temporarily to regain her powers of speech. When Lord Orville returns, Evelina answers him "readily . . . and with . . . little constraint" (263). Yet the return of her own abashed silence reveals her gesture as only momentarily effective, and after Orville leaves she exclaims, "Had I been blessed with any presence of mind; I should instantly have explained to him the accident which occasioned my being in such terrible company;—but I have none!" (265). Instead, it is her very presence of mind, her continued consciousness of both her improper position and the questioning stare of Orville, that binds her tongue. To affect her spectators, Evelina must forget both the audience that terrifies her and her own consciousness of display.

This alternative effectiveness of insensibility is demonstrated in the climactic reconciliation scene between Evelina and her father. When Mrs. Selwyn must physically lead Evelina into the presence of Sir John Belmont (Evelina states that she would have "withdrawn [her hand], and retreated" [413]), Burney depicts her heroine as again, unwillingly, on display. And again she suffers an excess of emotion, only this time her feelings result in physical collapse. Once before Sir John, she screams, covers her face, and involuntarily sinks to the floor; the ineffective letters and admonitions of Evelina's friends and guardians, urging Sir John to accept her as his daughter by the abandoned Carolyn Evelyn, are replaced by the "speechless, motionless" body (413). Yet the sight of her has an instantaneous impact; Sir John exclaims, "My God! Does Caroline Evelyn still live! . . . yes, yes . . . thou art her child!" (413).

While Evelina's fits and faints are involuntary, the documented sense that excessive emotion produces them, and that certain (repressive) situations are designed to produce this excessive emotion, constructs a chain of causality that informs the production and effect of *Evelina* itself. Burney would often characterize her own writing in terms synonymous with those surrounding female collapse, and she would describe the composition of *Evelina* as an involuntary reaction to emotional repression. Though she burned her early works, she insists that "the passion [to write] . . . though resisted, was not annihilated: my bureau was cleared; but my head was not emptied; and, in defiance of every self-effort, Evelina struggled herself into life."[18] In defiance of—or perhaps because of every self-effort? Burney's half-sister, Sarah Harriet Burney, attests that while Burney "looked and generally spoke with the most refined modesty . . . what was kept back and scarcely suspected in society, wanting a safety-valve found its way to her private journal."[19] As Burney's novel itself suggests, this carefully maintained "refined modesty" is exactly what produces the need for a "safety-valve," and her private journal was obviously not her only outlet.

Evelina, Burney's literary "outburst," made her a spectacle much like her title heroine. Though she published *Evelina* anonymously, her anonymity gradually wore off, and her journal is replete with descriptions of staring fans and the discomfort they cause her: "they stared at me every Time I came near them as if I had been a thing for a *shew,* surveyed me from top to bottom, & then, *again & again & again* returned to my *Face* with so determined & so unabating a curiosity, that it really made me uncomfortable."[20] She defends herself from any charges of voluntary display, maintaining that she never intended her authorship to come to light: "My *printing* it, indeed . . . tells terribly against me . . . but I had so little notion of being *discovered,* & was so well persuaded that the Book would never be *heard of,* that I really *thought* myself as safe, & *meant* to be as private, when the Book was at Mr. Lowndes's [her publisher], as when it was in my own Bureau."[21] Burney's professed discomfort and her defense demonstrate a need to convince others, and perhaps herself, that she was completely insensible of any audience when she wrote this book. Burney describes her novel, like Evelina's attention-getting swoon, as the involuntary product of desperately repressed emotion. Whatever effect the woman as spectacle can have on her audience is therefore something that she is not responsible for, a threatening result drawn from her obedience to the conventions of decorum. And yet, the novels and journals indicate Burney's awareness that the repression she maintains will produce the very result she professes to detest and avoid.

STAGING INSENSIBILITY: *THE WITLINGS* AND *CECILIA*

About a year and a half after the publication of *Evelina*, with the fact of her authorship now widely known, Burney records the following episode in her journal:

> While we were talking of our Brighthelmstone acquaintance, Mrs. Thrale told Mr. Fuller that I could imitate Mrs. Holroyd's voice & manner very exactly,—which, indeed, may soon be done . . . Mr. Fuller was highly diverted at the intelligence . . . he flew *to* me, & *at* me, eagerly entreating me to exhibit:—I could, however, *so soon bite off my own Nose* as stand forth to perform, at demand, any thing that I previously knew was to draw all Eyes upon me.[22]

While describing the events of a June afternoon at Streatham, Burney also testifies, in extreme terms, to her feelings about public display. When Mr. Fuller keeps pestering her, Burney finally protests, "I really had no *power* to offer myself for a *spectacle.*"[23] Burney's phrasing indicates that the idea of deliberate performance for the sake of display would render her a *spectacle,* and she emphasizes the term in a manner that suggests its most negative connotation.[24] But her additional emphasis on the word "power" suggests that more than distaste prevents her from complying with his requests. In entertaining Mrs. Thrale, Burney makes herself just as much a spectacle as she would have had she performed her imitations for Captain Fuller. The difference seems to be that, as Fuller demands the entertainment, she "previously kn[ows]" his attention will be fixed on her. When Fuller renews his demands a few days later, she finds herself physically unable to comply, despite noting that "he was so earnest that I was ashamed of refusing." She was "upon the point of trying 50 Times" to no avail, for "I have really no manner of command of my voice when I am not quite easy."[25]

Sophy Streatfield, socialite and friend of Mrs. Thrale, represents Burney's antithesis in these regards. Sophy (or, "the S.S." as Burney refers to her in the early journals) was famous for her "crying eyes": the ability, as Burney records, to shed tears on demand. After witnessing one of Sophy's tearful displays, Burney records the experience, in her typically detailed style, and at some length:

> Mrs Thrale: Yes, *do* cry, a little, Sophy . . . indeed, S.S., you *ought* to cry—
>
> Now for the wonder of wonders,—when Mrs. Thrale, in a coaxing voice, suited to a Nurse soothing a Baby, had run on for some Time,— while all the rest of us, in Laughter, joined in the request,—two Crystal Tears came into the soft Eyes of the S.S.,—& rolled gently down her Cheeks!—such a sight I never saw before, nor could I have believed;— she *offered* not to conceal, or dissipate them,—on the contrary, she really *contrived* to have them seen by every body. She looked, indeed, uncommonly handsome, for her *pretty face* was not, like Chloes, *blubbered*, it was smooth & elegant, & niether [sic] her Features nor her complexion were at all ruffled,—nay, indeed, she was *smiling* all the Time . . .
>
> Loud & rude bursts of Laughter broke from us all at once;—how, indeed, could they be restrained?—Yet we all stared, & looked & re-looked again & again 20 Times ere we could believe our Eyes . . .
>
> "There, now, said Mrs. Thrale, she looks for all the world as if nothing had happened,—for, you know, nothing *has* happened!"
>
> "Would *you* cry, Miss Burney, said Sir Phillip, if we ask'd you."
>
> "Lord, cried Mrs. Thrale, I would not do thus by Miss Burney for ten Worlds!—I dare say she would never speak to me again. I should think she'd be more likely to walk out of my House, than to *Cry* because I bid her."
>
> "I don't know how that is, said Sir Phillip, but I'm sure she is gentle enough."
>
> "She *can* cry, I doubt not, said Mr. Seward, on any proper occasion."
>
> "But I must know, said I, what *for*."[26]

Subsequent to this meeting, Sophy appears repeatedly in the early journals, fascinating and troubling to Burney for the ways in which she challenged the authenticity of the suffering female body.[27]

This anecdote indicates Burney's sense of how female distress can be, yet should not be, performed. Her account of Sophy's display shows she is bothered both by Sophy's ability to dissemble and by the idea that this woman is consciously making a spectacle of herself. Yet while Burney conveys her dislike, even fear, of this sort of attention, what she does *not* convey is her own sedulous abstinence from any such attention-getting activities. She instead asserts that these activities, be they entertaining imitations or tears, are for her impulsive and uncontrollable, that she does not draw attention to herself in a conscious, premeditated way. To make sense of the above scene, Burney decides that even Sophy must really be "insensible" to "the numerous strange, &, indeed, *impertinent* speeches which were made" in response to her tearful show.[28] As Burney defends her own spectacular positions as involuntary, she highlights that the genuine unconsciousness of the sufferer should protect her from charges of dissembling. The senseless female body disavows the disturbing disjunction presented by Sophy's crying eyes and smiling face.

*   *   *

Burney's next literary project represented a foray into a genre that would, theoretically, lend itself to concerns of staging and spectacle: she wrote a play. *Evelina* had left her public clamoring for more, though interestingly her literary contemporaries called specifically and repeatedly for a drama, not a second novel. Burney herself found the response notable: "how *amazing*, that this idea of a *Comedy* should strike so many!"[29] Various readers, from Sir Joshua Reynolds to Hester Thrale, stressed her skill with dialogue and characters as reasons to try her hand at this new genre; some, like Mrs. Cholmondely, even went around town acting out the role of Madame Duval.[30] When she did begin to write her comedy, Burney was encouraged in her pursuit by Richard Brinsley Sheridan, Dr. Johnson, Mrs. Montagu, and the playwright Arthur Murphy, who offered to help her in matters of stagecraft.

Yet despite such encouragement, her first play, *The Witlings* (1779), was suppressed by her father and Samuel Crisp before it could even take its chance on the stage. Possible reasons for this reaction include the speculations that Crisp, himself a failed playwright, was envious of Burney's success; that the play bore too close a resemblance to Molière's *Les Femmes Savantes* (a play that Burney maintained she had never read); that the characters of the witlings too closely resembled contemporary figures.[31] This last reason seems to be the most significant factor in the play's suppression, as Crisp and Charles Burney feared the satirical portrayal of the Esprit Party and its members could provoke some answering satire. For whatever reason, the play, which itself dwells on the suppression of female expression, reads as a self-fulfilling prophecy.[32] The heroine, Cecilia Stanley, becomes increasingly silent as the character Lady Smatter attempts to prevent her marriage, such that she spends a significant portion of time onstage without any dialogue at all.[33]

Comic drama, which draws its plot twists from sexual escapades and the difficulties within courtship and marriage, was already an "unladylike" genre for Burney to attempt, as a letter from Samuel Crisp to Burney suggests.[34] Crisp cautions Burney that "a great deal of management & Dexterity will certainly be required to preserve, Spirit & Salt, & yet keep up Delicacy" if she chooses to write for the stage.[35] To illustrate his point he recalls the following childhood event:

> Do You remember about a Dozen Years ago, how You Used to dance Nancy Dawson on the Grass plot, with Your Cap on the Ground, & your long hair streaming down your Back, one shoe off, & throwing about your head like a mad thing?—now you are to dance Nancy Dawson with Fetters on—there is the difference. . . . [36]

That Burney depicts a decorous, silent woman onstage represents one of the ways she sought to "dance Nancy Dawson with fetters on," or to make her comedy as proper as possible. Yet the compromises that Crisp proposes would finally be an impossibility, for as the outcome of *The Witlings* suggests, a completely proper comedy requires the repression of all expression—Burney's included.

Ironically, Cecilia's silent fortitude throughout this play means that she never affects her companions in the same instantaneous, powerful manner as her novelistic counterparts. Evelina's collapse convinces Sir John that she is his daughter; her acknowledged position as heiress is dependent on her physical presence. Cecilia Stanley, by comparison, might as well be invisible; her presence at the end of the play has nothing to do with her concluding good fortune. The cynical Mr. Censor engineers the resolution between lovers, giving Cecilia 5,000 pounds and blackmailing Lady Smatter into accepting her new daughter-in-law. This "happy ending" is rendered additionally ironic by her fiancé Beaufort's closing moral, "that Self-dependance [sic] is the first of Earthly Blessings; since those who rely on others for support and protection are not only liable to the common vicissitudes of Human Life, but exposed to the partial caprices and infirmities of Human Nature" (5.1054–58). Cecilia, who spent most of Act 5 trying unsuccessfully to become self-sufficient, stands silently onstage as Beaufort speaks this line. Both his statement and their union are undermined by her presence, for Burney has just described the difficulties a woman encounters in her attempts to be independent (a theme she will return to in *The Wanderer*) and the ways in which the dependent woman is manipulated and silenced by others.

Writing for the stage, Burney could not attain independence or expression either. The circumstances surrounding the failure of Burney's play reinforce the suggestion of the text, that a woman's dependence on others silences her. While Burney seems to agree that Lady Smatter and her ridiculous Witlings deserve to be quelled, she herself did not wish to be silenced for her literary aspirations. Her letters to her father and Samuel Crisp, after they vehemently insisted on suppressing *The Witlings*, show a rather desperate attachment to her play. She clings to her work, not realizing that making her play proper enough (in her daddies' eyes) for production would mean whittling it down to nothing at all. In response to their criticisms she proposes significant revisions until Crisp responds, "the omissions you propose are right, I think; but how the business of the piece is to go on with such omissions . . . it is impossible for me to know. What you mean to leave out . . . seems to have been the main subject of the play."[37]

Burney would not give up easily—she would write seven more plays—but the promise of the stage would for her always be frustrated by the dependence inherent in the genre. A playwright depends on the interaction and cooperation of playwright, actors, and theater manager; the script must circulate among all of these figures.[38] Burney's first play passed from her to her father and stopped there. As one who relied "on others for support and protection" she found herself "exposed to the partial caprices and infirmities of human nature": the very failure of her play proves the accuracy of its perceptions.[39] Like Cecilia at the end of her comedy, she had to stand by silent while her father fielded Murphy's and Sheridan's inquiries into the progress of Burney's play. Such repression carries with it the threat of collapse, but Burney would not suffer a complete breakdown (yet). She still had an outlet, and she uses her next novel to articulate what she could not onstage. Cecilia reappears and demonstrates what happens to women who are silenced.

*   *   *

Cecilia (1782), Burney's second novel, is a definitive rewriting of characters and events from her comedy. It also features a young heiress of the same name who loses her money and an authoritative woman (Mrs. Delvile) who tries to prevent the marriage of Cecilia and her lover (Mortimer Delvile, Mrs. Delvile's son), though this time for family rather than financial issues.[40] It also, rather significantly, put her audience in mind of a play: the famous actress Sarah Siddons reportedly told Burney that "there was no part which she had ever so much wished to act" as that of this new Cecilia.[41] But the novel is much darker than Burney's comedy, due in large part to Burney's fascination with the spectacle of the insensible female body. In this text, Burney presents physical suffering as more affecting (to spectators and readers) and more effective (in terms of conveying mental anguish) than any narrative explication of her heroines' internal consciousness. While Cecilia and Mrs. Delvile exercise such influence involuntarily, Albany's fiancée, a minor character in this novel, shows how this influence, if understood, can be manipulated. She is the first of Burney's heroines to demonstrate how suffering can be staged, as she plans and successfully carries out her own demise.

Scenes of collapse and insensibility are crucial to this novel, with the confrontation between a nearly insensible Cecilia and the passion-leveled Mrs. Delvile forming "the very scene for which [Burney] wrote the whole book," and the final insensibility of Cecilia enabling the novel's resolution (673–79; 912–17).[42] Albany's fiancée creates an important model by which these other scenes should be read. She is a nameless, easily overlooked woman who never actively participates in the novel's action (she has died long before the beginning of the plot, and the reader learns of her only through Albany's tortured reminiscing), yet her fate anticipates the fate of Burney's future heroines. When, toward the end of the novel, Albany is affected by the sight of insensible Cecilia, it is because he is haunted by the image of this other female body, a connection Albany makes as he exclaims before Cecilia, "my own wounds bleed afresh" (903).

We meet this woman in an earlier digression. Albany recalls falling in love with a young and innocent rustic, whom he must leave temporarily to claim an inheritance in Jamaica. His new setting and fortune cause him to forget his vows, and he lives a life of "licentiousness and vice" that only a near-fatal fever causes him to abandon (705). He returns to England to claim his fair one, to find that in his open-ended absence she has become a kept mistress. She admits to her undoing and begs his forgiveness; he beats her repeatedly and leaves again. In time he repents and spends two years searching for her, finally locating her in a brothel. The unfortunate woman seems again more tormented by his "rescue" than by her current situation. Once more before a gaze that she has experienced as judgmental and unforgiving, "she did not speak . . . but in two moments she fainted and fell" (706).

Up to this point, the pattern repeats a familiar emotional response. Observed in her improper occupation, the woman faints, much the same way that Evelina, in the company of prostitutes, almost swoons before her lover. (Evelina's ability to resist complete insensibility can perhaps be attributed to the fact that, while ashamed of her companions, she is not a prostitute and therefore does not suffer from the same degree of remorse or guilt.) The woman's recognition of her own spectacular position adds to her emotional turmoil—and leads to the collapse that renders her even more spectacular than before. Yet whereas the heroine's prostration in *Evelina* has the desired effect on her father, and Cecilia's insensibility will gain her Delvile's immediate forgiveness, the swoon in this case is not enough. While insensible, this woman afflicts Albany with remorse and escapes his painful gaze, but her fainting and its effects represent a temporary, transitory state. She is revived by others, then seized violently by her "rescuer": "I drew, I almost dragged her away" (707).

For this woman, the only solution is the permanent insensibility of death. Her fall has been too great, Albany's crimes, too heinous. He cannot rectify the situation by apologizing, like Delvile, or by acknowledging her lineage, like Sir John. When she does die, Albany exclaims, "I kept her loved corpse till my own senses failed me,—it was only then torn from me" (708). Again he grasps her, replaying the scenes of physical abuse, but now, finally, the influence is reversed. She causes him pain, and he remains tormented by her image in much the same way that Mr. Delvile will find himself "pursued by the pale image of Cecilia" (913). Her death relieves her of her crimes and his judgmental stare, while at the same time fixing his attention on her suffering in a way that will ensure his perpetual remorse.

Yet while the effect of her collapse on Albany is not unique, the method by which she attains it is. Even saying that she has a method to her death distinguishes it from the purely involuntary swoons of Evelina, or what Kristina Straub describes as the "living death that Cecilia, however irrationally, thinks she is fighting off."[43] From the brothel Albany takes her to the country and gives her lodging, servants, comforts, but "she would taste nothing but bread and water, never spoke, and never slept" (707). He pleads with her, yet "I spoke, however, to a statue,"

> she replied not, nor seemed to hear me . . . she seemed deaf, mute, insensible, her face unmoved . . . she sat constantly in one chair, she never changed her dress, no persuasions could prevail with her to lie down. . . . (707)

Only once she feels herself expiring does she acknowledge that "she had made a vow, upon entering the house, to live speechless and motionless, as a pennance [sic] for her offences!" (708).

Her confession, made when she feels herself dying, momentarily breaks her vow and links this transient freedom of expression to her approaching demise.[44] It also reveals her preceding stasis as consciously inflicted, her catatonic state as designed to result in death. Yet what seems to be striking behavior is really not striking after all: Margaret Doody notes that this woman "caricatures what men seem to want . . . anorexia, silence, a decorous forgettableness here turned into the macabre unforgettable."[45] Albany's fiancée merely enacts an exaggerated version of female decorum and extends the pattern of emotional repression and collapse that has manifested itself in all of Burney's novelistic heroines up to this point. The vow of repression that this woman adopts is an intensified version of Cecilia's attempts to hide her tears and assure Delvile that she is happy (678–79), her death, an extension of Cecilia's death-like insensibility toward the novel's end. But this woman is Burney's first heroine to recognize and purposefully manipulate the pattern; this episode is Burney's first explicit articulation of how emotional repression can be used to prepare for an effective, expressive (albeit dangerous and maybe deadly) moment of unconsciousness. Her later heroines continue to anticipate this moment, while expression itself continues to coexist with the involuntary behaviors of madness, insensibility, and death.

THE BACKLASH OF STAGED INSENSIBILITY:
THE COURT TRAGEDIES AND *CAMILLA*

Though the figure of an abandoned prostitute seems antithetical to the obedient, serious author who created her, Burney herself came close to adopting the method of expression and escape chosen by Albany's fiancée. Four years after the publication of *Cecilia,* Burney unwillingly accepted a court position as the Keeper of the Queen's Robes. She would be confined to court from 1786–1791; her experiences there require excessive emotional restraint and suggest that self-sacrifice might be the only way to escape servitude and express despair.

Burney's first introduction to the king and queen impressed her with the unnatural, theatrical behavior necessitated by court etiquette.[46] "It seemed to me we were *acting a Play,*" Burney writes to Susanna, and perhaps her most difficult role would be that of stoic servant.[47] In a much quoted letter to her sister Esther, Burney details directions for court behavior that seem a sadistic exaggeration of the restraint that must govern a woman's behavior elsewhere in society. All and any external manifestations of internal sensation must be repressed, at any cost:

> In the first place, you must not cough. If you find a cough tickling in your throat, you must arrest it from making any sound; if you find yourself choking with the forbearance, you must choke—but not cough.
>
> In the second place, you must not sneeze. If you have a vehement cold, you must take no notice of it . . . if a sneeze still insists upon making its way, you must oppose it, by keeping your teeth grinding together; if the violence of the repulse breaks some blood-vessel, you must break the blood-vessel—but not sneeze.
>
> In the third place, you must not, upon any account, stir either hand or foot. If, by chance, a black pin runs into your head, you must not take it out. If the pain is very great, you must be sure to bear it without wincing; if it brings the tears into your eyes, you must not wipe them off . . . If the blood should gush from your head by means of the black pin, you must let it gush; if you are uneasy to think of making such a blurred appearance, you must be uneasy, but you must say nothing about it. If, however, the agony is very great, you may, privately, bite the inside of your cheek, or of your lips, for a little relief; taking care, meanwhile, to do it so cautiously as to make no apparent dent outwardly. And, with that precaution, if you even gnaw a piece out, it will not be minded, only be sure either to swallow it, or commit it to a corner of the inside of your mouth till they are gone—for you must not spit.[48]

The letter is striking yet not unique in its violent images; the bursting blood vessel and the blood-blurred visage recall Mrs. Delvile's burst blood vessel in *Cecilia* (680), while the necessity for statuesque stillness is reminiscent of Albany's fiancée. The truly shocking nature of the letter rests in the author's blatant awareness of restraint as self-destructive: choking leads to bursting, leads to bleeding, leads to agony-inspired self-cannibalism. At the end of such directions the person in question is left standing, but probably not for long. Collapse, insensibility, even death seems a welcome alternative to such an existence.

This letter would prove prophetic. After several years of determined though miserable service to the queen, Burney began to get sick. By 1790 she had lost weight; she coughed; she suffered pain and insomnia. It will probably always be unclear whether her symptoms were prompted by a persistent viral infection or whether they were completely psychosomatic, though Burney seems aware of the potential for psychosomatic illness and desperate that her own sufferings not be interpreted as such. She notes that "illness here . . . is commonly supposed . . . [to] be willful, and therefore meets little notice, till accompanied by danger, or incapacity of duty."[49] Yet Burney's novels demonstrate that illness can be both willful and very real, a fact Burney's own decline seems to duplicate. She knew the significance of her symptoms and how to frame them to her advantage: she planned to retire from court service, and she drafted a statement of her resignation in the summer of 1790. But she did not present the document "until a rapid decline in both health and strength . . . made the necessity of the resignation palpable to all"—six months later.[50] Doody reads this as a subversive, though terrifying bid for freedom on Burney's part—subversive because Burney was finally expressing her misery, terrifying because to do so in the most proper, least willful manner meant that the external representations of her suffering could not be feigned.[51] If Burney felt that life at court was killing her, she had to make her point literally, by almost dying.

Burney had searched for other outlets before being pushed to this extreme, and again these outlets took the form of writing, specifically tragedies. These tragedies are generally considered as useful "occupational and emotional outlets" but literary disasters[52]—though even these readings do not explain why drama would become the "outlet" of choice. Burney suffered at court from the beginning of her appointment, but early in 1787 she made a resolution to "'be Happy!' . . . to curtail painful recollections and heart-searchings and to write a court-journal from the accumulated memoranda of the previous six months."[53] The court-journals therefore, while thorough and informative chronicles, contain much less of the personal introspection seen in her earlier diaries, whereas her tragedies respond more directly to her personal sufferings. When the King's illness confines Burney to Kew in 1788, she states,

> I have just begun a tragedy. We are now in so spiritless a situation that my mind would bend to nothing less sad, *even in fiction*. But I am very

glad something of this kind has occurred to me; it may while away the tediousness of this unsettled, unoccupied, unpleasant period.[54]

The artist's life creeps inevitably, admittedly, into her work. Burney's observation poignantly highlights the articulation of personal experience with what she frames as an escapist, fictional text.

This first tragedy, *Edwy and Elgiva,* was set aside, to be resumed in April of 1790—a time when Burney was again physically and mentally distressed. By August she had completed what she described as "an almost spontaneous work" that "soothed the melancholy of imagination for a while." Burney, who had not written for four years, had "done something at last," and "scarce . . . had this [*Edwy and Elgiva*] done with imagination . . . when imagination seized upon another subject for another tragedy."[55] Burney would write three complete tragedies (*Edwy and Elgiva, Hubert De Vere, The Siege of Pevensey*) and one fragment (*Elberta*) by the time she left court in July 1791. Her spurt of writing was self-described as compulsive and therapeutic: "the power of composition has to me indeed proved a solace, a blessing! When incapable of all else, that, unsolicited, unthought of, has presented itself to my solitary leisure, and beguiled me of myself."[56] Burney again portrays writing in terms synonymous with those surrounding insensibility—as an involuntary, expressive moment, "unsolicited, unthought of," that allows the sufferer to forget herself.

Yet Burney's interest in having at least one of these plays produced, and her continued attention to her play manuscripts, shows that the importance of these texts to her went far beyond the cathartic act of composition.[57] Indeed, her timely gravitation toward plays reflects on her own experience: that suffering had to be witnessed to produce any effect on an audience. Her father had to see his daughter in her weakened state before he would acknowledge what she had always known—that court life was not good for her.[58] Writing for the theater therefore provides Burney with more than a compositional outlet; it offers her a way to reify and control suffering. Whereas *The Witlings*, in an attempt make to the comic drama proper, celebrated feminine restraint, Burney's tragedies "emphasiz[e] the *progress* of enduring decay . . . female bodies bear tangible signs of drawn out physical and mental suffering."[59]

Such bodily suffering is most evident in her first tragedy, the play that Burney herself singled out by submitting it in 1794 to John Philip Kemble for production, reasoning that it was "more dramatic" than the others.[60] *Edwy and Elgiva* focuses on Edwy's attempts to overturn papal edicts that forbid his union to Elgiva on grounds of consanguinity (she is his cousin), while power-hungry monks use their king's transgressive marriage to encourage public discord and ultimately civil war. The play emphasizes visible, physical female agony, culminating in the dramatic stabbing of Elgiva. The heroine faints in Act 2 (2.3.49), reappears at the end of Act 5 for a public death scene, and then remains onstage for seven scenes as a corpse. Elgiva's final appearance onstage is, as Darby notes, "the most notable change Burney makes to her sources . . . none of which recalls any reunion with the king,"[61] and the sight of her body crucially moves Dunstan (the villain who has engineered her murder) to remorse (5.18.6–7, 10–11). Burney purposefully has her heroine return to remain in a state of visible, insensible suffering and frames Dunstan's torturous penitence, like Albany's, as initiated by the sight of the woman he indirectly killed.

Yet when *Edwy and Elgiva* was finally staged, these scenes of the insensible female body became perhaps the most mangled in an indisputably miserable production. This time Burney made it past the barriers of censorship, only to see her play performed poorly, her scenes misrepresented and misconstrued. The play premiered at Drury Lane on 21 March 1795 and featured some of the best tragic actors of the day, with John Philip Kemble as Edwy and Sarah Siddons as Elgiva. But in the climatic death scene, the suffering Elgiva, who was supposed to emerge from behind a hedge, situated in an area remote from any dwelling, "was brought from behind it [the hedge] on an elegant couch, and, after dying in the presence of her husband, was removed once more to the back of the hedge. The solemn accents of Siddons herself were no match for this ludicrous circumstance, and she was carried off amidst roars of mirth."[62] Apparently, viewers found the discrepancy between the proposed rural, remote setting and the ornate couch with its accompanying bearers, between the supposed physical suffering of Elgiva and the obvious nod to Siddons's comfort and privilege, too ridiculous too ignore.

Thus the genre that theoretically seemed so fitting to Burney's project of emotional expression proved frustrating in practice. After all, Burney was unaccustomed to the mechanics of theater. She never knew that when her brother Charles first read the script to the assembled cast, all the actors left.[63] Yet even if she had, she was nursing a baby and in ill health, unable to be any more involved with the rehearsal process. And the play contained many other flaws apart from Elgiva's death scene that Burney attributes to herself; she notes that it appeared "with so many *undramatic* effects, from my inexperience of Theatrical requisites & demands, that when I saw it, I perceived myself a thousand things I wished to *change*."[64]

Both Burney and her husband did craft extensive revisions to the play, which make the character of Elgiva even more visible and place an even greater emphasis on her bodily suffering.[65] While the play was never actually resubmitted to Drury Lane, her revisions, as a practical response to the play's public failure, show a much more resolute, determined Burney than the woman who would run and hide when she heard *Evelina* being praised. In a letter to her brother Charles, dated 10 June 1795, the supposedly shy and prudish author mocks herself rather crudely, then simultaneously toys with the ideas of publishing the play by subscription and beginning a new project:

Dearest Charles,
How are you? How are yours?
I am well. So are ours.
I begin with dignity, because I am going to write upon business.
But—"What's the Play to Night?"
Edwy & Elgiva?—
No!—'Tis out of sight!—
Well!—let that pass!
And
"Write me down an ass!"[66] . . .

So now to new matter. . . . I have had a long & warm & fervent exhortation from the good and wise seer Cambridge,[67] to print the tragedy by subscription. . . . And I have had a message to the same effect, with the same advice, in form & ceremony, sent me, openly & with great kindness, from Mrs. Montagu.[68] And—I have had a spirited anonymous letter urging ditto forcibly.

So Much for That.

Now—to *The* business.

All things considered,—& weighty are some of them!—have just come to a resolution to print my Grand Work, of which you have never yet heard,—by subscription.[69]

This new work was *Camilla,* and it seemed to replace Burney's work on her play. The plan to publish *Edwy and Elgiva* by subscription never materialized, and Burney's letter professes casual indifference to her play, dismissing it with a "so much for that" before announcing "*the* business." But she takes her time getting down to business; her lengthy account of the response to her play demonstrates a strong attachment to the genre and her previous project. While she would at least temporarily redirect her efforts from playwriting (or revising) to *Camilla* (1796), its composition is clearly intertwined with her theatrical experiences. And the content of the novel attests to this, as in it she presents the insensible female body the way she could not onstage.

* * *

Like Evelina, Camilla Tyrold is a heroine who spends the majority of the novel in a theatrical position, unwillingly on display before a public gaze that requires dissembling and restraint. She is told to feign an indifference to the man she loves, and even, at times and again in obedience to others' suggestions, a fondness for the men she does not.[70] The disastrous consequences of her behavior expose the danger of playing such parts; as in Burney's earlier novels, Camilla's near-death is the result of pages of emotional repression. But her breakdown also represents a much needed break from the restraint that produced it, and the "death" scene finally communicates her hidden feelings to her lover and parents. This scene is also presented as staged: unlike Evelina or Cecilia, and more like Albany's fiancée, Camilla is described as at least partially responsible for her own physical failings.[71]

The main conflict of *Camilla* involves the misunderstandings between Camilla and the hero, Edgar Mandlebert. Camilla and Edgar love each other, and they both recognize their own feelings relatively early in the novel. But Edgar has been counseled by his misogynistic tutor Dr. Marchmont not to declare his affections until he is sure of Camilla's, and Camilla, because Edgar has not verbally specified his intentions, cannot articulate hers. The lovers find themselves trapped in a vicious cycle, only perpetuated by Camilla's father. Mr. Tyrold, aware of his daughter's feelings yet fearful that the attachment is not mutual, tells her to "struggle against yourself as you would struggle against an enemy" and advocates a "strict and unremitting control over your passions" (358–59). As "there are so many ways of communication independent of speech," she must "shut up every avenue by which a secret which should die untold can further escape you" (360). Camilla, as the dutiful daughter and modest young woman she is, adheres to his instructions so successfully that Edgar leaves her, convinced she does not love him at all, and she almost carries her secret to the grave.

Thus it is that Camilla, abandoned by Edgar and separated from her family, finally prays for death. Like her Richardsonian precursors, Clarissa and Pamela, Camilla sees death as a chance to free herself from persecution and establish, once and for all, the legitimacy of her anguish. Just so, death offers Pamela a means of representing to Mr. B both her suffering under his advances and the truth of her protestations against them. Her demise, she imagines, will cause Mr. B to see that "she preferred her honesty to her life. She, poor girl . . . really was the innocent creature she pretended to be!"[72] What differentiates Camilla from these heroines is her desire that she not suffer unobserved. She writes to her parents that she is dying, hoping that her described illness will bring them to see for themselves.

So while Claudia Johnson notes that "the flagrancy of female suffering so copiously represented in these novels [of sensibility] . . . is surpassed only by the strenuousness of the heroines' inhibitions about articulating it,"[73] Camilla clearly wants to be seen, and she clearly considers how and when an audience will respond to her bodily symptoms. Indeed, her desire for an audience, and her fears about that audience's reception, actually lead her body to express more accurately the mental tumult inside it. Immediately after sending her letter, Camilla fears being accused of pretension, and the anxiety that "her friends might find her too well, and suspect her representation was but to alarm them into returning kindness" (866) keeps her awake despite her debilitating exhaustion. These psychological torments quickly trigger physical symptoms, much as Burney's mental distress affected her health while at court. Repeating what G.J. Barker-Benfield notes as a pattern among sentimental heroines, Camilla, "harassed with fatigue, and exhausted by perturbation . . . felt now so ill, that she solemnly believed her fatal wish quick approaching" (862).[74] Like Albany's fiancée, she soon has gone nights "without sleep, or the refreshment of taking off her cloaths" and finds herself "too seriously disordered to make her illness require the aid of fancy" (866).

If the relationship between mind and body is nothing new, Camilla's manipulation of this relationship is. Burney here asserts that a woman's body can express her emotions—and that she can to some degree control how and when this display will take place. Such control has its positive effects, for despite her very real suffering, Camilla does not die. *Camilla* has a happy ending, as the heroine's physical deterioration finally strikes Edgar with remorse, prompts her mother's forgiveness, and instigates a general reconciliation. But though redemptive, Camilla's display is not ultimately condoned by Camilla's spectators or Camilla herself. She is criticized for voluntarily creating her own illness; while the sight of her suffering and her more active role in engineering this spectacle are depicted as the only way to reunite the family, the staged, willful nature of her suffering remains unacceptable. As her sufferings increase, Camilla experiences a fear of death, a sense that "she had been presumptuous . . . her preparations had all been worldly, her impatience wholly selfish. She called back her wish" (873).[75] Her mother, while she forgives her daughter, also labels her sufferings as the product of "willing despair" (882). It does not matter to her audience that her sufferings are ultimately very real; they are recognized as voluntarily endured and displayed, and criticized as such. She is cajoled by her mother to "repress, repress . . . these strong feelings, uselessly torturing to us both" (881–82), though this self-inflicted torture seems to have been particularly useful in its own way.

Camilla articulates this conflict—between the effectiveness of staging one's feelings, and the critique that staging one's feelings in too obvious a manner sustains—without resolving it, signaling, perhaps, the impasse at which Burney found herself upon the completion of this novel. She wrote *Camilla* while still dealing with the frustration of *Edwy and Elgiva*, while still wanting to write and stage plays. As Burney would later tell her father, "the chance [to write for the theater] held out golden dreams," and *Camilla*, the novel she wrote at the expense of revising and possibly resubmitting *Edwy and Elgiva*, does not represent her explicitly theatrical aspirations.[76] Using the trope of staged insensibility, she has tried in first one genre, then the other, simultaneously to enact and efface the agency over expression that a theatrical display of feeling seems to imply. In her last creative works, she abandons such attempts. The dilemma, instead, becomes an impossible paradox, and one that can tear a woman apart. Burney splits her female protagonist into two people: Sophia and Joyce from her final play, *The Woman-Hater*, and Juliet and Elinor from her final novel, *The Wanderer*.

SPLITTING THE SELF: *THE WOMAN-HATER* AND *THE WANDERER*

The years between *Camilla* and Burney's final play, *The Woman-Hater*, were eventful ones. Thomas Harris accepted Burney's play *Love and Fashion* in 1799; production was scheduled for March of 1800. But then her sister and confidant Susanna died, and her father forced her to withdraw the play on the grounds that producing a comedy would be inappropriate in light of the family bereavement. Her stepmother had died, and her brother James and half-sister Sarah shocked the family with their supposedly incestuous affair. Burney's decision to keep writing and to return to comedies (she composed the comedy *A Busy Day* around this time as well) shows a new determination. This is not the same Burney who, overcome by despair, dabbled in tragedies and death as her only mode of escape—perhaps because, as the conflicted conclusion of *Camilla* demonstrated, such an outlet involves much pain and suffering for the woman without definitively clearing her from charges of willful self-display. Burney's last comedy, like her first one, does not feature female insensibility, but it does sketch out the potential for a different, less punishing and more collaborative approach to expression.[77]

Burney's final play contains clear echoes of her earlier work. Characters from the suppressed *Witlings* reappear only slightly revised (most notably in the part of Lady Smatter), and the main plot of *The Woman-Hater*, which involves the reunion between Wilmot and Eleonora and Wilmot's recognition of Eleonora's daughter as his rightful child and heir, resonates in obvious ways with the plot of *Evelina*. But whereas Burney's novel barely mentions the character of Polly Green, the false Evelina, here she devotes great attention to both the true Miss Wilmot, Sophia, and her imposter, Joyce. In a move that she will soon repeat in *The Wanderer*, Burney simultaneously polarizes and links her female protagonists.

These two women have radically different personalities—Joyce is loud and outspoken and ultimately lowborn, while Sophia, true daughter of Wilmot, demonstrates her pedigree through her consistent silences and self-effacing shyness—and yet both represent, for a time, the same person. Even the theater audience was meant to be confused. Burney disguises the true name and identity of Joyce until the fourth act, and the *dramatis personae* lists her as "Miss Wilmot" and not by her corrected, Christian name. She is referred to as Miss Wilmot in the stage directions until the Nurse has revealed her upbringing, and our first introduction to her does nothing to dispel the sense that she is the proper, decorous daughter of a well-born gentleman. In Wilmot's presence, the girl is, like her counterpart Sophia, deferential and almost completely silent, answering all his queries by monosyllable (2.1).

Yet the instant Wilmot leaves the room, we witness a dramatic transformation:

> Miss Wilmot (*peeping over the shoulders of the Nurse*): Is Papa gone?
> Nurse: Yes, Miss.
> Miss Wilmot: Are you sure?
> Nurse: Yes, Miss, up stairs to his own room.
> Miss Wilmot (*jumping up and singing*):
> Then hoity, toity, whiskey, friskey,
> These are the joys of our dancing days—
> Come, now let's get rid of all this stupefying learning! . . . (*throwing about the Books, and dancing round them*) (2.4.31–42)

Joyce loves the body and physical activity. She hates reading and study, but she loves, as she says and shows, dancing, singing, swinging, walking, running, jumping, and eating (3.10.73–121). Burney has created an exuberant, liberated heroine, who is endowed with freedom of speech and the freedom to marry the man she loves (Bob Sapling). After the suffering, repressed heroines of Burney's earlier works, it is tempting to read Joyce as Burney's rebellious solution to her own personal and literary experiences. The image of a young girl, dancing so giddily that spectators fear she is not quite right in the head (2.4.52–55), powerfully recalls Crisp's reference to the young Burney, who upon occasion used to "dance Nancy Dawson on the Grass plot . . . throwing about your head like a mad thing."[78] Joyce's concern with her "father's" perception of her and Wilmot's effect on Joyce recall Burney's deferential attitude toward her two "daddies" and her resulting silence, especially in the dramatic genre. Yet Joyce, with her antipathy toward books, reading, and study, makes a disturbing model for the woman who loved the literary life.

Indeed, neither Joyce nor Sophia represents, independently, a satisfactory solution to a woman's struggles for expression—yet together they successfully resolve the conflict of the play. The reconciliation scene between Sophia and her father recalls the similar scene in *Evelina;* in both scenes the rightful daughter displays herself silently before her father, Evelina by swooning and Sophia by kneeling. Yet whereas the sight of Evelina's face was enough to convince Sir John of her lineage, Wilmot looks straight at Sophia and exclaims "thou nameless Girl! I am not thy Father!" (5.15.20–21). The play insinuates that, were it not for Joyce's intervention, the silent Sophia would prostrate herself before her father "for nothing" (5.16.3). Joyce, now informed of her true birth, "a'n't afraid to speak to him now he i'n't Papa" (5.16.1–2), and she assures him he is not her father. Together the proper, silent heroine and the outspoken, indecorous heroine clear up the confusion. Sophia's quiet demonstrations of gentility and submissiveness (she kneels again to her father) reinforce the truth of what Joyce has announced—that Sophia is the daughter of Wilmot.

Yet this play ends with Sophia and Joyce going their very separate ways, and it ended up, like most of Burney's other plays, tucked away in some desk drawer. To resolve her play Burney had two different girls represent "Miss Wilmot," and as two distinct characters, Joyce and Sophia can interact only for a moment. As "Miss Wilmot" they both stand before their confused father, but the moment Sophia is defined as the true daughter, Joyce as the servant's girl, they split. Sophia is absorbed, silently, into the aristocracy, while Joyce, as a hopeful ballad singer and lover of Bob, is firmly entrenched in the lower class. They cannot permanently coexist, even onstage. This play momentarily links these two models of female identity, only to underline how firmly opposed they really are. The fate of this play reinforces the same divisions it describes: Burney's own family associated her dramatic endeavors with a Joyce-like indecorousness, her novelistic projects with the more proper model of female behavior. According to her family, she could not do both.

* * *

Burney's last novel also contains a commentary on the divided nature of female identity and a criticism of the customs, both social and professional, that perpetuate these divisions. Though *The Wanderer* was not published until 1814, after Burney returned to England with her husband, she says in the dedication that "I had planned and begun it before the end of the last century! but the bitter, and ever to be deplored affliction with which this new era opened to our family [the death of Susanna] . . . cast it from my thoughts, and even from my powers."[79] Her statement locates the early work on her novel as occurring simultaneously with her work on *The Woman-Hater*, and while her final play, like most of her court tragedies, would never reach a contemporary audience, these dual female protagonists reappear in the novel that she finally published.

Her novel, like her play, features two women with radically different temperaments, linked in this case through love of the same man and through a similar struggle to express this love: the reserved and mysterious Juliet Granville and the outspoken, volatile Elinor Joddrel.[80] Both women articulate their feelings at moments when the intensity of these same feelings leads to insensibility or at least self-absorption; the difference between the two women is that Elinor tries (with no success) to stage these moments, whereas Juliet does not. And yet Elinor's failure does not stand in simple contrast to Juliet's happy ending. Though Juliet marries Harleigh, the man both women love, chance, and not her own agency, is responsible for her good fortune. While the novel ends "happily," neither woman really achieves independent expression.

The performance given by Juliet for most of the novel is instead one of externally imposed restraint. The novel begins with her mysterious flight from France, and we learn much later that she has been forced to marry a brutal French commissary to save the life of her guardian. As a wife on the run, she must keep her true name and circumstances secret. She is, as other characters note, a veritable chameleon—transforming from a bandaged Creole (the disguise she dons for the boat ride back to England), to a fair-skinned harp-player, to a rustically dressed woman mistaken for the town slut. Yet she adopts all these disguises, not in an attempt to express anything about herself, but to avoid notice, to "say nothing."[81] How she feels is kept strictly in check (at one point she cries "I have no heart!—I must have none!" [341]) and who she is, Juliet Granville, is hidden from the reader until the fifth volume. We do not learn even her Christian name until Volume 3; she goes by the alias "Ellis" for the first part of the novel, an appellation imposed on her by company (81).

Under such constant restraint, Juliet, like Burney's earlier heroines, must and does break down. Her collapse is of a more temporary, less self-destructive nature than the sufferings of Cecilia or Camilla, but Burney unequivocally describes it as a moment that shows us Juliet's true nature and feelings. Reunited with Gabriella, a female friend from France who knows the circumstances of her unhappy marriage and flight, Juliet can at least briefly forgo aliases and abandon self-control:

> The feelings of Juliet, long checked by prudence, by fortitude, by imperious necessity; and kept in dignified but hard command; having once found a vent, bounded back to nature and truth, with a vivacity of keen emotion that made them nearly uncontrollable. Nature and truth,— which invariably retain an elastic power, that no struggles can wholly subdue; and that always, however curbed, however oppressed,—lie in wait for opportunity to spring back to their rights. Her tears, permitted, therefore, at length, to flow, nearly deluged the sad bosom of her friend. (390)

Juliet's tears, unlike the decorous, showy weeping of Sophy Streatfield, are uncontrollable, overwhelming, and real. Juliet's dignified repression cannot, ultimately, affect or change her true feelings: "nature and truth," represented here by "keen emotion," "spring back to their rights" in a manner that conjures up the noun form of Burney's verb. Juliet's virtuous oppression seems to increase the potency and inevitability of the emotional reaction that is "nearly uncontrollable" when it finally occurs.

But Juliet, at least, has waited for a proper, and safe, opportunity to vent. The question that this novel repeatedly asks is how and where a woman can find such opportunity, and one answer it presents is in theatrical performance. Juliet's other significant moment of expression occurs when she is in fact onstage. During a home theatrical, she captivates an audience with her portrayal of Lady Townly in Colley Cibber's *The Provok'd Husband,* and her performance, like her tearful collapse, is cast as a moment of involuntary expression. In an episode reminiscent of Burney's experiences playing the tragic Mrs. Lovemore, Juliet first feels fright "so great, as nearly to make her forget her part, and occasion what, hesitatingly, she was able to utter, to be hardly audible" (94). Yet the audience will ultimately read Juliet's disturbance as a practiced portrayal of inquietude, and as the play proceeds, Juliet becomes so absorbed by her feelings that she forgets, not her part, but the audience itself. "The state of her mind accorded with distress," and she expresses her angst through the part she plays (96). As the audience praises what they think to be the "deep research into the latent subjects of uneasiness belonging to the situation of Lady Townly," Burney insists that Juliet's performance was "nature, which would not be repressed; not art, that strove to be displayed" (95). Burney's emphasis on the "naturalness" of Juliet's feelings resonates with her emphasis, in her early journal, on the naturalness of her own. Circumstances for both women are "happily miserable":[82] while the audience believes they are witnessing the feigned emotions of a fictional character, the stage allows the performer a much needed emotional release.

Yet Burney does not present such performance as voluntarily chosen or as a viable solution to Juliet's "female difficulties." Juliet experiences a form of catharsis onstage, and Elinor suggests that acting could also allay Juliet's financial troubles. But while Juliet expresses her respect and admiration for the art, she adamantly refuses to profess it: "I think it [acting] so replete with dangers and improprieties . . . that, when a young female, *not forced by peculiar circumstances, or impelled by resistless genius,* exhibits herself a willing candidate for public applause;—she must have, I own, other notions, or other nerves, than mine!" (398–99; emphasis mine). Juliet's statement forbids a woman from consciously appearing before an audience, though her disclaimers excuse her own previous appearance as Lady Townly and her subsequent, financially motivated agreement to play the harp at a public concert. "Peculiar circumstances" (the pressures of other participants, financial necessity) pushed her into both these situations, but a woman should not, in her terms, willingly make a spectacle of herself.

Juliet's disclaimers also excuse her author's professional career, as Burney had often lamented the attention bestowed on her by her fans. To counter this effect, Burney described her writing process as impelled by something like "resistless genius." In a cancelled introduction to *Cecilia* she attributes the novel to mysterious "interior movements by which I [am] impelled . . .",[83] and her dramatic efforts were often described as the product of "unsolicited, unthought of" imagination.[84] In 1800, while she was working on both *The Woman-Hater* and *The Wanderer,* Burney defends her dramatic compositions to her father, claiming, "my imagination is not at my own controll [sic], or I would always have continued in the walk you approved [sic]. The combinations for another long work did not occur to me. Incidents & effects for a Dramma [sic] did."[85] To maintain her standing as a dutiful daughter and a woman of decorum, Burney portrays herself as a slave to her imagination and portrays her resulting interest in theater as forced upon her.

To perform "properly," both Juliet and Burney must be, or at least must depict themselves as, under another's control. Yet just as Cecilia Stanley's dependency complicated *The Witlings'* happy conclusion that "Self-dependance [sic]" is "the first of Earthly Blessings," so does Juliet's dependency complicate the happy ending of *The Wanderer*. It is she, and not Elinor, who marries Harleigh, yet she must express her love and pleasure from within "a chastened garb of moderation" (861), and even her modest avowals are allowed only because Harleigh's proposal has been authorized by her brother, her guardian the Bishop, and her uncle. Her beaming smiles couple ominously with the declaration that her love for Harleigh makes her "not so independent" (861). The happily married Juliet has not really progressed from the bandaged Creole we meet at the beginning; at both points she is trapped by manners and customs that she can only momentarily and involuntarily transcend.

Unlike Juliet, who waits for the opportunity for expression to present itself, Elinor Joddrel seeks "occasion to exhibit character; instead of leaving its display to the jumble of nature and of accident" (630). Her rebellious efforts accentuate the conditions that even a revolutionary such as Elinor must struggle against. In her words, women are taught to "subdue all . . . native emotions . . . to hide them as sin, and to deny them as shame" (177); Elinor, in response, boasts of her ability to "speak and act, as well as think and feel for myself" (154).[86] Yet despite her resolution, "something within involuntarily, invincibly checked her" (154); later she exclaims, "how tenacious a tyrant is custom! How it clings to our practice . . . How it awes our very nature itself, and bewilders and confounds even our free will!" (174). What she struggles to say, that she loves Harleigh, she cannot at first articulate even to Ellis / Juliet. The closest she comes is "I hate him not!" (157).

To resolve these difficulties, Elinor turns playwright. Elinor explains: "My operations are to commence thus: Act I. Scene I. Enter Ellis, seeking Albert . . . Scene II. Albert and Ellis meet. Ellis informs him that she must have a confabulation with him the next day" (157). The rest of her plot is "not yet quite ripe for disclosure. But all is arranged . . ." (157). Elinor hopes that her staged yet honest expression of love will be met with an answering declaration of love. But her affection is not returned. Her theatrical avowal displays, as Harleigh (in an echo of Burney's own "Daddy Crisp") claims, "spirit" without "dignity" or "delicacy" (189).

So Elinor, in a move reminiscent of Albany's fiancée and Camilla, plans to stage her own death. A staged death should technically combine spirit and delicacy; it would express her despair and her independent agency, while containing both by the life-threatening consequences that deny its repetition.[87] And yet, Elinor's death scene becomes one of the most repeated tropes in this novel. Elinor must try again and again to kill herself, and as she does so, her efforts come to affect critics and readers as humorous, ridiculous interludes, more than as tragic moments of despair.[88] Still, readers who mock Elinor for her ineffective gestures miss the seriousness of her attempts. She plunges a dagger into her breast so definitively that "the blood gushed out in torrents" and then prevents a surgeon from stanching the flow; later she aims a gun straight at her head (359, 580). The interference of others keeps her alive; it is only because she is not allowed to die that she must repeat her attempts, and it is only because of their repetitive nature that these attempts do not have the desired effect on either spectators or readers. Elinor, much like Siddons/Elgiva, becomes an object of mockery instead of a tragic figure, even as she is cajoled to adopt the habits of society that only perpetuate her despair. The true tragedy of Elinor's existence is not that death is her only option, but that she ultimately has no options at all.

Elinor's second suicide attempt is a perfect example of staged suffering gone awry. Disguised as a deaf-mute man, she gains admittance to the public concert hall where Juliet will (unwillingly) be playing the harp, but she unmasks before the suicide attempt: "the large wrapping coat, the half mask, the slouched hat, and embroidered waistcoat, had rapidly been thrown aside, and Elinor appeared in deep mourning" (359). She stabs herself, violently forbids the surgeon to close her wound, then finally faints from loss of blood. The swoon signifies that her performance is going according to plan; it is a testament to the sincerity and severity of her suffering and a precursor to the death she desires—except that once she faints, Harleigh bids the surgeon to "snatch this opportunity for examining, and . . . dressing the wound" (362). Elinor becomes the first Burney heroine to be taken advantage of while unconscious, so that Harleigh's life-saving ministries represent a violation of her body reminiscent of a rape. The men that save her life change the script of her performance, for she meant to bleed to death.

Though Elinor's swoon is genuine, Burney indicates that the staged nature of her collapse renders it ineffective, and she purposefully contrasts it with a spontaneous swoon to demonstrate how differently each affects the audience. When Juliet first comes onstage she catches sight of the strangely dressed deaf and dumb man whom she had noticed outside. "An horrible surmise . . . that it was Elinor disguised, and Elinor come to perpetrate the bloody deed of suicide" fixes her with terror, and she "sunk motionless on the floor" (358–59). Her fainting prompts instantaneous pity and movement in every spectator, especially Harleigh, who "overcame every obstacle, to force a passage to the spot where the pale Ellis was lying" (359). When Elinor suffers, by contrast, "the ladies . . . were hiding their faces, or running away; and the men, though all eagerly crowding to the spot of this tremendous event, [were] approaching rather as spectators of some public exhibition, than as actors in a scene of humanity"

(359–60). Because the audience perceives her suffering as indisputably staged, Elinor's performance cannot be understood for what it is: "a scene of humanity." Burney's statement with its theatrical terminology acknowledges that real, human suffering can be staged—and announces the audience's inability to credit this.

Whereas the end of *The Woman-Hater* accentuated the permanent split between the two heroines, and thus the inability for expressive agency and decorum to coexist, *The Wanderer* demonstrates the same impossibility, but by forcing Elinor into Juliet's role. With the marriage of Juliet and Harleigh imminent, Harleigh announces that Elinor will "fin[d] how vainly she would tread down the barriers of custom . . . she will return to the habits of society and common life, as one awakening from a dream in which she has acted some strange and improbable part" (863). The novel ends painfully, granting Elinor a final moment of unrestrained expression that goes ominously unacknowledged: "in the anguish of her disappointment . . . she cried, 'must Elinor too,—must even Elinor! . . . find that she has strayed from the beaten road, only to discover that all others are pathless!' Here, and thus felicitously, ended . . . the DIFFICULTIES of the WANDERER" (873). The conclusion is a striking juxtaposition of Elinor's despair with a statement of Juliet's happiness that answers Elinor's question, indirectly, "yes." At the same time, the juxtaposition asks us to find a closer antecedent for "the wanderer," an association encouraged by Elinor's own metaphorical reference to her wandering ways. Our wanderers merge, their "difficulties" at an end because they have nowhere, really, left to go.

* * *

At the time of its publication Burney's last novel, much like Elinor's sufferings, was criticized, dismissed, misunderstood, or ignored by most of its male readers.[89] In writing a novel that punished or denied staged insensibility, Burney wrote a novel that went on and on and on. Pages go by as Juliet waits patiently for an opportunity for expression to present itself; more pages go by as Elinor is once again saved from death. John Wilson Croker, Byron, Hazlitt, and Walter Scott all greatly disapproved of the book, and Hazlitt criticized it especially for its tedium.[90]

Evelina and *Cecilia*, in contrast, affected readers powerfully, instantly—theatrically. The reconciliation scene between Evelina and Sir John had readers bursting into tears (Burney's journals quote readers who describe it as "a scene for a tragedy"), and the spectacle of Mrs. Delvile, prostrate and bloody, prompted one reader to fling down the book and exclaim "I'm glad of it, with all my heart!"[91] While Burney's novelistic scenes of insensibility describe the power of the visual spectacle to affect the fictional characters involved in the scene, they also affected contemporary readers in an instantaneous, visual manner. This reaction is more typical, as Burney herself explained in *The Wanderer*, of the theater: "good acting" being "that skill which brings forth on the very instant, all the effect which, to the closet reader, an author can hope to produce from reflection" (95). By provoking a spontaneous response in both the fictional characters and the readers who "witness" them, Burney's swooning women create what David Marshall notes as a characteristic of many eighteenth-century novels, an experience of reading that is "analogous to the experience of becoming a spectator to a moving spectacle."[92]

Yet while *The Wanderer* features no effectively staged moments of insensibility, the text itself comes close to duplicating the trope that Burney expunged from it. Reviewer John Wilson Croker indicated the links among *The Wanderer,* Burney's early works, and Burney herself when he compared the novel unfavorably both to *Evelina* and to Burney's own, aging body:

> The Wanderer has the identical features of Evelina—but of Evelina grown old; the vivacity, the bloom, the elegance, "the purple light of love" are vanished; the eyes are there, but they are dim; the cheek, but it is furrowed; the lips, but they are withered . . . [93]

Croker draws the analogy to emphasize his claim that Burney "has been gradually descending from the elevation which the vigour of her youth had attained."[94] His analogy implicates Burney, personally and corporeally, in her writing; her decision to make the controversial Elinor abide by Juliet's model of propriety represents a kind of professional restraint that is, by Croker's terms, damaging to the author in a literary and physical sense. Yet in reading this final novel as an authorial performance of repression, we can see productive parallels between Burney's approach to authorship and the actions of all her suffering heroines. For if Burney recognizes extreme, consciously adopted restraint as that which leads ultimately to an expressive collapse, then Croker's critical comparison becomes unwittingly apt: he sees the author and the novel as a weak and suffering female body, the same type of body that in Burney's works finally, desperately, expresses its own frustrations.

FEMINISM AND FEELING: FROM BURNEY TO INCHBALD

The displays of suffering that predominate the creative work of Frances Burney characterize, in G.J. Barker-Benfield's assessment, the foundation of feminism: the central focus on suffering in late eighteenth-century literature by women represents "their awakening to self-consciousness as a group."[95] Yet Burney's sensible and conflicted heroines also illustrate how "self-consciousness" has shifted from a form of productive self-awareness (as demonstrated by Haywood's heroines) to take on the connotations of insecurity that it maintains today. And as even her heroines' insensible displays become hounded by frustration and criticism, they indicate what Claudia Johnson counters, that a "woman's presence in a sentimental public sphere is not to be confused with her empowerment there."[96] One objection to reading Burney's works as feminist is to problematize how effective this approach to emotional expression really was.

Another objection is to question how personal this approach really was. Adela Pinch makes the point that both the pro-feminism argument and its rebuttal present a critical tendency to assume that "when women wrote, it was of their sufferings as women," a tendency especially evident when the writing deals explicitly with suffering itself.[97] Since "emotion often appears to us to belong definitively to the realm of experience," when women write about feelings they are assumed to be writing about their own.[98] However misplaced this assumption is, it stretches all the way back to the early eighteenth century, at which time it was invoked by the writers themselves. Haywood's previously quoted disclaimer to *The Fatal Secret* is a case in point: "Love . . . requires no Aids of Learning, no general Conversation, no Application . . . this is a Theme, therefore, which . . . frees me from the Imputation of Vain or Self-Sufficient."[99] Haywood's assertion is somewhat tongue-in-cheek, a cover for her interest in contemporary politics and scandal. Yet while the caution against reading women's literary writings as exclusively about women's experience is merited, both the criticism that endorses and the criticism that counters this assumption neglect to question why this assumption might even exist: why would women bother to turn to fiction, as opposed to some more overtly autobiographical form of writing, to express their feelings?

The backlash against female suffering that surfaces in Burney's life and work can provide one answer, as it illustrates the danger in having fiction align too closely with personal experience. No matter how carefully they try to obscure the agency or intention behind emotional display, Burney's heroines—and, as Croker's critical analogy between *The Wanderer* and the aging authoress makes clear, Burney herself—are condemned for publishing sufferings that are too obviously their own. The unconscious nature of the swoon that erases the threat of conscious dissembling also insists "these are *my* feelings," and as the abandoned Elinor and chastised Camilla experience, the public is not always receptive to such assertions. No one likes a guilt trip or a pity party, even an unintentional one; it is more comfortable, as the response Sophy Streatfield's tears or Juliet's anxious Lady Townly indicates, to read suffering or discomfort as put on.

For a woman to claim, by adopting a theatrical role or by choosing to write fiction, that "these are not *my* feelings" thus becomes the safest and surest way for her to articulate that they are.[100] In the next chapter, Elizabeth Inchbald explores how emotions can be felt by individuals and yet channeled through multiple roles and personae, so that the distance between woman and role, between an expression of feeling and its origin, becomes much more overt. While Burney's staged swoons represent a similar effort to channel sufferings through carefully crafted displays, these moments are designed to appear completely spontaneous, to disguise the lag time between feeling and expression. Inchbald's approach demonstrates that, as the distance between these categories increases or is advertised, the emotional link between character and role becomes stronger: more effective and more compelling. If emotions seem to circulate, or seem hard to claim as one's own (per Pinch's observations),[101] it is less in Inchbald's case because of a questionable experiential origin to feeling, and more because the one who owns and expresses emotions can do so only by claiming distance or detachment from them.

Note that now, as opposed to specifying a passion such as desire or suffering, I associate an author with emotions—general and plural. Emotions in Inchbald's work are hard to pin down, again, not because they lack an experiential origin, but because so many emotions share the same one. Acting theory and the literature of sensibility alike treated the passions in a sequential and limited manner (for all its claims to general "sensibility," the melodramatic tendencies of such literature stem from the way in which characters respond to events in emotionally consistent and repetitive ways). While Inchbald shows characters attempting to do the same thing—to use role-playing as a way to detach themselves from complicated and overlapping passions, to disguise undesirable ones and convey only the discrete feeling of their choice—she also shows the way this strategy inevitably produces a very different result. The performances that are designed to distill, divide, and disguise the passions become the performances that conflate, connect, and express them. For Inchbald, gaps and categories are created only to be joined.

4   Acting as Herself
Elizabeth Inchbald and Mediated Feelings

In March of 1784, George Colman the Elder, manager at the Haymarket, accepted Elizabeth Inchbald's afterpiece *The Mogul Tale* for production. The piece would be an overnight hit, propelling Inchbald from her position as mediocre actress to one of the most successful playwrights of the late eighteenth century. Yet she and Colman exhibited caution when it came to publicizing this, her first accepted piece. Both took "the greatest care . . . to conceal that she was the author of the farce," and "the best mask they thought was to give her a part in it."[1] As a result, Inchbald attended the first reading of the play as an actress, not as the playwright. None of the other actors were told that she was the author, and her friend and fellow actress Mrs. Sumbel comments with some annoyance that during the reading Inchbald "corrected me in some of the passages which I did not speak to please her; which was by no means agreeable to me at the time, for I then conceived her very inadequate to the task."[2]

While the play was ultimately a rousing success, the anecdote illustrates provocative assumptions surrounding actresses and female playwrights at the end of the century. First and foremost, it emphasizes that beginning a career in the theater was still a risky and nerve-wracking business for a woman, enough to inspire the hopeful female playwright and the manager brave enough to take her on with extreme caution. Secondly, and as a result, it illustrates a strategically mediated form of personal expression.

As Ellen Donkin has described, female playwrights in the late eighteenth century tended to channel their authorial opinions through an appropriate spokesman: a respected male patron, such as David Garrick; a trusted male relative (as in the case of Frances Burney, who often relied on her brother Charles to deliver scripts and talk to casts); or the theater manager himself. And while the approval of the theater manager was essential to any playwright's success, the sense of debt among women "appears to have extended well beyond the practicalities of editing and producing, and to have worked its way into the creative mechanism itself."[3] The playwright "could expect either to have theatre personnel substantially alter her play for production or to be asked to provide revisions on tight deadlines"; this complicated dependence on the theater manager led to a kind of reverse mediation, a fear among women playwrights that "somehow [the manager] had written plays *through* her."[4]

Inchbald was unique in that, unlike many female playwrights, she did not rely so heavily on male patrons or go-betweens. Her early career as an actress familiarized her with the practicalities of theatrical performance—unlike Burney, she knew what kind of dialogue would work well on stage, for example—and put in her touch with many necessary contacts.[5] She was an insider, as this anecdote shows. Yet while she may speak her mind to her actors, she does so in this instance by passing herself off as one of them. She and Colman use the public role of actress to obscure her identity as playwright even as she, to her friend's consternation, expresses opinions befitting the author of the play. This strategy is curious in that Colman and Inchbald understand it to be an effective disguise: Inchbald the actress should "mask" Inchbald the playwright, as if she could be one or the other but not both (though there are precedents, Haywood for one, for this overlap). It becomes even more curious when we recognize that by separating her professional roles, Inchbald actually allows these roles to coexist. Inchbald's unique opportunity to advise her actors in person, to act like Inchbald the playwright, is contingent upon her ability to act like Inchbald the actress. An aspect of mediation remains, if less literally, as Inchbald channels the opinions of the playwright through the medium of the actress. In doing so, Inchbald connects the very roles that she presents as distinct, a kind of layering that lends complexity to every sentiment she articulates. No wonder Mrs. Sumbel was confused.

This story of Inchbald's performance in *The Mogul Tale* frames a discussion of what I term "emotional mediation" in Inchbald's life and work. The sections that follow offer readings of Inchbald's first novel (*A Simple Story*, 1791) and two of her later plays (*Wives as They Were, Maids as They Are*, 1797; *A Case of Conscience*, 1800). In each text, Inchbald exposes the inefficacy of direct communication and makes explicit the alternative that emotions be mediated through others—or through chosen roles. These texts also illustrate an increasing emphasis on female characters' ability to perceive and embrace the advantages of emotional mediation, an ability that corresponds to their increased influence over men. The constraints placed on women, or the subordinate positions that keep these characters at a distance from their tyrannical masters, necessitate those strategies of mediation that Inchbald presents as more effective than any alternative. In this context, limitations placed on female characters become assets, a formulation I test by returning to Inchbald's opening night appearance in *The Mogul Tale* and her onstage fit of stuttering that ensued. The speech impediment (that illustrates at once constrained expression and the excessive emotion that provokes it) becomes a final test case for the sense of impediments or limitations as empowering, and for the theoretical validity of reading a woman writer in the context of her texts. The stammer represents in my analysis both the necessity for emotional mediation and, by its position onstage, an act of mediation in itself.

As this chapter shifts between literal and more figurative forms of mediation, what constitutes direct or indirect communication bears clarification. Direct communication consists of face-to-face interactions between the person who has something to convey and his or her intended auditor. For Inchbald, direct communication is often signaled by physical gestures and expressions that drive home the bodily proximity of the participants. Yet in Inchbald's work, not only do such interactions lead to misunderstandings and ambiguity, but characters often treat their auditors as conduits for feelings that apply to someone else. Thus, even direct communication reveals itself upon examination to be indirect, a form of communication in which the interlocutor distances himself or herself from the object of his or her feelings. It is this distancing that can be very literal—signaled through the use of messengers or letters, and maintained through segregation and banishment—or more figurative. Performance, in the form of role-playing, injects the same sense of distance between feeling figures; in this case, role-playing involves an emotional masking or compartmentalization that substitutes for geographic space. In presenting emotions as merely "put on," characters gain the ability to act out the very feelings they would hide: feeling *as* they are allows them to feel as they *are*.

To read Inchbald's texts in the context of her career illustrates why this convoluted approach was necessary, and how various genres invoke this same literal and figurative relationship between distancing and expression. Even if they employed intermediaries, playwrights "risked public exposure in a way that was distinct from that of writers in other genres."[6] While negotiating print publication also demanded a certain amount of social mobility and interaction, negotiating the production of a play "required . . . a complex kind of sociability."[7] The forms of social networking required of playwrights forced a woman into the public eye, whereas the novelist could address her public at a greater remove, from the safety of her "closet."[8] Inchbald and many of her contemporary female dramatists often commented on the particular susceptibility to public criticism that resulted from this more direct form of communication. "The Novelist is a free agent. He lives in a land of liberty, whilst the Dramatic Writer exists but under a despotic government," Inchbald would claim,[9] while Hannah Cowley notes in the preface to *A School for Greybeards* that the dramatist feels "encompassed in chains" when she writes, which "check [her] in [her] happiest flights, and force [her] continually to reflect, not, whether *this is just?* But, whether *this is safe?*"[10]

What signifies effective emotional expression therefore also shifts in this chapter. In the previous analysis, an effective expression signified an alignment between what a character was feeling and what the audience understood the character to feel. Here, effectiveness represents more the character's (or author's) ability to act out his or her emotions safely—to express feelings yet remain exempt from criticism or retribution. Emotional mediation offers this combination of expression and protection, through the distance it injects between character and audience, and through the indeterminacy it preserves in a character's emotional state. Mrs. Sumbel's cranky response to Inchbald's authorial opinions reveals how mediated emotions are often confusing to those who witness them; auditors sense a complexity to the individual emotional experience that they can't quite explain.

These auditors sense subjectivity—the convoluted and unique interior life that Inchbald reveals through her adamant refusal to expose it. Inchbald crafts psychological depth not through her emphasis on internal or consistent character traits, but through descriptions of external and varied traits that lend freedom and continuity to the act of expression. By fragmenting their identities, characters in Inchbald's work gain the ability to mediate personal feelings through themselves. Inchbald's characters thus exhibit aspects of the protean and superficial identity supposedly characteristic of the earlier part of the century, even as these shifting personae enable the expression of consistently held, identity-defining passions more in line with romantic conceptions of the self.[11]

In her work on Inchbald, Terry Castle has provocatively concluded that "we do not yet know, perhaps, how to read her fully."[12] Understandably so, given her convoluted approach to expression. But in applying Inchbald's own strategic methods to her texts, this chapter attempts to make our readings of Inchbald a bit more complete. To appreciate the full complexity of this author, we must recognize, as Inchbald does, that every gap creates the possibility for connection, that every layer creates the possibility for depth.

MEDIATION IN THE NOVEL: *A SIMPLE STORY*

A Simple Story features daring subject matter for the time period: it tells the story of a beautiful ward (Miss Milner) who falls in love with her Catholic priest guardian (Dorriforth, later Lord Elmwood) and the effects of their love on the next generation. As Jane Spencer puts it in her introduction to the novel, "only Inchbald's extreme delicacy of handling could have made her theme acceptable to her readership," and Inchbald achieves such delicacy by what she does *not* say or describe.[13] As Inchbald's friend Maria Edgeworth writes, "by the force that is necessary to repress feeling, we judge of the intensity of the feeling; and you always contrive to give us by intelligible but simple signs the measure of this force."[14] The terms of Edgeworth's praise highlight several key elements of the novel, among which are the characters' consistent efforts to suppress their feelings and Inchbald's refusal as author to specify them (note that Edgeworth describes as intelligible the extent of the force exerted to control emotions, not the emotions themselves). Instead, as Nora Nachumi observes, "Edgeworth's opinion about the power of silence and 'simple signs' draws our attention to the way Inchbald dramatizes her characters' emotions through their bodies."[15]

This emphasis on physical rather than verbal expression is necessitated by the plot events that demand (an oft repeated word) "silence!" from the characters involved. In the first half of the narrative Miss Milner must hide her blossoming love for her guardian, not merely because confessing her love would violate the codes of female modesty, but because the object of her affections is a Roman Catholic priest. For the latter reason especially her love is unspeakable, and when she does finally admit her love, violently, passionately, to her confidant Miss Woodley, her friend interrupts her horror-struck, with the command of "Silence."[16] Their future interactions are marked by this order. When Miss Milner asks for her friend's advice, Miss Woodley can only sit, "still pale, and still silent" (73), and when they meet again later in the day "a silence ensued between her and Miss Woodley for near half an hour; and when the conversation began, the name of Dorriforth was never uttered" (76). Her love loses some of its impropriety when Dorriforth gains a title—Lord Elmwood—and is permitted to dispense with his religious vows, but Miss Woodley's early prohibition clings tenaciously to all interactions involving Miss Milner and her guardian; modesty still prevents Miss Milner from directly stating whom she loves.

As noted, Inchbald fills these silences in *A Simple Story* with descriptions of gestures, and most critics assert that the novel privileges gesture over speech as a clear, comprehensible method of communicating emotion.[17] Certain moments in the novel do seem to describe forms of wordless communication as more effective—more pointed, more forcible, more confirming—than the spoken word. Perhaps the most striking such interaction occurs between Miss Woodley and Lord Elmwood, when Elmwood finally realizes that he is the object of Miss Milner's love:

> He once more turned his enquiring eyes upon Miss Woodley.—He saw her silent and covered with confusion.—Again he searched his own thoughts, nor ineffectually as before.—At the first glance the object was presented, and he beheld *himself*.
>
> The rapid emotion of varying passions, which immediately darted over his features, informed Miss Woodley her secret was discovered—she hid her face, while the tears that fell down to her bosom, confirmed him in the truth of his suggestion beyond what oaths could have done. (130)

The silent, face-to-face exchange between Lord Elmwood and Miss Woodley conveys emotions "beyond what oaths could have done"—except the emotion in question is actually felt by someone else, the process of emotional communication actually mediated. Silent and confused under Lord Elmwood's stare, Miss Woodley unconsciously occupies the role of the absent Miss Milner, the modest maiden standing before her lover. Unable to convey her emotions directly to Lord Elmwood, Miss Milner has confessed her love to Miss Woodley who now, through her confusion and silence, expresses it to him. Lord Elmwood, too, sees Miss Milner's love by turning his mental eye inward; by examining his own thoughts and passions, he discovers the passions of someone else. Yet even as the interaction between Miss Woodley and Lord Elmwood highlights what Adela Pinch traces in other eighteenth-century prose as a "concomitant tendency to character-ize feelings as transpersonal, as autonomous entities that do not always belong to individuals but rather wander extravagantly from one person to another,"[18] this traveling passion acknowledges its source. The interaction proves crucial to the plot development because the love that is finally com-municated is very much Miss Milner's.

What the interaction also reinforces, though, is the impossibility for such passions to be expressed directly, though the attempt to do so, and the belief that this should be possible, lead to most of the misunderstand-ings that plague the novel. Inchbald's noted emphasis on gesture signals that characters who want to share feelings often deal with each other face to face, a circumstance that (contrary to what most critics claim about this novel) leads persistently to confusion. "It is not impossible I remain wholly unacquainted with your sentiments, even after you have revealed them to me" (55), Dorriforth complains of Miss Milner at one point, and gestures prove as unreliable a form of communication as words. While the narrator claims that "looks and manner alone express" (17), the verb remains curi-ously without an object, and the narrative continuously endorses gestures as expressive without clarifying of what. In the second chapter Mrs. Hill-grave, an acquaintance of Miss Milner, lifts up her hands and sheds tears at the mention of Miss Milner's name, which another guest reads as a sign of condemnation. When Miss Hillgrave speaks, however, she reveals that her gestures represented her sense of obligation: "'Miss Milner,' answered she, 'has been my benefactress, and the best I ever had'" (11). The minor episode reveals an important fact: that gesture can represent a multiplicity of different, often contradictory emotions and can therefore be interpreted in radically different ways by different observers. As Jane Spencer notes, "bodily signs which usually, in the literature of sensibility, speak more truly than words, are radically ambiguous in Inchbald's world."[19]

So while the long-distance relationship is typically bemoaned for the strain it puts on communication and intimacy, this ambiguity of gesture means that Lord Elmwood and Miss Milner actually communicate their feelings more effectively from a distance, and through intermediaries. After Lord Elmwood's meeting with Miss Woodley enables him to learn of Miss Milner's feelings for him (and to recognize his feelings for her), the two lov-ers enjoy a passionate, tumultuous engagement. Yet Miss Milner repeatedly tests the strength of Lord Elmwood's affections by challenging his admoni-tions, and when she attends a masquerade after he has explicitly advised against it, he breaks off the engagement and plans to leave the country. A silent interaction with her lover, when he apprehends her crying and leaves her with a bow, has convinced Miss Milner of "his total indifference" (181), while her flirtations with Lord Frederick have convinced him of hers. It is the priest and mentor figure Sandford who senses that both still possess great feeling for each other, and who intercedes at the last moment to propose that instead of parting, they forgive each other and marry.

Sandford advocates the physical proximity that should enable the lovers to express their love, yet while Elmwood's departure does not bode well for the relationship, the erasure of all distance between the lovers does not, either. With this happy reunion comes a renewed emphasis on gestures that remain tenuous and uncertain indicators of meaning. The wedding ceremony dictates that lovers' feelings be formalized through words, yet when Elmwood asks if Miss Milner will "show me that tender love you have not shown me yet?" she replies by "rais[ing] him from her feet, and by the expression of her face, the tears with which she bathed his hands, gave him confidence" (191–92). Elmwood at this moment does not need to be shown, he needs to be told, and without the performative "I do," Miss Milner's commitment seems uncertain. The fact that Miss Milner cannot say that she loves Elmwood testifies not necessarily to a lack of feeling (indeed, it indicates an excess), but rather to the difficulty in communicating it and the danger in refusing to acknowledge this difficulty. For even as Elmwood assumes he understands her looks, her tears, her tremblings, the ceremony is formalized with another physical symbol of love that ominously and inappropriately conjures a double meaning: "the ring Lord Elmwood had put upon her finger, in haste . . . was a—MOURNING RING" (193). Hands may touch while hearts and minds do not.

*　　*　　*

If the first half of the narrative suggests that feelings cannot be communicated effectively in a direct and physical manner, then its resolution should involve emotional expression that is more mediated or detached. And so, when the narrative resumes after the wordless marriage ceremony, seventeen years have passed: Miss Milner (now Lady Elmwood) has had a daughter and an affair; she and Elmwood have separated; she is living apart from him; she is dying. Many critics have criticized this transition as abrupt and artificial, with Jo Alyson Parker's response as indicative of the more general reaction: "the graft of the two parts seems mechanical . . . and the usual critical response has been to deplore the addition of the second half of the novel."[20] But as Inchbald's narrative structure strikes critics as not seamless, as an unnatural bridge over too wide a gap, the structure also mirrors the type of resolution that the second part will present. The genealogical narrative sets up a temporal detachment from the first half of the novel even as the second part posits the unnatural segregation of Lord Elmwood from his daughter as crucial to their reconciliation.

Distance characterizes the second half of the novel in the way that painful proximity and awkward interaction characterized the first half. Lord

Elmwood leaves for the West Indies and remains there for three years. Lady Elmwood, who in his absence has dallied with Lord Frederick, flees upon her husband's return, and Lord Elmwood's inexorable temper ensures that the two former lovers remain apart for the duration of Lady Elmwood's life. Lady Elmwood's last request, that Lord Elmwood provide some habitation for their daughter, Matilda, is granted on the condition that Elmwood never see her or have any evidence of her presence. The father and daughter skirt each other for the remainder of the novel, until an unexpected meeting between the two causes Lord Elmwood to banish her to an even more distant location.

In this summary, distance seems to create problems not solve them, especially as Lord Elmwood's three-year stint abroad apparently provides the stimulus for Lady Elmwood's affair. Yet even here Inchbald suggests that it is not his absence, or at least not *only* his absence, that so aggravates his wife, but his refusal to acknowledge the real reason (a severe illness) that he cannot return. Elmwood does not attempt to communicate his feelings from a distance—indeed he represses all mention of his physical or emotional well-being—so we cannot really judge how effectively his feelings would have translated from afar. And a contrasting example indicates that distance can do much, both to convey and inspire feeling. Lady Elmwood's final wishes are conveyed to her husband from two removes, via Sandford and via a letter. This letter, which causes Elmwood's tears to flow, moves her husband as it reinforces the distance that has come between them. First, she makes her request, that he shelter their daughter, on her father's behalf. The daughter is presented and welcomed as "the grand-daughter of Mr. Milner," an epithet that erases a generation and a conjugal bond (210). Secondly, she invokes her body as it rests in the grave, not as an expressive symbol of pain, but as a non-expressive corpse: "in my altered face there is no anxiety . . . my whole frame is motionless" (211–12). The effectiveness of the letter rests in its insistence that the language of gesture is at an end; vivid as this image is, its potency lies in its assurance that she is forever beyond his sight and reach.[21]

But whereas Lady Elmwood's letter demonstrates how emotions may bridge physical distance, and that separation indeed encourages an emotional communication not possible in more intimate interactions, distance is more commonly understood to forestall any emotional connection. This understanding forms the basis for Lord Elmwood's conduct. His emphatic need to separate himself physically from his wife and daughter is described as a strategy to suppress emotional bonds: "prudence he called it not to remind himself of a happiness he could never taste again . . . prudence he called it, not to form another attachment near to his heart" (202). The prohibitions that he issues to others, never to see these women, never to be reminded of these attachments, are actually "as much a means of controlling himself" as a means of controlling the people to whom these orders are issued.[22] Any necessary communication with the objects of his displeasure tends to be conducted through forms of expression (letters, messengers) that allow him to maintain a physical distance between himself and those with whom he communicates.

While Elmwood enforces this distance and detachment through physical separations, he also creates space between himself and this audience through a bizarre kind of role-playing, signaled first by Inchbald's use of theatrical terminology. Like an eighteenth-century portrait of Dorian Gray, Lord Elmwood's appearance changes with his behavior. The Dorriforth of Volume 1 is handsome because "on his countenance you beheld the feelings of his heart . . . on this countenance his thoughts were pictured" (8); by contrast, the tyrannical Lord Elmwood of Volume 2 is often described as "masked" (153). "Why persuade Lord Elmwood to put on a mask," cries Miss Milner, when Miss Woodley suggests he attend the masquerade as a grave and serious character, "just at the time he has laid it aside?" (153). The term refers to the new static, hidden element of Elmwood's countenance. It labels him as a performer who seeks to disguise his feelings from other characters—and from himself.

That this is role-playing, or a form of performance, is reinforced by the narrator through a subtle rhetorical device. When the Lord Elmwood of Volume 2 selects library books for "Miss Woodley," he clearly knows that Miss Woodley will carry these books to his daughter. Yet he is described as choosing the books as carefully "as the most cautious preceptor culls for his pupil, or *a fond father for his darling child*" (272–73; emphasis mine). A rhetorical device that "sets up a comparison—creates a space,"[23] the simile reproduces the same idea of distance and detachment represented by the living arrangements, by Miss Woodley's (and not Matilda's) presence in the library. Described by the narrator *as* a father, Elmwood makes his emotions role-like, and his behaviors seem consciously adopted to drive a wedge between who he is and how he feels. The grammatical construction of the sentence suggests that if Elmwood acts "as" a certain role, he cannot "be" that role. If Elmwood can "put on" the father's behavior, he can also take it off; he may perform signs of paternal tenderness and yet remain the stoic individual.

The simile reveals an underlying supposition about performance, that the behaviors of the performer are feigned or dissembled, and so about why Elmwood adopts the kind of behavior that he does. But the simile stands out because Elmwood is, of course, the father he acts "as," and it signals to us how Elmwood's strategies of detachment and disguise ironically enable him to express the very feelings he would deny. By separating himself from the objects of his affections, physically and rhetorically, Elmwood actually becomes better able to communicate these feelings. In the first half of the novel, he can show kindness to Miss Milner by showering affection on her favorite, his young nephew Rushbrook. In the second half, he can be kind to Matilda via Miss Woodley. Rushbrook and Miss Woodley become conduits for his emotions; they enable him to express feelings that would otherwise be repressed. He can act on the feelings he acts out.

And although Elmwood's methods of indirect emotional expression are disturbingly "unnatural"[24]—and unintentional—the novel never presents any viable alternative to Elmwood's methods of indirection. He cannot act "as" a father unless he is separated from his child, and when finally faced with his daughter he must reestablish a separation between them before he can communicate paternal emotion. Supposedly twenty miles away from his house, Lord Elmwood returns unexpectedly one afternoon, just in time to catch Matilda walking down the stairs. Matilda starts, screams, and falls senseless into her father's arms:

> He caught her, as by that impulse he would have caught any other person falling for want of aid.—Yet when he found her in his arms, he still held her there—gazed on her attentively—and once pressed her to his bosom . . . Her name did not however come to his recollection—nor any name but this—"Miss Milner—Dear Miss Milner."
> . . . at this instant Giffard, with another servant, passed by the foot of the stairs; on which, Lord Elmwood called to them—and into Giffard's hands delivered his apparently dead child; without one command respecting her, or one word of any kind. . . . (274)

With his attentive gaze and close, protective embrace, he momentarily looks like the father he truly is. Yet the daughter in his arms brings the image of his wife before his eyes, and he cries out to his senseless girl the words he could never articulate to his faithless lover.[25] And while his conjugal feelings may be mediated through Matilda, he no longer has that physical distance that allows him to "put on" his paternal emotions. Lord Elmwood therefore "masks" himself once more, reasserting the separation between father and child that in turn implies (to himself and to the watching servants) a separation between the father and the feelings of a father. Matilda's hand unconsciously grips the side of her father's coat, and Lord Elmwood commands the servant to pull it off: "it fell—and her father went away" (274).

After pulling himself away, Elmwood increases the distance between himself and his daughter by banishing her from the house and by conveying his orders indirectly via letter, in much the same way that he broke off his engagement with Miss Milner. He reasserts his prohibitions to other characters that Matilda cannot be mentioned in his presence. And it is Matilda's banishment—the reinforced separation between father and child—that again allows Lord Elmwood to act as he is. Separated from her father, Matilda finds herself a "defenceless woman" (319), capable of being abducted by the rakish Lord Margrave. Her abduction gives Lord Elmwood, once more, the opportunity to "prove [him]self a father" (324), this time by becoming her rescuer. Again the unnatural, un-paternal distance

Elmwood establishes between himself and his child enables the formation of that very paternal bond Elmwood seeks to erase.

Yet this method of emotional conveyance provides a decidedly unsatisfying solution to characters' communication problems, in part because it provides a decidedly temporary one. The typical "happy ending" that involves the reunion of separated lovers and kin also involves a reunion of bodies and a return to the language of gesture that is in this case uncertain and ambiguous. The return of Matilda to her father and the suggestion of a union between Matilda and Rushbrook do away with the literal distance between characters, and almost instantly we are presented with a series of misunderstandings left pointedly unresolved by the narrator. Rushbrook, long in love with Matilda, finally has the opportunity to propose, yet Matilda does not understand Rushbrook's intentions, and when he tells her that he wants "a wife," she turns pale, sags against a nearby desk, and is silent. Rushbrook, in turn, either misunderstands her reaction or purposefully glories in this proof of her emotion, though again, the exact emotions signified by her bodily changes remain unclear. His question, "What means this change?" (337), represents the governing uncertainty of the novel and is unaccompanied by any narrative gloss on his or her internal feelings. When Rushbrook clarifies his request, Matilda, like her mother, provides no answer to Rushbrook's proposal; instead, the narrator steps in with a final, ambiguous flourish:

> Whether the heart of Matilda, such as it has been described, *could* sentence him to misery, the reader is left to surmise—and if he supposes that it did not, he has every reason to suppose their wedded life was a life of happiness. (337)

The outcome recalls Miss Milner's marriage ceremony and subsequent troubled marriage; even if the reader chooses to suppose that Matilda and Rushbrook marry, Catherine Craft-Fairchild notes that "there are many reasons given in *A Simple Story* to suppose that no wedded life is a life of happiness for the woman."[26]

But proposing detachment and mediation as the alternative solution to emotional communication troubles us on a more intuitive level. In a "Gift of the Magi" kind of paradox, we are offered physical proximity without emotional intimacy, or emotional intimacy without physical proximity, neither of which seems sufficient. Inchbald's "resolution" undermines the value we place on direct, unmediated emotional contact as more personal and therefore more honest, a value reflected in the traditional romance plot that presents the ability to convey affection only through intermediaries or disguise as the obstacle the hero or heroine must overcome. By reversing this usual trajectory, Inchbald's novel suggests that mediated, performed feelings may actually be more effective, sincere representations of one's true emotional state. This suggestion recalls the work done in the previous chapters to establish theatrical performance as self-expressive, precisely because it is approached by spectators and performers as an instance of feigning. What Inchbald explores in greater detail is the emotional complexity conveyed, and perpetuated, through theatrical performance. As she does so, she revises the contemporary theatrical conventions that codified emotion, and she makes the stage, more like the novel, a place for interiority and character depth.

*   *   *

Of all the authors considered in this study, Inchbald had the greatest amount of acting experience and theatrical exposure, and so would have been very familiar with contemporary theater's treatment of emotions as sequential and discrete. The stage dealt with the passions one at a time, manifested in the dramatic technique of "pointing." "Pointing" refers, as Lisa Freeman defines it, "to the practice of bracketing off a set speech from the course of action and directing that speech, along with a set of gestures, at the audience."[27] Perhaps one of the most famous "points" was Hamlet's meeting with the ghost of his father. In enacting this scene, David Garrick would "stan[d] rooted to the spot" with "both his arms, especially the left . . . stretched out nearly to their full length, with the hands as high as his head, the right arm more bent and the hand lower, and the fingers apart; his mouth is open."[28] Joseph Roach observes that "Garrick held this tableau for so long that some spectators wondered if he needed prompting."[29]

This technique was the practical application of current theories that codified gesture and associated emotions with a specific repertory of poses, in which each pose possessed a fixed meaning. Theatrical manuals of acting and stage handbooks contained descriptions and illustrations of the passions; in fact, in lieu of stage directions the theater manager often glossed the margins of plays with the names of individual passions, and the actor or actress would then simply pick the corresponding pose and adopt it at the specified point in the dialogue.[30] Such poses were carefully notated or drawn: mirth "opens the mouth towards the ears; crisps the nose; half-shuts the eyes, and sometimes fills them with tears"; surprise is conveyed when the eyes and mouth open up and the nostrils widen.[31] Garrick's stance when faced with Hamlet's father's ghost adheres to the directions for astonishment as specified in *A General View of the Stage* (1759): "the whole body is accentuated; it is thrown back, with one leg set before the other, both hands elevated, the eyes larger than usual, the brows drawn up, and the mouth not quite shut."[32]

Critic Alan McKenzie notes that these conventions of gesture were so widespread "that their signifyings could be taken for granted by painters, actors, and writers alike."[33] This interdisciplinary ability to communicate through gesture alone is emphasized by the illustrations of actors that proliferate in contemporary manuals on both acting and rhetoric.[34] While the appearance of the actor in guides to oratory underlines a link between the body and language—indeed, contemporary politicians flocked to plays to learn rhetorical skills, and Thomas Erskine, later the Lord Chancellor, acknowledged that "his best deliveries owed something to the harmony of [Sarah Siddons's] periods and pronunciation"[35]—the distillation of the actor's craft into a series of drawings indicates it was bodily language that entranced spectators above all else.

In fact, these eighteenth-century texts on acting, painting, and rhetoric consistently stress physical, gestural expressions as more reliable than words. James Burgh's *The Art of Speaking*, a popular eighteenth-century manual on oratory first published in 1761, describes the significance of the appearance or countenance that accompanies speech:

> Nature has given to every emotion of the mind its *proper* outward expression . . . from hence, that is, from *nature*, is to be deduced the whole art of speaking properly. What we mean does not so much depend on the *words* we speak, as on our *manner* of speaking them; and accordingly, in life, the greatest attention is paid to this, as expressive of what our words often give no indication of. Thus nature fixes the outward expression of every intention or sentiment of the mind.[36]

According to Burgh, outward expression, be it facial position, body position, or the inflection placed on words, is a more sincere testament to the emotion being conveyed than the words used to convey it. In fact, words can often be misleading, or give "no indication" of the sentiment being experienced by the speaker. In contrast, the straightforward semantics of the physical poses (note that Burgh maps "every emotion" onto "its proper outward expression") meant that, as Diderot claimed, words were not even necessary for the audience to interpret the passions depicted onstage. Diderot himself would often watch a play with his fingers stuck in his ears, to prove that he could follow the changing passions of the actors without the benefit of words.[37] Burgh, too, concludes this portion of his essay with the definitive statement that "a whole play can be represented without a word spoken."[38]

Such anecdotes indicate that the theater presented the passions as not only expressed but experienced with what Roach calls a "taxonomic rigidity": even as "all passions may be represented pictorially as essences and not analogically as processes . . . their formality denies the idiosyncratic, the fortuitous, and the *emergent*."[39] True, the so-called "naturalism" of Garrick's acting style stemmed in part from his celebrated ability to shift rapidly among these poses;[40] Sarah Siddons, one of the greatest tragic actresses of the time and one of Inchbald's close friends, was also known for her innovative ability to move almost seamlessly from gesture to gesture.[41] And yet an actor such as Garrick, who would famously run through an entire series of facial expressions to demonstrate the passions in rapid-fire succession, was merely creating the illusion of emotional simultaneity.[42] Even those innovators of the stage, Garrick and Siddons, were bound by eighteenth-century theatrical conventions that prevented emotions from being dynamic, variable, coexistent.

Inchbald's reliance on gesture in her nondramatic prose is undoubtedly suggested by her own theatrical training and her extensive professional and personal connections to the stage.[43] But if, as the previous section has detailed, Inchbald puts her reader in the theatrical position of interpreting what he "sees," gestures in Inchbald's work are rife with ambiguity, and misunderstandings arise because characters assume they can read bodies in the model of Diderot. The reliance on physical expression and the use of role-playing throughout the novel show characters acting on and acting out their feelings—but these performances signify emotional experiences and displays that are anything but discrete and sequential.

Gestures are for Inchbald unstable signifiers not merely because one gesture can suggest more than one feeling (Miss Hillgrave's look skyward signifies gratitude though it is interpreted as exasperation), but because more than one feeling can simultaneously motivate a gesture. Inchbald signals this concept of emotional complexity in various ways throughout her novel. Her narrator relies regularly on the conjunction "or," highlighting the different possible interpretations of gesture without specifying any. "What she said was spoken with an energy . . . joined with a real *or* well-counterfeited simplicity" (15); "she trembled—either with shame *or* with resentment" (28); "his lordship g[ave] himself up to the rage of love, *or* to rage against Dorriforth" (61); "the sensibility of Miss Milner had now reversed that prospect [of marriage] to perpetual spring; *or* the dearer variety of spring, summer, and autumn" (137; emphases mine in all examples). Similarly, the narrator uses indefinite terms such as "perhaps" and "probably": "what passion thus agitated Lord Elmwood . . . it is hard to define.—Perhaps it was indignation . . . perhaps his emotion rose from joy . . . perhaps it was perturbation . . . perhaps it was one alone of these sensations, but *most probably, it was them all combined*" (162; emphasis mine). This sense of emotional complexity is brought home when the distraught Lord Elmwood catches his swooning daughter, and his face is "agitated with shame, with pity, with anger, with paternal tenderness" (274).

Presented in this manner, Inchbald's repeated emphasis on the ambiguity of physical display stands as a testament to the complex interior life of her characters, a technique that contrasts with how critics generally understand the novel to signal psychological depth. Unlike the drama, the novel should present characters "whose emotions and motives [are] freely and completely available to scrutiny"; the novelist, in delineating these feelings, reveals "[the] rich and varied interior life" of his or her characters.[44] Yet Inchbald's narrator does not describe the exact emotions behind physical expressions, and therefore endows her characters with an endless emotional potential. Her narrator repeatedly reveals the rich and varied interior life of her characters—not by describing it—but by refusing to.

More specifically, Inchbald depicts this emotional complexity as expressed and perpetuated by forms of theatrical performance, and by the theatrical conventions of gesture that should function so differently on the stage. It is human nature, Inchbald tells us, to feel many passions at the same time. Elmwood's role-playing, then, is not unnatural so much for the distance it injects between himself and other characters, but for the distance it posits among his own emotions. Elmwood, with his static face and his carefully compartmentalized feelings, is a poster boy for the traditional, theatrical display of feeling. But as we recognize him as unnatural, and as we recognize how his attempts at rigid and static deportment break down, we are also forced to reevaluate how emotions can be experienced and expressed on the stage. In contrast to contemporary theatrical conventions, Inchbald shows that performing the passions encourages the experience of multiple emotions, and that physical expressions express this ambiguity as they indicate the presence of emotions without clearly demarcating them. Understood in these terms, theatrical performance becomes the most accurate way by which to represent the human condition of emotional flux.

Of course, Elmwood does not understand his performances in these terms; readers and author recognize what Elmwood does not. If this novel refuses to give the reader complete access to its characters' thoughts and feelings, it also describes the characters as ignorant of the dimensions of their own emotions, either unaware or not in control of the ways in which they perform their feelings through others. Characters find themselves forced into forms of indirect expression in response to unreasonably strict external dictates (Miss Milner, Matilda) or unwittingly exposing their true feelings while engaging in forms of indirect expression that they adopt to disguise these same emotions (Lord Elmwood). Yet in describing the ways her characters misunderstand performance and thus each other and themselves, Inchbald highlights her own awareness of how emotions may be performed. In this novel, Inchbald acknowledges mediation, not as a limitation or restriction, but as productive of the emotional complexity that renders an author's work realistic and compelling and of the emotional ambiguity that renders work safe. She reclaims the cultural constraints that force a woman to communicate her emotions as if they were not her own: from a distance and through others, through her fictional writing, through performance.

MEDIATION IN THE PLAYS: *A CASE OF CONSCIENCE; WIVES AS THEY WERE, MAIDS AS THEY ARE*

But if theatrical performance constitutes a form of mediation, the logistics of writing for performance threaten to undo whatever benefits mediation may convey. As noted, the female playwright already relied heavily on intermediaries, both as a way to navigate the complicated social network of the playhouse and as a way to deflect public criticism. Yet even with these strategies in place, Inchbald and other female playwrights found the drama constraining, especially when compared to the novel. Generic conventions dictated that the drama be bound by space and time limitations; as William Godwin observes to Inchbald, "It seems to me that the drama puts shackles upon you, and that the compression it requires prevents your genius from expanding itself."[45] And, as Inchbald observes in her essay for *The Artist*, the legal ramifications of the Licensing Act dictated that plays be limited to a few accepted topics: "A dramatist must not speak of national concerns, except in one dull round of panegyrick [sic] . . . whilst the poor dramatist is, therefore, confined to a few particular provinces; the novel-writer has the whole world to range, in search of men and topics."[46] On top of these constraints, the playwright is "the very slave of the audience," who can determine through their reactions the run of a play, whereas the novelist "assumes a freedom of speech to which all its readers must patiently listen."[47]

And yet—with two novels and twenty-one plays to her name, Inchbald was primarily a playwright. Not only that, she transposed characters and events from *A Simple Story* into a play. The heroine of her 1797 comedy, *Wives as They Were, Maids as They Are*, was, in Inchbald's own words, "formed from the same matter and spirit as compose the body and mind of the heroine of the 'Simple Story.'"[48] Inchbald's determined and successful participation in the very genre she laments as limiting provides yet another example of how she embraced vexed modes of communication to achieve the expression these same forms of communication would seem to efface.

Two of her later plays, *Wives as They Were, Maids as They Are* (1797) and her never-performed drama *A Case of Conscience* (1800), have specified links to Inchbald's first novel. Both feature tyrannical fathers and husbands and like her novel depict the effectiveness of mediated expression. Yet now we see a more explicit split in gendered approaches to emotional communication, as her male characters mediate their feelings unconsciously, her women, by choice. The potency of her misguided men is accordingly diminished as they misunderstand their own emotional complexity. Tyrannical male behavior, which seeks to limit the emotional range of both the individual and his associates, is in these plays less influential than the subordinate female approach that acknowledges emotional conflict and conveys it through mediated channels. To accentuate this difference, I focus first on the male characters from both plays and then the female ones. The contrast demonstrates what I suggest above, that women productively embrace a mediated form of expression depicted as more effective than its alternative—and ultimately as characteristic of fiction itself. In the process, staged characters take on an interiority and complexity more typical of their novelistic counterparts.

The title alone of Inchbald's 1800 play, *A Case of Conscience*, indicates the idea of an internal monitor or guide, while specific scenes attribute the now familiar misunderstanding of others' gestures to emotions harbored by the character who views them. One of the few plays Inchbald never had performed (it was sidelined due to complicated negotiations among Sheridan and the Kembles), *A Case of Conscience* tells the story of the tyrannical Marquis Romono, who has become convinced that his beloved wife Adriana was not virtuous before their marriage, and that his beloved son Oviedo is therefore not his own.[49] The play gradually reveals Adriana to be faithful, the Marquis, a victim of a plot arranged by her still jealous former suitor, Salvador (Duke Cordunna).

But in an echo of Lord Elmwood, Romono has difficulty modifying his own harsh assumptions. Stage directions indicate at one point that Romono looks upon his (innocent) wife "with a kind of agonizing inquiry. His emotions now evince that her embarrassment and confusion . . . are evidences which confirm all his fears of her guilt" (329). His misreads his wife's expressions, not simply because they represent a complex emotional state, but because he projects his own feelings onto the gestures he sees. Similarly, Adriana's spurned (and disguised) lover eagerly questions her physical response to the mention of Cordunna's name: "why does [your heart] throb? Why does the colour fade upon your cheek, and trembling seize your frame?" (326). While Cordunna's questions expose the ambiguity at the heart of Inchbald's project (Adriana feels guilty at this moment, not passionate), his character poses them rhetorically. Cordunna lists a series of gestures that should be unambiguous on the stage, and he questions her confidently, as a prompt for Adriana to verbalize the love he believes her physical response to indicate. Cordunna and Romono, persuaded by their own emotions to read Adriana's unambiguously, take decisive and disastrous measures. Cordunna reveals himself and proposes an elopement; Romono turns Oviedo over to the Inquisition.

As a revision of Lord Elmwood, the Marquis Romono also recalls Sir William Dorrillon, the bullying father in Inchbald's 1797 comedy, *Wives as They Were, Maids as They Are.*[50] In this play, business travels have kept Sir William abroad. In his absence his daughter, Miss Dorrillon, raised by his friend Mr. Norberry, has matured into a flirtatious, witty, beautiful woman—sexually virtuous, but fond of gambling and an extravagant lifestyle. The action begins when Sir William returns home disguised as Mr. Mandred to determine objectively his daughter's character. Yet although Sir William describes his disguise as "a stratagem by which . . . [to] ga[in] a knowledge of [his daughter's] heart" (4), he also seems to have personal reasons for keeping his identity a secret. His actions toward Miss Dorrillon—he dictates her current behavior, advises her as to her companions, and chastises her for her past actions—are justifiable from a father but not from a mere acquaintance, and Miss Dorrillon, thinking he is merely a friend of her guardian, responds with an indifference or anger that provokes her father even more. But every time Mr. Norberry offers, even begs, to end this vicious cycle by revealing Sir William's status to his daughter,

Sir William adamantly refuses with a rigour that reminds us of Lord Elmwood: "If you expose me only by one insinuation to her knowledge, our friendship is that moment at an end" (10). His objections now are rather curious, since when the play begins he has already had a month in which to observe his daughter's character.

Much like Lord Elmwood, then, Sir William sees the role of Mr. Mandred as a way that he can "pla[y] the role of father without publicly recognizing his paternity";[51] his role is designed to compartmentalize various feelings of paternal tenderness and indulgence, displeasure, regret, and guilt over his own neglect of his child. As long as he is Mr. Mandred, he can act with a father's authority toward his daughter and yet "leave the kingdom and her for ever—Nor shall she know that this indignant merchant whom she despises, was her father" (3). His statement, meant to emphasize Miss Dorrillon's potential misfortune in losing a father (and a father's fortune), also functions as a personal reassurance that he has the ability to abandon her. He can keep his identities distinct, and with them, his emotions: the authoritative merchant does not feel the emotional bonds that would tie a father to his child.

But as Inchbald will reinforce in *A Case of Conscience*, Sir William is fighting a losing battle. Familial relationships and the feelings they inspire are portrayed as innate and inescapable. "If I could trust the power [Oviedo] has over my heart . . . But, 'tis Cordunna's son at my feet . . . !" (339), Romono cries, and explains away his pangs of love and remorse: "he called me father, till I have imbibed all the feelings of a parent" (346). Yet the fact that Marquis Romono is completely wrong—"my reason . . . has erred: my heart always acknowledged [Oviedo]" (350)—shows Inchbald challenging the idea that emotions can be conditioned. Likewise, despite the practiced behaviors and rigid determination of Sir William, both father and daughter are constantly surprised by unsolicited feelings of kindness toward each other. Miss Dorrillon comments that "what is very strange, [Mr. Mandred] has taken an aversion to me.—But it is still more strange, that although I know he has, yet in my heart I like *him*" (17–18). Even his "aversion" isn't certain, as she senses that "if any serious misfortune were to befall me, he would be the first person to whom I should fly to complain" (18). Certain cues signal that Mr. Mandred is just as susceptible to this involuntary liking: "Sometimes indeed I have traced a spark of kindness," notes Miss Dorrillon of her companion, "and have gently tried to blow it into a little flame of friendship; when, with one hasty puff I have put it out" (17). Later, when she is encouraging a reconciliation between Mr. Mandred and one of her suitors, she claims "Now, as I live, Sir George, Mr. Mandred's hand feels warmer and kinder than yours—he tried to draw it back, but he has not the heart. [*Sir William snatches it away as by compulsion.*] Thou art a strange personage!—thou wilt not suffer me either to praise or dispraise thee" (53).

Sir William's attempts at rigid self-control also mirror the conventions of the eighteenth-century stage, which require characters to distill and distinguish the emotions. Yet again the inefficacy of this attempt, the way in which the characters' performances both reveal and increase their emotional turmoil, contradicts the sense that the eighteenth-century stage was limited to a "world of artifice, surface, masking."[52] In this play and in *A Case of Conscience*, hubristic attempts to condition and contain feelings through roles become the source of further internal conflict, a tragic pattern that culminates when the Marquis, in resistance to his feelings, condemns Oviedo to death. The moment he believes the execution to be complete, he exclaims "Dead! Oviedo dead! . . . how has a moment changed me! The sentence, 'he is no more,' has made me feel as if I would give the universe he were in existence!" (345). Sir William, in an effort to compensate for a sympathetic expression that involuntarily crossed his face, sends his daughter to jail for her gambling debts. He then "walks proudly" across the room, murmuring "this is justice—this is doing my duty—this is strength of mind—this is fortitude—fortitude—fortitude," only to "thro[w] his head into [his handkerchief]" (68).[53] The contradictory emotions that make these characters hard to read point to the kind of deep subjectivity that does not complicate the surface of a Joseph Surface. Not surprisingly, other characters see them as unpredictable, incomprehensible—as Miss Dorrillon puts it, "strange."

Yet these same conflicted characters misunderstand themselves as static and unfeeling, and in the process they become increasingly susceptible to manipulation. The insensible Matilda destroys all of Elmwood's emotional defenses, the beleaguered Adriana becomes comforter during Romono's sudden and to him inexplicable onset of remorse, and the swooning Miss Dorrillon sends Sir William into a tailspin of passion. As emotional instincts in these plays are portrayed as more trustworthy than reason, the ability to recognize the complex nature of the human heart is associated with a subtle power shift.

When Norberry does finally disclose Sir William's identity to Miss Dorrillon, the argumentative man can only utter "My daughter!—my child—! . . . I perceive that, in spite of philosophy, justice, or resolution, I could follow you all the world over" (86). Sir William's dictatorial influence proves temporary and groundless, and in a striking role reversal he follows his nearly insensible daughter off the stage. The happy endings of both plays depend on the discovery that feelings are trustworthy and inescapable, and that emotions dictate identity, rather than the other way around. But Inchbald's investment in the layered and coexistent nature of emotions endows the characters who acknowledge this capacity with a liberating range of behaviors and expressions. Those characters who embrace the complexity of the human heart thus embrace an identity that is both innate and varied. And it is consistently her female characters who exhibit the emotional intuition that renders them more powerful than the men who would control them, and the feelings they inspire.

But if owning up to your emotions means agency and power, women (who can't own much of anything at this point in time) should be at a distinct disadvantage, especially as women's emotions are communicated through channels and formalized through bonds that would seem to subsume them completely. "I had rather be your slave than his [Cordunna's] legal wife," cries Adriana to her husband, "only be kind to me *as* a slave, and I will conform to vassalage in the strictest sense" (342). The woman as slave, never an equal, always at a remove, is destined to enjoy her master's kindness from a distance, and Adriana correspondingly sees her son's return as the solution to her marital discord. Oviedo, she hopes, will "prove . . . an advocate for me with my dear Romono, and bring back those happy times, when you and I were by turns the mediator with him for each other in all my female, and your boyish, faults" (324). Instead of lamenting this scenario, Adriana indicates that even in happy times, feelings (and failings) are explained most effectively through intermediaries.

The previously demonstrated efficacy of mediation explains why the limitations forced upon women become strengths: the subordinate position that fosters emotional conflict also provides the only effective means to convey it. Lady Priory, the titular "wife as they were" from the subplot of Inchbald's 1797 comedy, similarly welcomes the subordinate position that necessitates mediated or indirect expression. A model of chastity and devotion, she explains that men "are *all tyrants*. I was born to be the slave of some of you—I make the choice to obey my husband" (59). Betsy Bolton points out that "while a woman has no choice but to be a slave . . . [her husband's] power depends on her choice—a fact which Lord Priory recognizes only belatedly, and promptly forgets."[54] In this play, Lady Priory's position of enslavement endows her with an influence over men that is consistently absent in the stubbornly independent and outspoken Miss Dorrillon.

At first, Lady Priory seems an obvious victim. Married to a jealous and officious man, she is also repeatedly molested by the libidinal Bronzely. Surprised by the rake in a dark passageway and embraced with an ardor that nearly smothers her, she can barely articulate the anger that such treatment inspires. Yet her final words—"'Don't hope to conceal yourself; I shall know you among the whole concert-room, for I carry scissors hanging at my side, and I have cut off a piece of your coat'" (31)—undermine the influence that this speech should assert. Her proclamation alerts Bronzely to his missing fabric: he swaps coats with Sir William, and lets him take the fall. Lady Priory would have been better off to remain victimized and "fairly speechless" (30), to let his appearance speak to her abuse.

Thus it is that silence, so often interpreted as a sign of feminine submission or oppression, becomes in this play an influential form of indirect expression. When Lady Priory, later abducted by Bronzely, is returned to her husband, Lord Priory questions her in front of the company.[55] "Boldly pronounce," he insists, " . . . that you return to me with the same affection and respect, and the self-same contempt for this man . . . you ever had" (92). Lady Priory does not answer, and his further prompts are met again with silence. Her non-answers become answers; her speechlessness indicates that she does not love her husband, that she has some feelings (and her silence leaves these tantaliz-ingly vague) for her abductor. When she does finally specify that gratitude "is the only sentiment [Bronzely] has inspired" (94), Lord Priory forgets the existing silence on the question of her feelings for himself. She has said noth-ing that can implicate her, yet by saying nothing, she has said much.

Silence, indirection, and self-effacement, all characteristics that should represent "the explicit disavowal of . . . self-expressive behaviors,"[56] in this play constitute conscious methods of self-expression that preserve most accurately the complexity of a woman's heart and communicate most safely (because most ambiguously) these multiple feelings. In this context, Miss Dorrillon's sentimental faint when she learns the true identity of "Mr. Mandred," is less a submissive demonstration, and more—in the tradition of Burney—an effective shift from her bossy ways. "Exact what vow you will on this occasion," our once spirited heroine tells her guardian, "I will make and keep it" (86). But her faint, which follows Norberry's command that she implore her father's forgiveness, excuses her from this action and her promised vow. That "we never learn what vow may have been exacted" is as telling as Lady's Priory's conscious silence.[57]

Miss Dorrillon's final lines, "a maid of the present day shall become a wife like those—of the former times" (95), therefore resonate as an asser-tion, not a concession. A statement purposely formulated to associate her with Lady Priory, Miss Dorrillon's declaration connects but does not con-flate these characters. Instead, the generalizations that characterize her final speech, and the tenses that simultaneously associate and contrast past and future states of being, introduce conceptual gaps that preserve the pos-sibility for mediated expression modeled by Lady Priory herself. Miss Dor-rillon isn't a Lady Priory yet, and even when she is, she will be similar but not a clone. These final lines demonstrate, not a lesson of submission, but a lesson about deferral and detachment—and the emotional connections that these characteristics enable.

The final lines also recall the title of this comedy, *Wives as They Were, Maids as They Are*, a title that posits the comparative and temporal divi-sions so characteristic of Inchbald's work. The comma that separates "were" from "are" mirrors the generational divide in *A Simple Story*, while wives and maids are described redundantly in terms of a state of being, much like Lord Elmwood who, in acting as a father, acts as he is—though not neces-sarily as he should be. This final point is brought home by a play title that recalls the corrective impulse behind Jacobin texts such as Godwin's *Things As They Are* (1794), or Robert Bage's *Man As He Is* (1792). The parallel rhetorical construction signals that neither things as they are, men as they are, nor maids as they are, are as they should be.

But instead of proposing a return to ancient domesticity, or, like her Jacobin colleagues, mourning the discrepancy between the real and the ideal, Inchbald stresses that "as" enables "is." The ideal and the innate are, in Inchbald's texts, achieved and expressed through the adopted and the put-on. Miss Dorrillon's celebrated reformation rests less in her adherence to a past model of decorum, and more in her final mastery of the Lady Priory-like role. The woman as she should be recognizes that she can be this woman only *as* she is.

Rhetoric and performance here unite. The strategy of mediation, represented by this tiny preposition, bridges the gap between character and role without filling it and posits the distance between character and role that makes connection possible. "As" and "as if" call attention to "substitutions" as comparisons; they highlight both the process by which these comparisons occur and the fact that there remain two roles, two objects in play. Just so, Lord Elmwood can be a father only as a father; his identity as father depends upon keeping the role of father discrete. Just so, too, with the workings of fiction: for fiction, according to the French critic Marthe Robert, also survives exclusively on the "as if" (though at certain points in the eighteenth century, "it tries very hard to make us forget it").[58] Always a form of dissembling, fiction communicates to its readers from a distance, at a remove—much like the characters within it. But to what end? If, by Inchbald's terms, "as" ultimately reveals "is," we as readers must rethink the function of fiction. By Inchbald's terms, the discrepancy between reality's "is" and fiction's "as" constitutes fiction's theatrical nature—and allows us to read fiction as an authorial performance.

INCHBALD ON INCHBALD: SELF-CRITIQUE

In critical terminology, the phrase "authorial performance" responds to poststructuralist effacements of writers, which "while provocative within the terms of historiographic theory, fail to provide a theoretical tool with which to investigate how women writers sought to shape authorship for their own purposes."[59] Thomas Crochunis specifically applies the concept to Inchbald, an author who consciously juxtaposed her various public roles. Inchbald, like Haywood, demonstrated a remarkable flexibility in her professional life, working as a playwright, an actress, a novelist, a translator, and a drama critic. Yet less like Haywood, who often used her theatrical roles to reflect on her novelistic heroines, Inchbald kept her professional personae quite distinct. For Inchbald, the sense of conscious shaping that marks Crochunis's idea of authorial performance is implied in her choice to move among different literary genres, and becomes explicit in her work as a critic and an actress. As a critic, she reflects objectively on her own dramatic compositions; as an actress, she performs in plays to disguise her own authorship of them. Inchbald's self-presentation in both cases calls attention to the discrepancies among her professional roles.

In contrast to this claim, straightforward conflations of Inchbald's fiction with her life run rampant in Inchbald criticism. Her contemporary biographer, James Boaden, claims that the masquerade incident in *A Simple Story* recalls Inchbald's own 1781 masquerade appearance in male attire.[60] Jane Spencer reads the Miss Milner/Dorriforth relationship in terms of the charged friendship that existed between Inchbald and John Philip Kemble, and Misty Anderson sees the harassment of Lady Priory in *Wives as They Were* as a retelling of Inchbald's own near-rape experiences at the hands of Thomas Harris.[61] Indeed, Inchbald herself sometimes connects an author with the characters she creates: she describes her meeting with Madame de Staël, for example, under the heading of "Meeting between 'Corinne' and Miss Milner," and she once submitted a play manuscript under the pseudonym "Mrs. Woodley."[62] All these associations are suggestive, but they also threaten to collapse the space that (if they ring true) Inchbald carefully creates by repositioning personal experiences in her novels and plays. By doing so, Inchbald simultaneously associates herself with and distances herself from her various personae. Inchbald presents role-playing—fragmentation—as essential to self-expression, even as this role-playing results in self-reflexivity and coherence.

Early in 1806, Inchbald signed a contract with the Longmans, in which she agreed to write a series of prefaces for plays to be published in *The British Theatre*. This collection was taken from the current performances at Drury Lane, Covent Garden, and the Haymarket, and as many of Inchbald's plays were in the contemporary repertoire, this project gave her the opportunity to comment on several of her own works.[63] *The British Theatre* includes the texts of, and Inchbald's prefaces to, her plays *Every One Has His Fault, To Marry or Not to Marry, Such Things Are, Wives as They Were, Maids as They Are,* and *Lovers' Vows* (her translation of August von Kotzebue's play *Das Kind der Liebe*). In considering her comedy *Wives as They Were*, Inchbald writes that "the first act promises a genuine comedy," but "she has had recourse at the end of her second act to farce . . . she then essays successively, the serious, the pathetic, and the refined comic; failing by turns in them all, though by turns producing a chance effect."[64]

Inchbald's commentary here is typical of her other critiques, in that it shows her to be an objective critic of her own work. The third-person pronoun separates the playwright from the critic, though as Inchbald's authorship of these plays and prefaces was public knowledge, the pronoun cannot be read as an attempt at humility or disguise. Instead, Inchbald uses this rhetorical technique to create critical objectivity, while concurrently encouraging readers to sense, as Crochunis points out, "the complicated dialogue between [Inchbald's] two voices."[65] We are meant to recognize how these different personae permit Inchbald to critique her own work, even as the associations between personae make it impossible to read these critiques in a straightforward manner.

Inchbald's rhetorical strategy recalls the techniques of emotional mediation that proliferate in her plays and novels. It also recalls my opening anecdote, on Inchbald's and Colman's decision to disguise Inchbald's identity as

playwright of *The Mogul Tale* by casting her in the play itself. Here too we
see a carefully preserved distinction between associated roles that endows
Inchbald with the unique opportunity to critique her fellow actors as the
playwright she actually was. Yet on the opening night of this performance,
the seasoned actress lost her cool:

> While [Inchbald] was standing in her natural alarm upon the stage,
> as Selima,[66] in the second scene, she heard a cue from another char-
> acter . . . after which she was *herself* to speak. The cue was, "Since
> we left Hyde Park Corner." She had merely to reiterate as an excla-
> mation, "Hyde Park Corner!" but terror had robbed her entirely of
> utterance; she turned pale, and remained for a time in a suspension of
> mute amazement. At length, with that stammer which in private only
> attended her, she slowly, and in a sepulchral voice, ejaculated, "Hh-yde
> Pa-ark Co-orner!"[67]

More curious than Inchbald's fumble is Boaden's assertion that by stammering, she "nearly betrayed both author and piece."[68] While Inchbald
was well known for her speech impediment, it is unclear why her stammer
would identify Inchbald as both actress *and* playwright.[69] But the onstage
stutter nearly conflated the roles that Inchbald was working so hard to keep
distinct, for soon after this incident, the audience began to whisper that the
stammering actress might actually be the author of the play.[70]

Her stammer illustrates the necessity for emotional mediation on several levels. Most generally, a speech impediment often forces the sufferer
to communicate through intermediaries, and Boaden asserts that in her
youth Inchbald's stutter was so severe as to "render her speech indistinct,
and intelligible only to those who had become skilful interpreters."[71] She
avoided society as a child, writing letters instead of seeing company, or having those close associates who could understand her speech translate what
she was saying to listeners. Her disability forced her to communicate from
a distance or through others—until she took to the stage. An acting career,
with its heavy emphasis on personal interaction and the spoken word, would
not seem to cater to her strengths, but Inchbald apparently discovered that
"stage declamation, being a raised and artificial thing, afforded more time
for enunciation; and that it is, for the most part, the eagerness and hurry of
conversation that, in the stammerer, provoke the desire, and obstruct the
performance."[72] Boaden's wording suggests that not only the pace, but the
emotional immediacy involved in spontaneous conversation work to hinder
the stammerer's expression. Stage declamation, as that which is "raised and
artificial," can proceed at a slower and more manageable speed—but it also
introduces a discrepancy between what is said and the speaker's "desire"
that frees the speaker's tongue. Getting some distance from her emotions,
either through writing or through rehearsed dialogue, becomes for Inchbald essential to their expression.

Her onstage stammer then represents a reversion to her youthful struggles for expression. It reveals a loss of the emotional detachment that Inchbald needs to speak clearly, which in turn, according to Boaden and her other biographers, signals the loss of that professional detachment that had been the foundation for her varied involvement in this play. The stammer signals an excessive nervousness—more than could reasonably be expected from a experienced actress—that apparently convinced the audience of her extra attachment to this production. The flubbed line startles her not only because it affects her performance, but because it affects the presentation of the entire piece, and she, as playwright, would be invested in the play as a whole.

Yet the asserted fact that the stutter caused the audience to think of Inchbald as the playwright opens up another, equally suggestive way to read her stammer: as a feigned re-creation of a defect for which she was well known that serves, perhaps, as a purposeful yet subtle puff for her play. Inchbald, who knew that she was known for her stutter, would have understood this break in character to advertise her identity to audience members. And as one who struggled with a genuine speech impediment, she would have known what the defect implied and how it could be read: as a sign of involuntarily expressed emotional turmoil suggesting—subtly, decorously—to her audience that her involvement with the play might transcend her role in it. Instead of representing a breakdown in emotional mediation, the stutter itself could be staged.

The above is necessarily speculative, but Inchbald's treatment of the stammer in her own plays reinforces the idea that a speech impediment could be consciously and productively employed. In her early comedy, *Such Things Are* (1787), Inchbald depicts the congenital stammer as a chosen means of expression and as a defect adopted to circumvent improper speech:

> TWINEALL: . . . [W]hen a gentleman is asked a question which is either very troublesome or improper to answer, he does not say he *won't* answer it, even though he speaks to an inferior; but he says, "Really it appears to me e-e-e-e-e- [*Mutters and shrugs*]—that is— mo-mo-mo-mo-mo—[*Mutters.*]—if you see a thing—for my part—te-te-te-te—and that's all I can tell about it at present.
> SIR LUKE: And you have told nothing.
> TWI: Nothing upon earth.
> LADY [TREMOR]: But mayn't one guess what you mean?
> TWI: Oh, yes—perfectly at liberty to guess.[73]

Twineall is a bit of a buffoon, and like most of Inchbald's misguided men, he reveals as much as he hides. While he prides himself on his deceptive performance, his affected muttering inevitably conveys the ignorance and unspecified insecurities that require him to resort to stammers instead of exact answers. Yet his performance also reveals how the stammer, assumed to be involuntary and incapacitating, can instead be feigned and advantageous. In preventing the articulation of emotions, the stammer simultaneously attests to their presence and preserves them in all their unspecified complexity. Paradoxically the stammer that grants us the perfect "liberty to guess," grants Inchbald a perfect liberty to express.

For behind Twineall lurks a stammering female playwright, who approaches this character with a necessary level of self-consciousness.[74] Stage declamation was supposed to stop Inchbald's stammer by distancing her from the immediacy of the emotions that triggered it. The danger, though, as Sir William, Elmwood, and Romono have all experienced, is that our emotions can be kept at bay for only so long. They will inevitably resurface to disturb our carefully constructed personae, our carefully controlled expressions. Inchbald's choice to *stage* the stammer represents a recognition of, and response to, this scenario. By acknowledging a personal defect, she may distance herself from a behavior that is involuntary and innate, then recast it as something she can adopt at will.

Emotional mediation thus revises our late-eighteenth-century picture of the individual to that of a unified self, consciously fragmented, so that it may be unified again and more firmly than before. Inchbald shows characters and author alike split into roles that allow them to re-approach emotions and traits as if they were not their own. This process renders these feelings more personal than if they remained suppressed or went unacknowledged. The concept of selfhood that emerges in Inchbald's work is contingent upon a dynamic process: being as you *are* depends on being *as* you are. Ontology becomes dependent on performance.

Another word for this performance is fiction, as this same sense of strategic distancing informs our understanding of how fictional genres can work. Furthermore, if the dynamic process that constitutes subjectivity for Inchbald also characterizes her literary compositions, then fiction and fictional texts could become, not a threat to selfhood, but useful epistemological models for it. Just so, contemporary critic David Richter asserts that reading literature has made him better able "to understand those who are Other to me" and that his "training in empathy has come from the practice that fiction and poetry have given me in taking on other selves, other lives."[75]

Yet the sympathetic identification with fictional characters that Richter applauds, as that which encourages us to broaden inevitably individual perspectives, served in the eighteenth century as the basis for much anxiety about novels, theater, and social mobility. Especially at the end of the century, the ability to "take on other selves, other lives" represented not a beneficial open-mindedness, but a threat to the social hierarchy otherwise determined by inherited and inherent characteristics—birth, race, sex. And while plays modeled this kind of subversive "identity play" (to use Dror Wahrman's term) quite explicitly, novels too came under fire for the very emotional effect that Richter praises.[76] Readers, caught up in these other, fictional lives, thereby lost touch with their own responsibilities and feelings: "I have actually seen mothers, in miserable garrets, *crying for the imaginary distress of an heroine*, while their children were *crying for bread* . . . I have seen a scullion-wench with a dishclout in one hand, and a novel in the other, sobbing o'er the sorrows of a *Julia* or a *Jemima*."[77]

Both Richter and Inchbald thus approach fiction from their own historical context. Writing from within a culture anxious to foster tolerance and diversity, Richter naturally praises fiction for encouraging these same traits. In Inchbald's approach, we likewise see a savvy defense of fiction that responds to the very different anxieties of her time. For while Richter uses fiction's difference and otherness to snap out of an introverted state of mind, Inchbald uses these same characteristics to snap into it. An author and actress whose professions consisted of "taking on other selves, other lives," Inchbald disarms the potentially threatening "otherness" of fiction, as she illustrates that the ability to experience multiple roles ultimately gives one the capacity to understand and be oneself.

TRIAL AND ERROR: FROM INCHBALD TO EDGEWORTH

How we learn about ourselves from fiction, or how fiction relates to education, forms the central connection between Elizabeth Inchbald and my final case study, Maria Edgeworth. The 1780s and 1790s "saw the effective beginning of mass education" in England,[78] a response in part to late-eighteenth-century anxieties about ungoverned sensibility. Education was believed to mitigate the dangerous, misleading effects of emotional indulgence, supposedly experienced most frequently by the uncivilized or the ignorant. Mass education also responded to the contemporary political and social turmoil produced by two revolutions: the climate of the late 1790s demanded collective social change, and general theories of education offered one way to effect it.

Inchbald's first novel ends with just such a gesture, closing with a rather heavy-handed moral: "and Mr. Milner, Matilda's grandfather, had better have given his fortune to a distant branch of his family . . . so he had bestowed upon his daughter A PROPER EDUCATION" (338). While the conclusion of Inchbald's first novel offered eighteenth-century readers a familiar formula, it has often struck contemporary readers as out of place in Inchbald's sentimental tale. According to a modern editor, it introduces a theme that "seems hardly to be integral to the development of the work" and presents the theme in a dictatorial manner at odds with the speculative, ambivalent stance characteristic of the narrator elsewhere.[79] This abrupt change in tone and focus also foreshadows what critics see to be the differences between Inchbald's first novel and her second, *Nature and Art* (1796). Dubbed in an early version "The Prejudice of Education,"[80] this novel is a satiric exploration of contemporary pedagogical methods, represented in the text by near-caricatures of the Rousseauvian "man of nature" versus the "man of art." In Inchbald's second novel, interest in the individual seems subsumed by an interest in the broader ills of society and in how these ills could be produced or rectified by education; the shift from Inchbald's first novel to her second, with its satiric project and flat, type characters, seems to exaggerate the political and social undercurrents of its time.

Yet despite the above description, Inchbald's second novel contains more than its fair share of sentiment. Ostensibly a study in the contrasting upbringings and personalities of brothers William and Henry Norwynne (and their like-named sons), *Nature and Art* nonetheless spends many pages on the character of Hannah Primrose, an innocent rustic seduced and ruined by the younger William. While readers categorically dismiss this subplot as extraneous and harmful to Inchbald's larger project,[81] the scenes featuring Hannah number among the most moving, and most memorable, in Inchbald's work. Shawn Maurer labels the "most famous passage" in this novel as the moment when "William, now a London magistrate, unknowingly sentences to death the woman whose ruin he had himself precipitated":[82]

> [William] summed up the evidence—and every time he was com-
> pelled to press hard upon the proofs against her, she shrunk, and
> seemed to stagger with the deadly blow—writhed under the weight of
> *his* minute justice, more than from the prospect of a shameful death.
>   The jury consulted but a few minutes—the verdict was—"Guilty."
>   She heard it with composure.
>   But when William placed the fatal velvet on his head, and rose to
> pronounce her sentence—she started with a kind of convulsive mo-
> tion—retreated a step or two back, and lifting up her hands, with a
> scream exclaimed—"Oh! not from *you*!" [83]

The very potency of these moments makes it difficult to see them as extraneous to Inchbald's overall focus on education, and what I find more interesting is our difficulty in reconciling such scenes with the main thrust of the narrative. As we separate the sentimental from the satiric, we reveal fixed views about what constitutes teaching and what merits being taught. Hannah's trial stands out from the rest of the narrative since it is not about tangible evidence or quantifiable facts, but emotions. And how are we to determine and communicate emotional truths?

Inchbald's choice to locate the emotional center of her novel in a trial scene is provocative. Emotions are traditionally not the prerogative of justice, and the late-eighteenth-century backlash to sensibility (advocated it seems by Inchbald's own novel) involved the societal anxiety that truth and justice would get lost in this new focus on the passions.[84] As an irate Mary Wollstonecraft would claim, "sensibility is the *manie* of the day, and compassion the virtue which is to cover a multitude of vices, whilst justice is left to mourn in sullen silence, and balance truth in vain."[85] By contrast, Inchbald in this scene highlights the relevance of emotions to conceptions about truth and justice, and illustrates the difficulty, yet necessity, for emotions to be included in a realm of testing and deduction. The flaw in Hannah's trial becomes clear when William prods the accused, "Have you no one to speak to your character?" Hannah's answer, "No," is accompanied by a flood of tears as she "call[s] to mind by *whom* her character had first been blasted" (137). Technically, she is guilty of the theft for which she has been arrested, but because the emotional motivations for her conduct are not a subject for court, we sense that the trial is unfair, and that justice has not been done.

And in the eighteenth century, emotions were put on trial. Eighteenth-century legal practice insisted that the accused summarize his or her own defense, as the speech and mode of speaking would provide the court an opportunity to assess "truthfulness." Indeed, how the defendant spoke was more important than what he said, a sign that guilt or innocence were considered to be emotional states, attested to by the defendant's poise, elegance, mannerisms, and expressions. A kind of early polygraph test, these scenes become an acceptable way for the defendant to demonstrate, and the audience to test, the legitimacy of human emotions. Feeling, not fact—or, feeling *as* fact—was at stake in these summary defenses.[86]

These speeches were also appreciated by defendant and audience as theatrical performances, a fact that did nothing to diminish their effectiveness. In the 1775 treason trials of Robert and Daniel Perreau, Robert's defense was composed for him by the playwright Richard Cumberland, and he delivered it with feeling enough to convince audience member (and famous actor) David Garrick of his innocence. Again, who actually authored the speech was irrelevant to observers, for they "judged the power of the performance rather than the source of the words."[87] If eighteenth-century legal trials, with their emphasis on audience, presentation, trappings, and rhetoric, represent a form of theater,[88] this is a type of theater as invested in its emotional effects as its empirical project—or, a type of theater that illustrates emotions as central to empirical inquiry.

And if the courtroom had a theatrical dimension, the stage correspondingly came to have a deductive one: the trial scene in Inchbald's novel, a theatrical and emotional forum, develops in Edgeworth's work to theatrical performance as a place of trial. The subsequent chapter explores this fluid relationship between testing and staging, such that a trial can mean both a test and a theatrical scene, and a theatrical scene can provide both an emotional display and a test of these emotions. Essentially, then, my final chapter challenges the traditional opposition between thinking and feeling, the grounds for which challenge rest in long-standing associations among educational, legal, and scientific practice. All three of these provinces share a common goal, the discovery and dissemination of fact. In the eighteenth century, all three achieve this goal through the process of "trial," a term that signifies most generally the process of experience itself. Yet "trial" also connotes the act of experimentation, or the repeated testing used in scientific inquiry to ascertain authenticity. A legal trial can be read as a more specific version of this latter approach, referring to the "test" of due process designed to examine evidence and determine truth as it relates to a person's guilt or innocence. In each case, as facts are established through observation and careful testing, intangible qualities such as the emotions should necessarily be exempt from analysis.

Yet disciplines that today represent reason versus sentiment were, in the eighteenth century, interrelated. In particular, theatrical metaphors pervaded the realms of law and science; courtroom theatrics were essential to the judicial process, while to perform a dissection in an anatomy theater meant more than just to do it—the audience and display were crucial to the project. And in the transition from Inchbald to Edgeworth, we see how deductive practice similarly pervaded the theatrical world. Theatrical performance too becomes a way to test and discern, so that the stage or the act of staging thus comes to serve a pedagogical function. But theatrical performance remains a very unique testing ground, as what are tried and experienced there are not tangible facts, but feelings.

5 Pedagogical Performance
Maria Edgeworth's Didactic Approach to Fiction

Theater, trials, and education unite once more in an anecdote from *Practical Education*, the volume on educational practice that Maria Edgeworth coauthored with her father:

> (February 1797.) A little theater was put up for the children, and they acted 'Justice Poz.' When the scenes were pulled down afterwards, S_____ [Sneyd, Edgeworth's brother] was extremely sorry to see the whole theatre vanish; he had succeeded as an actor, and he wished to have another play acted. His father did not wish that he should become ambitious of excelling in this way at ten years old, because, it might have turned his attention away from things of more consequence; and, if he had been much applauded for this talent, he would, perhaps, have been over stimulated.[1]

At first this passage seems antitheatrical in its sentiments, a testament to the seductive power of the stage. But if we read carefully, we note that Edgeworth presents the home theatrical as condoned, even encouraged by the family—not, as it will be in *Mansfield Park*, condemned. A little more research reveals that "Justice Poz," their play of choice, was written by Edgeworth herself, while their father, Richard Lovell Edgeworth, constructed this theater, as well as others.[2] The negative reaction Richard has to his son's fascination with acting reveals that theatrical performance should not be enjoyed for its own sake, yet his willingness to have his son act, and his own involvement in the theatrical process, indicates that the practice must have some utilitarian function.

What this function could be surfaces as the anecdote continues. Instead of chastising Sneyd for his reaction, Richard attempts to distract him with a new set of ideas. A neighborhood trial catches Sneyd's attention, and his father engages him in a discussion of justice, power, and punishment (things of "more consequence" than acting). But while his father's stratagem works, and Sneyd "looked fully as eager hear a trial, as he had done, half an hour before, to act a play," this conceptual transition is encouraged by the fact that "in the little play in which he had acted he had played the part of a justice of the peace, and a sort of trial formed the business of the play; the ideas of trials and law, therefore, joined readily with his former train of thought" (427). Sneyd's acting experience has given him the framework he needs to comprehend these real-life events and their philosophical and moral significance. The play, then, represents a crucial step in Sneyd's learning process, while "much of the success of education depends upon the preceptor's seizing these slight connexions" (427).

Maria Edgeworth consistently associates pedagogy with theatrical performance, a statement that may surprise critics well versed in her nondramatic fiction and her work on education, but unaware of her dramatic compositions. While Edgeworth framed many of her well-known novels and short stories in terms of the experimental studies, *Practical Education* and *Professional Education*,[3] that she coauthored with her father, she was also captivated by the idea of writing plays and in having these plays performed. This chapter demonstrates that Edgeworth's fascination with drama influences her educational ideals and asks us to reevaluate what it means for her fiction to illustrate—or enact—these precepts.

The idea that plays could be teaching tools was not a new one. James Quin, an actor in the mid-eighteenth century, also served as tutor to the children of the Prince of Wales, and as part of his job, Quin encouraged the children to act out characters and parts from their readings.[4] A more immediate precursor to Edgeworth, the French writer and educator Madame de Genlis also features the performance of comedies as a central component of childhood education. In de Genlis's long exposition on educational theory and practice, *Adèle et Théodore, ou Lettres sur l'éducation* (1782), the Baroness d'Almane claims that "children must have natural and lively images before them, which may strike their imagination, touch their hearts, and be engraved on their memories," and so composes "Dramas for the use of children, and young persons."[5] "It appeared to me," states the Baroness,

> that children, by amusing themselves in this manner, may exercise their memory, improve their pronunciation, acquire grace in their speaking, and lose that foolish kind of embarrassment, to which they are so subject. When they have acted a part, filled with goodness, delicacy, and generosity; they will blush to be perverse, or insensible. (146–47)

While she stresses performance as an elocutionary exercise, de Genlis also hints at its potentially efficacious emotional effect. As the Baroness states elsewhere, children "will adopt, what they have been taught to represent" (146); for this reason, she encourages them in renditions of admirable characters. By the same token, she cautions the reader that there are also "very dangerous parts to be acted" (146) and expunges any violent passions from her home theatricals.

This example has a special significance to Edgeworth. Her first professional literary attempt was a translation of this same work, and she shares de Genlis's belief in the pedagogical potential of plays.[6] But for Edgeworth, theatrical performance has a very different emotional motivation and effect. While "Justice Poz" would qualify as one of de Genlis's "admirable characters," Sneyd's initial skill in performing this part demonstrates an enthusiasm for themes of law and justice that predates his exposure to an actual trial, so that the play allows Sneyd to identify and later explore latent interests that may have been unknown even to himself. And by including an account of this play within *Practical Education* (unbeknownst to Sneyd), Edgeworth turns Sneyd's acting into a sort of pedagogical demonstration, staged by herself and her father, for the benefit of her reading audience. Edgeworth's anecdote at once explicates and embodies the didactic potential of performance.

In both her creative and theoretical work, Edgeworth emphasizes education as the process by which we come to understand our own desires, and she depicts theatrical performance as the most effective way to fulfill this goal. The phrase "pedagogical performance" thus refers to moments in Edgeworth's writing when characters stage scenes and adopt roles that represent their feelings. The unique development, and what makes these displays pedagogical as opposed to merely self-expressive, is the motivation of the performer and the effect of these displays on their target audience. In Edgeworth's work, staging emotion becomes a test by which the performer may discern otherwise convoluted personal sentiments, and these displays in turn prompt the observer to analyze and articulate feelings otherwise repressed. The performer stages feelings not merely from a need for catharsis or communication, but to verify his or her own emotions, and to put spectators in touch with theirs. And as Edgworth's nondramatic fiction illustrates this process, it suggests that we consider her fictional works as these same types of emotionally honest performances, capable therefore of stimulating readers' feelings for productive, not corruptive, ends.

To reach these conclusions, I first demonstrate the centrality of interaction to Edgeworth's theories of educational practice and suggest that she presents both her dramatic and nondramatic fiction as potentially didactic in that they establish this crucial prerequisite to learning. I then move to two of Edgeworth's early works, a childhood fable titled *The Mental Thermometer* (ca. 1784) and her first published work, *Letters for Literary Ladies* (1795), both of which emphasize emotional analysis as a component of pedagogy but expose the shortcomings of traditional scientific methods to perform such analysis. The subsequent section, an extended reading of her home theatrical *Whim for Whim* (1798), shows that theatrical performance fulfills both these goals, as it provides a testing ground for the passions. Finally, I use a reading of her novel *Belinda* (1801) to illustrate that as Edgeworth's nondramatic fiction implements similar scenes of pedagogical performance, it reflects upon the mechanism and effect of its own production. Edgeworth effectively counters contemporary anti-novel sentiment and defends her own fictional work as didactic by portraying it as an enactment of her pedagogical ideals.

EDUCATIONAL PRACTICE AND FICTIONAL ENTERTAINMENT

As a family, the Edgeworths were interested in more than educational theory. They embraced the problems of actual teaching, and *Practical Education* (1798) had its origins in Richard Lovell Edgeworth's own experiences with his children. The book was a communal project, based on a work privately printed in the 1780s by Richard and his wife Honora. The first edition attributes the technical chapters (such as those on Grammar, Geography, and Mechanics) to Richard, the Introduction to Chemistry to Richard's son Lovell, and the chapters on "Toys" and "Tasks" to family friend Thomas Beddoes. The second edition, in contrast, attributes all but the Introduction to Chemistry to Maria Edgeworth.[7] But Edgeworth herself was consistently adamant about her family's contributions to the project, perhaps because familial interaction formed the basis for their conclusions. According to Marilyn Butler, the point of the volume "was not to devise another 'system' of education, or to discuss the merits of existing systems, to adjudicate between the school of Locke and the school of Rousseau. As scientists they [the Edgeworths] felt that the need was to establish facts."[8] They did so by using real life observations to suggest ways of interacting creatively with young minds.

As just such a suggestion, the anecdote concerning Sneyd establishes the function of the teacher supported throughout the text. The job of the preceptor, as the conclusion of the anecdote makes clear, is to identify and illuminate the "slight connexions" between childhood entertainment and everyday life. The preceptor, then, is not a dictator so much as a guide, a tenet that remains consistent across rationalist and romantic ideas of education alike.[9] Above all, the Edgeworths believed learning to be active. Students do not learn when they passively absorb information, nor when they memorize by rote; instead, learning occurs when students "think and reason for [themselves]."[10] The educator, then, does not disseminate facts, so much as lead students toward a personal discovery of fact. As a teacher, Richard Lovell Edgeworth "would sit quietly while a child was thinking of an answer to a question, without interrupting . . . without a leading observation or exclamation, he would wait till the shape of the reasoning and invention were gone through, and were converted into certainties."[11] Teaching, for the Edgeworths, is about process more than precept: their educational program teaches students how to teach themselves.

Such an educational program was anything but a solitary endeavor. As Susan Manly notes, "encouraging and equipping children to invent or imagine how something works . . . foregrounds not facts, but the process of coming to know, and doing so through conversation emphasizes the sociality of knowledge."[12] The social aspect of education was crucial to the Edgeworths, and in this they repudiate the Rousseauvian belief that society was a corruptive influence on young minds.[13] (An early disciple of Rousseau, Richard Lovell Edgeworth had already put these principles to the test; he raised his first son according to the tenets set forth in *Emile* with disastrous results.) *Practical Education* stresses the importance of communal interaction, and to encourage this process the Edgeworths liked to study *en famille*. "All would gather around the big table in the library at Edgeworthstown House, talking, reading, and writing," and indeed, a visitor to the Edgeworths' home was quite startled to see the famous writer herself "sitting in a corner of the sofa, writing at her miniature desk, while the children read, talked or played around her."[14] While the Edgeworths do not suggest that all interactions are pedagogical—far from it, as the educational treatises and fiction often juxtapose a didactic interaction to a deceptive or ineffective one—they do establish interaction as a crucial prerequisite to their educational projects.

Edgeworth's anxiety to claim her father as coauthor to this work, to present *Practical Education* as "as founded in communal exchange, creative community, correspondence and conversation—not as the theoretical or speculative work of a solitary author,"[15] may then be less a sign of insecurity or self-effacement, and more an attempt to make her work enact the precepts it presents. Edgeworth was a famously self-effacing author, and many critics remain uneasy about Richard Edgeworth's influence on, or interference with, Edgeworth's writing.[16] That she and her father both claimed Edgeworth's fictional tales, published under her own name, as "illustrations" of the more abstract principles published in "his" educational studies, has earned Richard Edgeworth "a reputation as an egregious egotist."[17] Yet for Edgeworth to present her writing as the application of the ideal makes it a closer, more perfect representation of the family's educational ideals than the ideals themselves. Above all, the Edgeworths wanted to avoid "wander[ing], in the shadowy land of theory";[18] if Edgeworthian education is meant to be "practical," her illustrative fictions embody her theory of "practice."

As do her plays. On the most basic level, Edgeworth's dramas created a forum for communal interchange recognized as essential to learning. Her plays encouraged the family to act, and to interact. Her father "loved the energy and bustle of a performance in which all the children could participate," and Edgeworth composed her plays so that there were parts for every Edgeworth child old enough to learn lines.[19] Richard was fond of contriving the stage effects, while her stepmother, Frances, helped with the set and costuming. Of *Whim for Whim*, Frances Edgeworth notes that "Mr. Edgeworth's mechanism for the scenery, and for the experiments tried on the children, were most ingenious" and adds, "I painted the scenery, and arranged the dresses."[20]

As Sneyd's experience illustrates, these theatrical activities prove pedagogical when they provide "connexions" to aspects of the practical world. The stress placed upon connection underlines how learning for the Edgeworths was a process of perceiving links, not distinctions. Though Edgeworth divides her educational writing into chapters on individual skills or subjects, she presents such divisions as organizational strategies rather than theoretical decisions: "the division and subdivision of different parts of education . . . must tend to increase and perpetuate error," states Edgeworth, "these intellectual *casts* are pernicious."[21] "Connection" has been a crucial concept throughout this work, as a way to describe links between categories that nonetheless remain distinct, and Edgeworth in particular associates categories, like fact and fiction, that would seem to exist in opposition to each other. Critics who note this tendency in her work often criticize Edgeworth for "blurring" or breaking down epistemological and generic boundaries.[22] But the idea of "blurring" collapses the gap—the discrepancy between character and role, or theatrical scenario and real life—that is necessary for Edgeworthian performance to function in a pedagogical manner. When we read Edgeworth, we need to keep her own educational philosophy in mind, and to recognize that distinctions enable the connections she sees as essential to learning.

EMOTIONAL ANALYSIS

The place to start this investigation is with the contemporary connections between art and science. As Jenny Uglow states, "the age of reason was also one of sensibility," and Maria Edgeworth was raised in a family particularly captivated by the links among science, experimentation, and art.[23] Her father was a prominent member of the Lunar Society, a remarkable grouping of artistic and scientific innovators who met every month on the Monday nearest the full moon,[24] and Richard's fascination with invention and testing characterizes his scientific, social, and literary pursuits. Maria's creative compositions likewise show the influence of this scientific background; her literary productions do not merely record scientific procedures, but often serve a scientific function themselves.

The Edgeworths were self-described "experimentalists" in the field of education, a term that Alan Richardson notes "refers not to the plethora of guided experiments in their educational scheme but rather to the principle of child study on which it is based."[25] Richard Edgeworth describes how his wife Honora

> . . . thought if proper Experiments were made upon different Children from their earliest years, if these Experiments were registered, if the answers & questions of children at different ages, Capacities and Educations were preserved & compared . . . some knowledge of the effects of different instruction might be acquired . . . the success or failure of different Experiments might lead to some certainty upon a Subject of such extensive importance.[26]

A compilation of individual experiments, the collection is itself an experiment to establish "certainty" about modes of childhood education, and one which depends on the lived reactions of the subjects involved.

In the eighteenth century, the term experiment was still interchangeable with the term "experience," and both terms derive etymologically from the Latin *experiri*, meaning to test or try out.[27] In stressing connections between education and experimentation, the Edgeworths want to underline that all their own conclusions are based "entirely upon practice and experience . . . to make any progress in the art of education, it must be patiently reduced to an experimental science."[28] Within their treatise, the children who learn through experimentation carry out the Edgeworthian ideal of active learning, and as an experiment itself, the treatise becomes an illustration of their ideal.

But the idea that these children are part of an ongoing experiment may give us pause. The shared etymological root meant that, in the eighteenth century, the verb "experiment" could also mean "to have experience of; to feel, suffer."[29] While the Edgeworths' methods were very humane—they would, for example, give their children different types of books to read at different ages, and then ask them how much they remembered from each type of book and at each age—experiment carries with it the threat of physical suffering. The Edgeworths' friend Thomas Day went to just such extremes in his education of "Sabrina," the orphan girl he had adopted to raise as his ideal wife (again a disastrous tribute to Rousseau). Day decided that the perfect woman must learn fortitude and stoicism, and to encourage Sabrina to withstand pain and fear he would drop hot sealing wax on her arms, or fire pistols at her petticoats.[30] Today these methods would qualify as child abuse, clearly unacceptable as they cause physical pain. Yet the emotional manipulation behind Day's project could also have been painful, an aspect of Day's experiment that Edgeworth criticizes more specifically in the Clarence Hervey/Virgina subplot of *Belinda*.[31] Edgeworth, like her father and his friend, was fascinated by experimentation, but her work shows she was not always fascinated by the affinities the elder Edgeworth and Day saw between mechanical and social engineering. Precisely because they have feelings, people should not be tested in the same way that objects may.

Edgeworth's interest in emotion dates back to an early age, as one of the first creative pieces she ever wrote was a "dialogue on happiness" in response to an assignment from Day.[32] Day's request obviously struck a chord with the young girl; though this early fable does not survive, her correspondence and other juvenilia, written around the same time, show she remained interested in this theme. In a letter to her school friend Fanny Robinson, Edgeworth writes, "surely there is nothing ridiculous in a girl of fifteen's attending to the feelings of her own mind & endeavouring to find out what makes her more or less happy?"[33] But as Edgeworth and many of her fictional characters discover, knowing "the feelings of [one's] own mind" is never easy—nor is it the self-absorbed, purely sentimental project that it seems.

Instead, science and sentiment overlap in Edgeworth's first attempts at emotional analysis, a surprisingly common conjunction for the time. In her book *The Female Thermometer*, Terry Castle notes a "deep tendency in Western culture since the Enlightenment to animate the unfamiliar products of modern scientific technology with human sentiments and capabilities," and as her title indicates, this tendency often manifests itself in joke thermometers or barometers, capable of measuring "fanciful changes of all sorts—fluctuations in sexual desire, physical or emotional excitement, religious enthusiasm and so forth."[34] One of Edgeworth's early fables, "The Mental Thermometer" (ca. 1784), capitalizes on this theme. In the process, it attests to a human need to quantify, scientifically, what Castle terms these "fanciful changes."

In the published version of the tale, two characters, an old man and a young boy, discuss happiness.[35] The young boy believes the old man to be the happiest person he knows, and he attributes this happiness to the man's great knowledge. The old man says the boy is correct, but that he is also in possession of a secret that has contributed to his knowledge: a magical thermometer, which, when worn next to the heart, will register the exact degree of pleasure or pain experienced by the wearer. While the boy does not at first understand why an external instrument is necessary, the old man observes that, "guided by the opinion or examples of others, [people] mistake the real objects of happiness" (382–83), and so makes a present of the thermometer to the boy. Then the fable suddenly ends. The young man thanks his mentor for the present, "clasped the golden chain around [his] neck, and resolved to begin, as soon as possible, a series of observations upon [his] *mental Thermometer*" (384).

But a manuscript version at the Bodleian Library continues beyond the rather abrupt conclusion of the published tale. In both versions, the boy's first description of the thermometer notes the two most extreme points on the tube: "Perfect felicity! and Despair." The older man cautions in return that "those extreme points . . . though apparently so far distant from each other, are equally dangerous, for beyond them the liquor can neither rise nor descend, without bursting the instrument" (382). In the manuscript, the old man's warnings prove prophetic. The boy does begin his series of observations or experiments, and the first man he approaches is a metaphysician who presses the thermometer to his heart. The fluid within rises *almost* to perfect felicity, and the metaphysician announces that if he owned such an instrument, he "could solve problems the most interesting to men and physicians; he could perfect his theory of the human mind." The boy decides the thermometer will be more useful to this man than to himself and grants his wish. But

> at that instant the liquor rose to the point of *perfect felicity* with such violence that the tube burst with a sudden explosion: and I & the world & the metaphysician were deprived of our intended experiments on the Mental Thermometer.[36]

While the published version of the tale preserves the thermometer as a potentially useful tool, the manuscript version of the tale makes a joke of its efficacy, and the completed fable reflects on the insufficiency of science and scientific tools to do this type of work.

Yet for all its flaws, the thermometer represents an investment in the passions that we may presume outlasts the destruction of the instrument. What Edgeworth's tale does not mock, in either version, is the importance of reflecting on one's feelings. More than this, Edgeworth associates the potential to discern our own sentiments with the ability to educate and influence others. This is the secret to the old man's influence over the young boy, and this is part of what the metaphysician (in the manuscript version) finds so attractive about the instrument: it will enable him to form more general theories about the human mind. Self-knowledge, for the Edgeworths, was a crucial prerequisite to teaching. "Before any person is properly qualified *to teach*," Edgeworth states in *Practical Education*, "he must have the power of recollecting exactly how *he learned* . . . he must . . . have acquired a knowledge of the process by which his own ideas and habits were formed."[37] This fable defines self-knowledge in terms of the emotions and underlines that to teach others, we must first understand our own feelings. What it does not resolve is how we are to do this.

Edgeworth's pedagogical theories, especially her ideas on women's education, were greatly concerned with emotional analysis. According to Catherine Gallagher, Edgeworth "never admonished women simply to obey or stoically accept their given lot. Rather . . . she recommended that women be educated to make rational decisions about their lives based on a Benthamite calculation of pains and pleasures."[38] Essentially, Edgeworth is advocating a version of what neuroscientist Antonio Damasio has again recently proposed, that "emotion [is] in the loop of reason, and that emotion c[an] assist the reasoning process rather than necessarily disturb it."[39] Damasio, like many an eighteenth-century heroine before him, admits that he "had been advised early in life that sound decisions came from a cool head, that emotions and reason did not mix any more than oil and water," advice he seeks to disprove through scientific experiments and observation.[40] Edgeworth, it would seem, eschews scientific experimentation and decides to write fiction, instead. Yet as her fictional texts explore the necessary relationship between reason and emotion, and are correspondingly designed to spark both thought and feeling in their readers, they become akin to the experiments she supposedly abandoned.

For example, while most critics read her first published work, *Letters for Literary Ladies* (1795), as a straightforward endorsement of reason, the tale in fact restates the importance and challenges of studying one's feelings. The middle section of the work consists of a correspondence between the rational Caroline and the sentimental Julia, in which Caroline tries to dissuade Julia from her emotional and self-destructive tendencies. In a potentially paradoxical solution, Caroline attempts to curb Julia's emotional indulgence by encouraging her friend to "reflect upon [her] own feelings . . . Analyse [her] notions of happiness . . . explain . . . [her] system."[41] Instead of denying her emotions, Julia needs to take a more focused look at them: a mental thermometer seems to be just what Julia needs.

Yet if Julia's claim that "my notions of happiness cannot be resolved into simple, fixed principles" (39) speaks to her overly emotional nature, it also recalls the power and reach of the passions that destroyed Edgeworth's fabulous instrument. As Edgeworth's early fable shows, the largest, most intricately demarcated thermometer in the world could not have represented—or contained—the true range of human feelings. And if the emotions resist quantification by scientific analysis, Caroline's categorical defense of science, in which any shortcomings derive from "the *insufficiency,* not the *fallacy,* of theory" (43), exposes her as a misguided advisor. Though the conclusion of their correspondence—Julia dies an ignominious death, while Caroline remains secure in her position as a respectable wife and mother—supports Caroline's own choices, Julia's disgrace also reflects on the efficacy of Caroline's didactic technique.

Granted, Julia must and does shoulder much of the blame, but many of Edgeworth's other educational tales (such as *Angelina, The Good French Governess,* and "The Mimic") show intractable, sentimental students of all ages responding positively to didactic lessons. So why isn't Caroline a more effective teacher? Perhaps because she endorses an idea of emotional experience that contradicts Edgeworth's didactic messages elsewhere. Despite her early advocacy of emotional analysis, Caroline ultimately encourages her friend to produce happiness through the parts she plays. When Julia writes to her friend, saying that she has married a vain, proud man who does not love her, Caroline encourages her to suppress despair and conduct herself as if she loved him: "Perform the duties, and you shall soon enjoy the pleasures of domestic life" (53). Edgeworth's subsequent fiction is haunted by images of characters who try to do just this, with disastrous results. As another Caroline, the heroine of Edgeworth's home theatrical *Whim for Whim* (1798), will lament, "how painful to wear the mask of gaiety with an aching heart."[42] Edgeworth's short story "The Mimic" (included in *The Parent's Assistant,* 1796) anticipates Caroline's plaint, when the seemingly gay child Frederick compares himself to the "man in the mask . . . the actor—the buffoon . . . who used to cry behind the mask, that made every body else laugh."[43] Edgeworth later uses this identical image to characterize *Belinda's* Lady Delacour: "at home, [Lady Delacour] is wretched; abroad she assumes the air of exuberant gaiety, like the man who wept behind the mask which made others laugh."[44] The persistence of this phrase, in near-verbatim forms, depicts the anguish experienced by characters who adopt roles that contradict their feelings. Edgeworth's work establishes a belief in intrinsic emotions that may be masked but can never be transformed.

Julia suffers, then, because she separates emotions from any rational process: "in vain, dear Caroline, you urge me to *think; I* profess only to *feel*" (39). Yet Caroline's advice occupies the opposite extreme, as she assumes that reason can vanquish present emotions and produce new, often antithetical ones. Neither position is quite correct. But without a mental thermometer, how can one think analytically about one's feelings? Theatrical performance provides an unexpected resolution to this problem, and an unexpected alternative to more typical scientific experimentation. In her home theatrical *Whim for Whim*, Edgeworth endorses performance as capable of defining and disseminating the passions. In so doing, she does not discount scientific practice so much as redefine what this practice could consist of—and include the emotions as a viable subject for analysis.

EXPERIMENTAL PLAYS: *WHIM FOR WHIM*

When Edgeworth was only fifteen, the same age at which she professes interest in "attending to the feelings of her own mind," she sent Fanny Robinson some sample scenes from a play she had just written. In the accompanying letter, she demands to know if Fanny thought the play "would . . . *take* on the stage."[45] Edgeworth's early query shows a specific enthusiasm for the genre, as her question concerns how her first play might function in performance, on the stage. She followed this early composition with a home theatrical, *The Double Disguise*, which was acted by the family at Christmas in 1786.[46] *Old Poz*, the only play included in the 1796 edition of *The Parent's Assistant*, was probably composed in the early 1790s, and a letter from Edgeworth to Sophie Ruxton, referencing "Old Poz's little theatre in the dining room," indicates that it was performed by the family at least once.[47]

In November of 1798 she composed perhaps her most elaborate drama, *Whim for Whim*. While her father busied himself with making the intricate props for this play, the playwright herself kept careful tabs on the practical issues of staging. On page fifty-one of the manuscript version, Edgeworth pasted in a note to explain that " . . . a bag of sand was to be drawn up over a pulley which Chrysse [daughter to one of the main characters] was to pull too high & to draw over the pulley so as to overwhelme [sic] herself in a shower of sand—Bran to be used instead of sand."[48] In the final version, neither bran nor sand is used. Edgeworth's note suggests that small changes were made to the script based on experiences in rehearsal: perhaps the shower of sand or bran made the stage too messy for the next scene; perhaps the child actors were not able to perform the required task. Either way, the note frames rehearsal as experiment. Adjustments to the production were obviously made in response to the trials and errors of run-through, and the final script reflects the conclusions gleaned from the play's various enactments. The plot of the play reinforces this idea of performance as experiment, as it outlines how staged scenes are used to test the reactions and emotional capacities of their participants.

Whim for Whim centers on the reformation, or re-education, of two characters: the dissipated Mrs. Fangle and the gullible and enthusiastic Opal.[49] Mrs. Fangle, a rich and whimsical widow, spends the play flirting with Sir Mordent Idem (an older baronet who hates anything new) and the Count Babelhausen (who represents much that is new and different). But Babelhausen is also a mercenary con man who tries to convince both Mrs. Fangle and Opal, Sir Mordent's nephew and heir, to donate their riches to the cause of Illuminatism.[50] The comedy traces the Count's machinations, and the process by which Opal and Mrs. Fangle finally disentangle themselves from them. Babelhausen's plots are complicated by Opal's affections for Caroline, a sensible heiress and ward of Sir Mordent, and Caroline's climactic role at Mrs. Fangle's masquerade finally convinces the two disciples that they have been misled.

Throughout the play, more traditional methods of teaching and education are mocked and undermined. The play opens as the numerous masters in Mrs. Fangle's service clamor for attention: the master of botany, the master of anatomy, the master of elocution, the master of geometry, the master of attitudes, and the music master spend the first scene talking over and around each other. Those who should be imparting knowledge become, in Mrs. Fangle's household, associated with social pandemonium. And Mrs. Fangle's first pedagogical action is to add yet another (inappropriate) person to the mix. She appoints a new governess for her children, one Mademoiselle Fanfarlouche, who, unbeknownst to her, is the Count's conniving French sidekick.

Mrs. Fangle is also the proud owner of an elaborate "gymnasticum," which represents her "*new* course of experimentation in Education" (3.6.349). In her gymnasticum, she teaches her children by subjecting them to exercises that transform abstract concepts and terms into physical trials. But her children emerge shaken and bruised from these "lessons":

> Chrysse: [Helle] hit me a great blow with the club of Hercules because I said I would knock down the man of straw first—and you know Mama he's my man of straw—my own, own man of straw!
> Helle: Yes but Chrysse you pushed me off the path of danger—And look Mama at the great bruise on my forehead—I hate the path of danger. (2.1.314)

Though the scene is constructed as comic, Helle and Chrysse clearly suffer under this form of pedagogy. Mrs. Fangle's approach raises the question of to what extent the education of people may productively be an experimental science.

But the idea of experimentation is understandably attractive in a play that is all about how we distinguish "the *true* from the *false*" (5.4.383). A subplot, involving the theft of Mrs. Fangle's diamonds, illustrates just how useful experiments can be. In a scheme masterminded by two of the Count's servants, Felix and Mlle. Fanfarlouche, Mlle. Fanfarlouche convinces Mrs. Fangle that the gems she intends to wear to her masquerade are dirty and should be cleaned. When Mrs. Fangle sends them off with Felix, he substitutes fake stones, then gives the fakes to Opal's blackamoor servant Quaco to return. Felix assumes that if anyone detects the cheat, Quaco will receive all the blame. Yet the scheme backfires because the supposedly ignorant savage knows much more than Felix does about diamonds. Opal rescued Quaco from hard labor in the diamond mines, and the blackamoor is immediately suspicious of the imitation stones. Even more surprisingly, Quaco knows a test to distinguish real diamonds from fakes: "Ahh Quaco know good way to try de good diamons—dey cold to de tongue—me try [*puts the false diamonds to his tongue*—] no cold!—no diamons!" (4.2.361).[51] Quaco's detective work, which he reveals to Caroline, begins the process by which the Count and his henchmen will be exposed. Without Quaco's quick thinking, it seems likely that no one would have noticed the swap.[52]

Unfortunately for Mrs. Fangle and Opal, the Count and his cronies cannot be subjected to a "tongue test": as the disaster of Mrs. Fangle's gymnasticum makes clear, one cannot experiment on people as one would do on things. And yet, one cannot take people at face value, either. Much like Felix's "paste ornaments" that are "so like Mrs. Fangle's diamonds that none but a knowing one could tell the difference" (3.2.331–32), the Count dissembles so convincingly that only those privy to his schemes are certain of his evil motivations. Somehow, people and their feelings must be tested, and Edgeworth presents a preliminary solution to this dilemma in her final scene. The Count plans to use Mrs. Fangle's masquerade to culminate his deceptions; instead, the masquerade affords Caroline the opportunity to verify both the Illuminati doctrine and the truth of Opal's love for her.

Mrs. Fangle and Opal have each come to the masquerade planning to meet the "divine Aspasia," the love interest chosen for Opal by the Count, and, as we alone learn in a previous scene, Mlle. Fanfarlouche in disguise. Yet despite Opal's fervor for the Count's doctrine, he has trouble warming to his costumed Illuminée: "I *must* see her face—I never swore I could love any body in a mask—If I could see her eyes, or any one of her features!—. . . Oh Caroline, Caroline! Why cannot I force myself to love another?" (5.4.381). In a tantalizing fashion, Aspasia then shows her features one by one, drawing aside her veil to show one eye, covering her eye to expose her nose. Opal greets each revelation with exclamations of "beautiful nose [or other exposed feature]—as beautiful as Caroline's!" Suddenly the woman throws off her veil to reveal, to the shock of Opal, the Count, and the theater audience, that the divine Aspasia *is* the very Caroline that Opal has been wishfully imagining. The costume change between Mlle. Fanfarlouche and Caroline has happened offstage and is explained only after Caroline's unmasking; her revelation comes as a surprise to characters and theatergoers alike.

Caroline has thus beaten the Count at his own game. While she has spent the play telling Opal and Mrs. Fangle that the Count's philosophies are lies, to no effect, her demonstrated and convincing ability to occupy the Aspasia role unequivocally undermines the sacred symbolism of Illuminatism on which those philosophies are founded. But the demonstration does more than simply illustrate her point. The goal of any teacher in the Edgeworth philosophy is to "induce [the student] to think and reason for himself,"[53] and Caroline's performance embodies this pedagogical goal. She guides Opal to her intended revelation in stages (symbolized by the way she unmasks bit by bit), but allows him—and us—to experience the epiphany of her unveiling for himself.

Her appearance as Aspasia also enables both Caroline and Opal to explore Opal's true emotional commitments. Faced with the Illuminée he believes to be his future wife, Opal becomes aware of, and able to articulate, his still-constant love for Caroline. Caroline's subsequent and calculated unmasking tantalizingly fans this flame, latent all along. Caroline's performance works because it works Opal up to an emotional pitch, then delivers. Her theatrical display encourages neither catharsis, nor even sympathy. Opal experiences something more psychoanalytic, as the act of witnessing Caroline's performance brings his own buried passions to the surface and forces him to come to terms with them.

Of course, performance becomes pedagogical only under specific conditions. As Aspasia, Opal's destined love interest, Caroline adopts a role that represents her own feelings. She performs her part with an unexpected emotional honesty, and her influence over Opal derives from the fact that, as with so many of Inchbald's protagonists, Aspasia is not only *like* Caroline, she *is* Caroline herself. Opal, on the other hand, does not know he is witnessing (or participating in) this performance until Caroline unmasks, and for the typical theater audience tucked safely behind a fourth wall, the conditions of performance are both more apparent and less interactive. Yet in Edgeworth's texts, performance shifts from entertaining to instructive when it is crafted so that the intended student audience is at least temporarily unaware of the performance's crafted nature. The act of obscuring performance conditions renders what would otherwise be merely a display into something experimental.

Practical Education, professedly an experiment, contains this same element of performance, as stressed in the Edgeworths' final apology. "We hope," the Edgeworths solicit, "that candid and intelligent parents will pardon, if they have discovered any desire in us to *exhibit* our pupils" (429; emphasis theirs). What makes this exhibition admissible, according to Julia Douthwaite, is that "its use-value dominates its entertainment-value."[54] The Edgeworth children are displayed for experimental purposes, a congruence that can be maintained only because "the following notes were never seen by the children who are mentioned in them, and though it was in general known in the family that such notes were taken, the particular remarks that were written down were never known to the pupils; nor was any curiosity excited upon this subject" (*Practical Education*, 410).[55] For the student to learn by experience, he must be able to react to a staged circumstance with his own emotions, and the good teacher both creates and obscures the conditions that enable this emotional reaction to occur.

Ironically, Edgeworth herself was often compelled to obscure her involvement in the theater. In particular, she frequently revised unsuccessful plays into novels, a tendency that has caused biographers to read her as nothing more than an insecure playwright, one who "still thought of her plays as experiments, and . . . neither wanted them performed nor raised to the status of her established tales."[56] And perhaps she did "[think] of her plays as experiments"—just not in the sense that she was still honing her talents as a playwright. Edgeworth employs theatrical performance scientifically in all her writing; both her dramatic and novelistic characters act out their own emotions in a manner that encourages spectators to analyze and act on their own. In this respect, Mrs. Fangle and Quaco form important pre-texts for Lady Delacour and Juba in Edgeworth's next novel *Belinda*, while Opal's theatrical wish-fulfillment prefigures Virginia's bizarre epiphany at this novel's end. Edgeworth's revisions strategically channel her professional frustrations, as they move the trope of experimental performance from the playhouse, to the page.

Yet the new generic frame, and the new assumptions surrounding it, do make a difference. In seeming contrast to her play, which depicts theatrical performance as pedagogical when its theatrical, staged nature is obscured, *Belinda's* highly stylized conclusion calls attention to the novel's conventions. Within her novel, Edgeworth shifts from a form of theatricality that endeavors to disguise its theatrical nature, back to a version of theatricality that admits of itself as such. In so doing, *Belinda* takes advantage of current anti-novel sentiments that encouraged readers to dismiss contemporary novels as empty, escapist entertainment. As Edgeworth's theory of pedagogy depends on disguising one's pedagogical aims, *Belinda* ultimately highlights its own fictionality as a way to maintain its didactic purpose.

DIDACTIC FICTION: *BELINDA*

Edgeworth's early attempts to stifle her interest in the theater are at once morbid and comic. When the young Edgeworth sent a copy of her first play to Fanny Robinson, it met with such emphatic disapproval that Edgeworth "immediately destroyed every sheet of the play except one, which was required to do penitential duty as a paper pattern for a cap."[57] Yet the response, meant to cure her of the "Mania of Playwriting," exhibits a "mania" of its own.[58] The complete account of her reaction illustrates an excessive violence reminiscent of passages from Burney's letters. "First then know," Edgeworth writes to Fanny

> that the unfortunate scenes are devoted to the flames saving one which has been reserved for a more lingering though not less ignominious fate; being previously stretched upon a catgut rack it was bored through with

sharp instruments having a head to protect the fingers of the unfeeling executioner then clipt by slow degrees with a pair of enormous shears, till at length after repeated Efforts it was wrought into the pattern of a cap in which degraded form it for the present exists. . . . [59]

The account is one of primitive torture, a curious fate for a genre encouraged by her family and endorsed by Edgeworth herself as having pedagogical potential.

While her other plays were exempt from such treatment, she did repeatedly disguise her dramatic attempts. A very successful family performance of *Whim for Whim* led her to submit the play to Richard Brinsley Sheridan, the theater manager at Drury Lane. He rejected it, and she did not include a copy of *Whim for Whim* in her collection *Moral Tales* (1801) as she had perhaps originally planned.[60] Shortly after Sheridan's rejection, she revised another play, *Angelina*, into a short story.[61] In fact, we owe some of Edgeworth's better-known fictional tales to her frustrated interest in theatrical production. In 1811 the Beddoes family enthusiastically applauded an Edgeworth family performance about an Irish landlord who returns to his estate in disguise and uncovers the dishonesty that has gone on there in his absence—*The Absentee*. Another submission to Sheridan, another rejection, and the play became her well-known novel of the same name.[62]

That Edgeworth would dress her plays up as novels is almost as curious as her attempts to turn them into clothes. She shared Madame de Genlis's rationale about pedagogical plays (that "children must have natural and lively images before them, which may strike their imagination, touch their hearts, and be engraved on their memories" [*Adelaide and Theodore*, 146]), and she was ambivalent about reading as an instructive activity. She believed that the good student should not read passively, but she also admits that this skill is hard for younger readers to master.[63] "Written explanations," she states, lack the advantageous "expression of the countenance . . . the sprightliness of conversation . . . and the connexion [sic] of the parts of the subject" so apparent in verbal instruction—and in dramatic performance.[64]

And while reading in general had its drawbacks, Edgeworth considered reading fiction to be particularly dangerous; she repeats much contemporary anti-novel discourse in her own nonfictional and fictional work.[65] *Letters for Literary Ladies, Angelina,* and parts of *Belinda* all illustrate the warnings articulated in *Practical Education*, that the emotional reactions of novel readers are passive sensations, directed at no real person and toward no real situation.[66] Novel reading, cautions Edgeworth, would diminish " . . . the sensibility of the heart . . . the imagination, which has been accustomed to this delicacy in fictitious narrations, revolts from the disgusting circumstances which attend real poverty, disease, and misery"; such reading "indulges all the luxury of woe in sympathy with fictitious distress, without requiring the exertion which reality demands."[67] The dangerous attraction of fiction rests both in the fictional descriptions that are impossibly, unrealistically moving, and in the fictionality of those descriptions that exempts the reader from any kind of responsibility to react more than sympathetically to them.

For Edgeworth to claim her own fiction as didactic, then, is to indicate that her writing has an educational capacity that should set it apart from other, corrupting novels. Edgeworth carefully termed *Belinda* a "moral tale," not a novel, the sort of decision Jane Austen would criticize as founded more in terminology than technique.[68] But if, as Gallagher claims (in what could be a summary of Edgeworth's own anti-novel sentiment), fiction's dangerous influence rests in its "having no 'real' substance . . . being nobody's actual story,"[69] Edgeworth's new appellation suggests that pedagogical fiction serves a different function. Within her novels, characters adopt fictional roles to enact their own sentiments, or cite fictional texts to articulate their own feelings. These characters thus provide an alternative to reading fiction as an escapist fantasy; they make nobody's story into their own. This technique also enables us to think of Edgeworth's fictional texts as a useful epistemological model for personal experience. While anti-novel discourse critiques the emotional response elicited by fiction, Edgeworth takes up this emotional connection as a strength. Because fiction creates an emotional connection, it can manage or channel the emotions of its readers in a positive, practical way.

Written three years after *Whim for Whim, Belinda* also deals with the education and reformation of several key characters, yet in the process overturns many assumptions about how such education occurs, and who should be doing the educating. Ostensibly it is the story of young Belinda Portman's early forays in romance and society, but Belinda is less naïve than the typical *bildungsroman* heroine as she negotiates her early affection for Clarence Hervey and her later esteem for the rich Creole, Mr. Vincent.[70] It is her first mentor, the vivacious socialite Lady Delacour, who seems most in need of reform. Yet it is also the theatrical Lady Delacour who ultimately untangles Clarence from his engagement to his sheltered ward and educational project, Virginia St. Pierre, while Mr. Vincent, the suitor endorsed by the Belinda's alternate mentors, the Percivals, is exposed as a dangerously impulsive gambler.[71]

While readers are quick to catch the obviously theatrical elements of Edgeworth's novel—the references to plays, Lady Delacour's characterization as an actress, the theatrical masquerade costumes, the staged, final tableau—the many connections between theatrical performance and enlightenment are often overlooked. These connections in *Belinda* perpetuate the pattern established in *Whim for Whim*, as performance in *Belinda* becomes pedagogical when the intended student audience "gets into the act" unawares. Edgeworth is a Lockean educator, one who simultaneously guides the student and disguises her own acts of guidance. For both theorists, experiential learning is coupled with covert tutorial observation, so that, in Locke's words, "though you have your Eyes upon [the pupil], to watch what he does with the time which he has at his own disposal . . . you must not let him perceive, that you, or any body else, do so. For that may hinder him from following his own Inclination."[72] Edgeworth, like Locke, "makes the initial tutorial or parental role essentially passive" in order to assure that the student follow his own "inclinations."[73] But the educator is also responsible for shaping circumstances so as to incite specific inclinations, a behavior that Frances Ferguson dubs "Locke's policy of 'cozening' or 'cheating' the child into useful knowledge."[74] This manipulation of setting and scene turns educator into dramatist, education into performance—with a twist. As Richard Barney puts it, "in the Lockean amphitheater, where pedagogical rule-giving is taboo, the pupil/actor must proceed, painfully enough, with *no idea* what his lines are . . . ideally he should be unaware that the spontaneity of this theatrical education is in fact an illusion."[75]

Painfully enough is right, as we see in one of the more obvious pedagogical moments in *Belinda.* In an episode generally read as the triumph of science over the uncivilized, overactive imagination, Belinda re-creates a mysterious, flaming obeah woman that has been terrorizing Vincent's blackamoor servant Juba.[76] Belinda suspects (correctly) that this voodoo ghost is really a phosphorous outline drawn by the devious Harriet Freke, but her method of educating Juba initially seems rather cruel. Without warning the servant of her plans, she orders that another phosphorous figure be drawn on Juba's bedroom wall, and the next morning Juba emerges in a state of extreme terror. Assured that she has determined the cause of his fright, Belinda then advises some of the children to "show him the phosphorous, and . . . draw some ludicrous figure with it in his presence" until Juba is "convinced that no obeah woman was exercising over him her sorceries" (222).[77]

Juba's epiphany is thus the result of suffering. Learning here is linked to emotional experience, a pattern that is perpetuated rather brutally throughout the novel. When Clarence Hervey later takes up the job of simultaneously ascertaining and correcting Mr. Vincent's gambling addiction, he states, "to save him a few hours of remorse, I will not give up the power of doing him the most essential service. I will let him go on—if he be so inclined—to the very verge of ruin and despair; I will let him feel all the horrours of the gamester's fate, before I tell him, that I have the means to save him . . ." (421–22). Hervey's strategy works, but it is a risky one, and at the last minute he must dash into the ruined gambler's chamber to prevent Vincent's desperate suicide attempt. Belinda's experiment on Juba could be similarly fatal, as Vincent acknowledges "the astonishing power, which the belief in this species of sorcery has over the minds of the Jamaica negroes; they pine and actually die away, from the moment they fancy themselves under the malignant influence of these witches" (221–22). Even a slight miscalculation in timing, or a slight misjudgment of the student's emotional limitations (think of the ruined mental thermometer), and an epiphany ends in death.

Edgeworthian education seems dependent on these risks, though, and on the need for characters to experience their own emotional extremities. This centrality of emotional experience to learning qualifies the relationship of reason to passion, usually posited by Edgeworth's critics as one of opposition. Edgeworth's treatment of obeah, for instance, does not belittle Juba's emotions or beliefs. As it prompts Juba to acknowledge and articulate his fear, Belinda's educational display, much like Caroline's in *Whim for Whim*, actually depends on Juba's superstitions, and the emotions they incite, for effectiveness.

Importantly, characters such as Opal, Vincent, and Juba can only reach these emotional extremities when the premeditated, theatrical "scaffolding" employed by their educators is obscured. Edgeworth's novel *Leonora* (1806), by contrast, includes an example of what happens when the staged nature of a scene becomes too visible to the experimental subject.[78] Olivia, the passionate anti-heroine of the tale, seduces the husband of her friend Leonora, then tries to inflame her lover's fading affections with an elaborate "death"-bed scene. At first, her plan works. Mr. L_____ admits "she never looked more beautiful—more fascinating . . ."; he becomes "agitated" with emotion (2: 208, 209). But when Olivia calls attention to her careful preparation of the room, she makes a mistake. Her lover is unfortunately as well read in romances as she, and Mr. L_____ writes that, "at this instance . . . a confused recollection of Rousseau's Heloise, the dying scene, and her room ornamented with flowers, came into my imagination, and destroying the idea of reality, changed suddenly the whole course of my feelings" (2: 210–11). When Mr. L_____ recognizes that Olivia has staged her scene from a book, the effect instantly changes from tragedy to farce. He realizes he is being worked upon, and his feelings shift from love to raillery.

Mr. L_____'s reactions prove again that for pedagogical performance to function effectively, the intended student audience must not see themselves as the student audience. But the initial power of Olivia's scene proves Mr. L to be slightly mistaken in his belief that the enactment of a fictional scenario must form a straightforward counterpoint to "the idea of reality." While Richard Barney points to the theatrical metaphor as "carry[ing] with it the greatest sense of artifice in the Lockean canon of tropes,"[79] theatrical performance for Edgeworth is a crucial tool for distinguishing the real from the false. Indeed, pedagogical performance works by re-appropriating the fictional or imaginary for didactic aims. Just as Caroline's "real" Aspasia depended on the "false" model proposed by the Count, Belinda's obeah woman depends on its fictional precursors for effectiveness: Juba must suffer through multiple obeah women to conclude that there are none. Belinda's "ghost" simultaneously obscures and embodies its new, pedagogical intent as it successfully reenacts Juba's superstition; Belinda ultimately convinces Juba of the trick that has been practiced on him by showing him the effect and mechanism of his ghost's fictionality.

Similarly, other characters in *Belinda* enact fictional scenarios to express their feelings and to educate others as to their own. When Clarence Hervey returns to Lady Delacour's house after a long absence, he returns to courtship chaos. Belinda is engaged to Vincent, but Lady Delacour suspects Belinda still has feelings for Hervey and that Hervey has feelings for her. Hervey, though, is rumored to have a mistress (Virginia), even to be engaged himself. To unravel this tangled web, Lady Delacour creates a scene in which Hervey may demonstrate, not simply describe, the condition of his heart and conscience. Instead of asking Hervey to state his feelings and asking skeptical observers to accept such a statement, Lady Delacour asks him to read aloud a poem by Thomas Day, in which the poet sympathizes with a young woman who has been abandoned by the man she loved. If Hervey does in fact have any "sins unwhipt of justice," she reasons, he should not be able to read this poem without faltering. And he does not falter. He reads the lines with "so much unaffected, unembarrassed energy, that Lady Delacour could not help casting a triumphant look at Belinda" (351). As a witness to this display, Belinda may work through some of her own feelings toward Hervey: "that reserve, which had been retained, as long as she had any suspicion of his having acted dishonourably, was now dissipated" (351).

Lady Delacour's test and Hervey's execution of it demonstrate, as Andrew McCann describes it, "Hervey . . . after all, only reading—literally performing his sincerity by rehearsing a preexisting model of sincere expression."[80] McCann's formulation is intended to be skeptical, to undermine the integrity which Lady Delacour reads into Hervey's effusions. But *Belinda* shows again and again that performance functions to communicate emotional truths more effectively than a straightforward assertion of sentiment. When Edgeworth has Lady Delacour don a costume of Queen Elizabeth in a showy attempt to disguise her physical and emotional distress, the costume conveys the sentiments it is meant to obscure. Physical and emotional suffering conflate, and in a telling revision of the mental thermometer experiment, the queen's large ruff vibrates with Lady Delacour's pulse to reveal that her heart beats at an unhealthy, unnatural rate (115). For Hervey, the "costume" is the poem he reads, but he is likewise a man who conveys his own feelings by "literally performing" a fictional role. In Hervey's case, his ability to share the poet's detestation of female seduction supports Lady Delacour's interpretation that his own romantic scenario does not duplicate the one being criticized. Hervey's reading thus becomes utilitarian and expressive, not escapist. The results of this reading revise how other fictions in the novel can and should be read.

Specifically, we should be cautious when we encounter *Belinda's* Virginia St. Pierre, the too innocent rustic whose unsupervised novel reading causes her to fall in love with the picture of a man she has never met. Initially, Virginia seems to emphasize all that is problematic and typical about novels and the women who read them. She plays upon those fears that reading "emphasizes the secretive eroticism of the passive female reader . . . [and] leaves [her] vulnerable to seduction."[81] Virginia explains how she has translated the image from a miniature she once saw into the fantasies from her novels: "when I read of heroes in the day, that figure rises to my view . . . when I go to sleep at night I see it . . . in my dreams; it speaks to me, it kneels to me" (468). Her reading seems to encourage what Gallagher terms an "unrestrained and diffuse sensibility"; Virginia is so in love with her fantasy man that she can feel nothing more than gratitude for her guardian, Clarence Hervey.[82] She fits into Gallagher's generalizations of female readers, who "spend their emotional energy on nonentities and [are] then too exhausted to respond to real people."[83]

But Virginia, renamed for a character in a romance, is a conscious testament to how fictions can be enacted. Hervey, no fan of her given appellation "Rachel Hartley," derives the more acceptable "Virginia St. Pierre" from the surname of a celebrated writer (Jacques Henri de Saint-Pierre) and the heroine from his celebrated romance (*Paul et Virginie*). Hervey later extends these connections when he decides to have Virginia's picture painted in a scene from that same tale. When Virginia finally reads St. Pierre's novel, then, it is because she knows that "her own name had been taken from this romance; Mr. Hervey had her picture painted in this character; and these circumstances strongly excited her curiosity to read the book" (380). She reads with the understanding that she herself has been cast as a living representation of a fictional character. Indeed, this understanding motivates her to read; her act of reading thus gains a practical, deductive valence.

Likewise, though Virginia is in love with a man she does not know, her fantasy love is not really Gallagher's "nobody." While reading stimulates Virginia's emotions, the "fatal picture" that incites them is a representative work of art, an actual portrait of an actual man. And much like Opal from *Whim for Whim*, Virginia is rewarded with the tangible manifestation of "her vivid dreams, the fond wishes of her waking fancy" (476). Lady Delacour tracks down one Captain Sunderland, the man from the miniature, and has him sit for his picture in the character of Paul, the hero of St. Pierre's romance. Like Hervey's portrait of Virginia, Lady Delacour's creation of this "fictional" scene, and her subsequent ability to produce the man who sat for it, complicate the typical critical statements, both modern and contemporaneous, on the craft of fiction and its effects. Virgina's reading has stimulated and defined her own latent passions. "I do not distinctly know my own feelings," claims Virginia, yet a passage from her reading (in this case, the very novel for which she was named) catches her attention, and she ponders "whether it was the description of—love" (381). In casting Captain Sunderland as Virginia's "Paul," Lady Delacour directs Virginia's seductive fictions, so that the girl's clarified emotions have an application and an object.

As one who fits real people to previously imagined roles, it is no accident that the final role Lady Delacour adopts is one of playwright. She jokes that she "shall . . . finish the novel" (477) then debates various and typical novelistic endings, only to shift genres suddenly:

> Now I think of it, let me place you all in proper attitudes for stage effect. What signifies being happy, unless we appear so? Captain Sunderland—kneeling with Virginia, if you please, sir, at her father's feet. You in the act of giving them your blessing, Mr. Hartley. Mrs. Ormond clasps her hands with joy—nothing can be better than that, madam—I give you infinite credit for the attitude. Clarence, you have a right to Belinda's hand, and may kiss it too. Nay, miss Portman, it is the rule of the stage. Now, where's my lord Delacour? He should be embracing me, to show that we are reconciled. Ha! here he comes. Enter lord Delacour, with little Helena in his hand. Very well! a good start of surprise, my lord. Stand still, pray, you cannot be better than you are. Helena, my love, do not let go your father's hand. There! quite pretty and natural! (478)

Critics such as Susan Greenfield read this scene as an oxymoron: "the final line of the passage highlights the artificiality of the moment, which must be staged to seem 'natural.' Concerned only with appearances, Lady Delacour mockingly proclaims, 'what signifies being happy, unless we appear so?'"[84] But Lady Delacour's tableau also demonstrates again that performance can be a place for appearances and feelings to align. While Greenfield reads Belinda's pose negatively—"if Belinda is forced to let Clarence kiss her by 'the rule of the stage,' what are her real desires?"[85]—theatrical performance throughout the text has provided an outlet for desires that are very real, though otherwise repressed.

Greenfield's response is useful, though, since her desire to read this final scene as artificial and unnatural shows Edgeworth to be once more re-appropriating a setting that is typically understood to be unreal, to be fictional in a pejorative sense. The theatrical nature of the conclusion is glaringly obvious to characters and readers alike, and its effect here seems anything but pedagogical; most critics dismiss the ending in a manner that reflects on the assumptions of artifice we immediately associate with the stage. And yet I'd suggest that there is a performance behind a performance going on here, and that our rush to dismiss the ending, a reaction the author herself encourages, is a conditioned response we have to a much more complicated kind of staging, and exactly the reaction we need to have to engage the text in a critical, as opposed to a passive manner. The obvious theatricality of the ending, with all its "scaffolding" exposed, encourages us to dismiss this as a didactic moment—yet the moment we do so is the moment Edgeworth accomplishes her didactic goal. Convinced that this is only an act, we get into it, as Edgeworth the pedagogue grins from behind the scenes.

For, like the characters within her novel, Edgeworth in this final tableau appropriates a fictional role for a pedagogical purpose. As Lady Delacour theatrically and self-consciously resolves the novel, Edgeworth asks us to make a connection between character and author that Greenfield reads as "a play on performance implying that perhaps neither of them trusts the final 'pretty' picture."[86] Not quite—for the reference to performance reminds us of how this "final 'pretty' picture" ought to be read. Edgeworth uses Lady Delacour's overt performance to hide her own, much more subtle one; she exemplifies the pedagogical strategies she outlines in her text by making Lady Delacour at once her mouthpiece and her disguise. If didactic epiphanies in this novel occur when imaginary characters ("Paul," Juba's "ghost") are revealed to stand in for real people or things (Captain Sunderland, a supply of phosphorous), we should recognize that the same process occurs in this final conclusion. In reflecting back on her author, Lady Delacour, herself a fiction, announces the representative, illustrative function that renders her, and her work, and her author's work didactic.

Mitzi Meyers claims that "if texts are acts, one way to rethink 'didactic' authors is to read them as writers who really believe that the world might be changed through the writing of texts."[87] Lady Delacour's tableau asks us to think of the text it concludes as an act, in the theatrical and practical sense. As *Belinda* deploys performance for didactic aims, it reveals (like Juba's lessons in ghosts) the mechanism and effectiveness of its own production, and the production more generally of didactic fiction. The final lines of *Belinda*, a theatrically conventional couplet, remind us that moments of performance in the text are models for how to read the text itself, and remind us that the emphasis of didactic fiction is on process, not precept: "our *tale* contains a *moral*, and, no doubt, / You all have wit enough to find it out" (478). This couplet is not coy, but deceptively direct. The moral is exactly as stated, that we will have wit enough to contemplate, on our own terms, a moral application of fiction—an epistemological ability modeled for us, and produced within us, by the novel itself.

CONSTRUCTING THE CLOSET: EDGEWORTH TO AUSTEN

As a novel, *Belinda* then pays a tribute to the stage. And yet Edgeworth's shifts between the drama and novel also indicate that by the early nineteenth century attitudes toward theatrical performance were changing—not as definitively as scholars once assumed, but changing nonetheless. While recent critics such as Julie Carlson, Catherine Burroughs, and Jane Moody have uncovered the prevalence of staged drama at the turn of the century, and established the "closet" as a theatrical space, the idea that drama belonged in the closet was gaining ground.[88] With an eye to Edgeworth's later correspondence and Jane Austen's seemingly antitheatrical *Mansfield Park*, I offer a select explanation for the evolution of this assumption.

In 1816 Richard Edgeworth wrote to the publisher Rowland Hunter, urging him to accept a volume of his daughter's plays. Hunter had already produced much of Edgeworth's work, but he apparently needed a little more encouragement this time around. Richard expostulates

> What you say with respect to many persons objecting to their young peoples acting plays—I agree with entirely. I would therefore in the title-page point out that these dramas were not intended *to be acted, but to be read.*—I would give them some such title as "*Juvenile Dramas not intended for representation.*"[89]

Richard's plea must have worked, for the plays were ultimately published by Hunter in 1817, under the title *Comic Dramas*. But Richard Edgeworth had more to say on this topic; in his preface to this volume, he asserts that "Miss Edgeworth has declined to risk a bolder flight. But encouraged by her father, without venturing onto the stage, she publishes the following little Comic Dramas, to feel her way in this new career."[90] He also sent a copy of the plays to their friend Elizabeth Inchbald, along with a letter indicating his hope that "the public will read the preface to these dramas, and will have the candor to believe, that they were intended for the closet, and not for the stage."[91] Packaging these plays as closet dramas—dramas not meant to be performed—now seems crucial to their public presentation and marks a drastic change from Edgeworth's (and her father's) earlier experiments on the stage.

These qualifications mark a generic and a methodological shift. First, the appellation "closet drama" takes away the expectation of performance and erases one of the crucial differences between plays and novels. More curiously, even as performance and the associated behaviors of observation and participation became central to a romantic program of education, the novel and the closet drama (genres that do not require performance) became the dominant genres for conveying pedagogy.[92] Edgeworth's collection of plays fits into the plethora of "academic dramas" that marked the end of the century, a proliferation of dramatic dialogues that were seen as "lesson[s] in the guise of play[s]," though plays that were never meant to be performed.[93]

This shift reveals, I believe, that the key to romantic pedagogy is not embodiment, per se, but mediated experience: physical observation or interaction is ultimately less crucial to romantic pedagogies than the notion that we learn about ourselves through others. Mediation, the act of conveying ideas or thoughts via intermediaries, is a defining component of playacting and a characteristic of theatricality. But on the stage, this process is all too overt, especially if the theatrical nature of performance must be obscured for it to function in a pedagogical manner. Closet dramas (and, as I discuss in my epilogue, an "antitheatrical" novel such as *Mansfield Park*) insist that the theatrical process itself be mediated. In essence, they *restore* the theatricality to drama, and with it, its pedagogical potential.

Yet the pedagogical potential of mediation comes at a price, one we can see exacted in the publication history of Edgeworth's plays. By 1817 Richard Edgeworth was in poor health and desperately wanted to see another of his daughter's novels in print before he died. Her novel *Harrington* was completed but was not long enough to be published on its own, and Richard wanted to ensure a quick publication by combining *Harrington* with the prepared manuscript of *Comic Dramas*. Edgeworth adamantly refused. Though she did later publish the *Comic Dramas* as an independent work, she chose to publish *Harrington* in conjunction with *Ormond* (a completely new tale). Her decision involved much extra work and produced significant stress; she states that one of her father's letters on the matter "threw me into utter and helpless despair."[94] Yet her refusal to publish her *Comic Dramas* in the same volume as a short novel shows, not an insecurity in her plays (especially since she did publish the work soon afterwards), so much as a desire to treat this work as a separate entity.

Still, emphasizing the distinct nature of her plays comes at a personal and professional cost, as it compromises the pedagogical interactions these plays were supposed inspire. In publishing these plays separately, Edgeworth essentially severed the literary partnership she maintained with her father, a partnership that symbolized their educational ideals. More generally, Edgeworth's personal correspondence reveals a solitary existence that belies her interests in community and connection. While Edgeworth's letters reveal a desperate desire to strike up correspondence with her fellow women writers (and a particular desire to make "Miss Burney's" acquaintance), they also underline her loneliness and isolation.[95] Later in life she did initiate a correspondence with Elizabeth Inchbald, who herself grew more ascetic with age. When Mme. De Staël once asked Inchbald why she shunned society, Inchbald answered "Because . . . I dread the loneliness that will follow."[96] Edgeworth sympathizes with this feeling in a letter: "I remember once . . . I was just in the solitary, melancholy state you [Inchbald] describe; and I used to feel relieved and glad when the tea-urn came into the silent room, to give me a sensation by the sound of its boiling."[97] Shortly after her father's death, Edgeworth received a note from Inchbald that criticized one of her novels and contained not a word of sympathy for her loss. Edgeworth was struck by "the harshness, the total want of human, not to say feminine feeling in writing in such a way to a daughter in such circumstances."[98] They never corresponded again.

The "want of . . . feminine feeling" shown in the correspondence, or lack of correspondence, among these authors represents exactly what these women turned to performance to provide: the missing outlet and missing community for "feminine feelings." But the forms of performance advocated by these women deny closeness even as they enable communication, and their professional accomplishments—their ability to explore in fiction the same issues that troubled their own lives—do not resolve the social constraints that led them to theatrical performance in the first place. These literary and personal strategies had a flip side that Austen explores, for, as we see both in Edgeworth's letters and in the narration of *Mansfield Park*, to perform the emotions effectively is to express oneself in a manner that is necessarily mediated, indirect, detached.

Epilogue
Generic Revolutions: *Mansfield Park* and the "Womanly Style" of Fiction

Throughout this study, self-expressive performance has operated on a fine balance of connections and distinctions. As distinctions (between authors and their texts, between performers and their roles) were assumed by an audience, or made obvious by an author or actor, strategic and expressive connections between these same categories became possible. Yet as these connections were explored and became more evident, the strategic aspect of theatrical expression threatened to disappear—distinctions had to be redefined. The Haywoodian heroine, for all her overt theatricality, yields to the "transparently" sentimental woman of Burney's work, while the same audience that embraces the swooning heroine as an antidote to female dissembling will in time come to criticize her swoons as feigned. This response reactivates an earlier form of theatricality, and the cycle begins anew. The pendulum slowly swings back and forth: the authors in this study maintain a consistent approach to self-expression even as they navigate, and manipulate, a shifting audience response. And they do so by moving between the genres that cue these audience expectations in complementary ways.

By the time we get to *Mansfield Park* (1814), the pendulum has started to swing once more, as Austen's novel tracks a shift in popular assumptions about gender and the generic forms associated with it. My own book began with the assertion that women were often "portrayed . . . as duplicitous, deceptive, costumed, showy, and thus as a sex inherently theatrical."[1] In other words, women were often associated with a particular kind of behavior or appearance—a particular kind of style—and this style has long been labeled as "theatrical." In the restoration and early eighteenth century, the association emphasized the duplicitous, deceptive nature of both women and the stage, and the showy façades that characterized theater and women were signs of their ability to ensnare, deceive, seduce. And yet, the showy, costumed, flamboyant women in Austen's novel seem to manifest what we today mean by "personal style"—their trappings represent an intensification of their personality traits, their individual desires. Concurrently, the stage becomes a space on which characters may act out idiosyncratic quirks. Mary Crawford and Maria Bertram have a penchant for the stage that almost undoes them: while acting, they lay their souls *too* bare.

It makes sense, then, that critics of the genre—from Richard Edgeworth to Sir Thomas Bertram—now condemn the performance of plays more than the genre itself. While at Mansfield, Henry Crawford's recitations from Shakespeare pass as acceptable amusements,[2] and though the young actors of Mansfield Park agonize over the potentially risqué content of their chosen text (Elizabeth Inchbald's *Lovers' Vows*, her translation of August von Kotzebue's *Das Kind der Liebe*, or *Child of Love*), their intention to perform, more than their chosen subject matter, earns them rebuke. "I come from your theatre," states Sir Thomas, in near disbelief, before he even asks them what it is they intended to stage. "I had not the smallest suspicion of your acting having assumed so serious a character" (154). Serious here is not a compliment, especially as the frivolous flock most quickly to this amusement. The privileged character in this novel is instead the self-effacing figure who does her best to eschew the theater and theatrical practices, and who seems to have no style at all: the heroine Fanny Price, the narrator, and behind her, perhaps, Austen herself.

Mansfield Park is the story of Fanny's long-suppressed love for her cousin Edmund, and her resistance to the courtship of the charming yet hypocritical Henry Crawford. It is also, thanks to the disastrous home theatricals that end the first volume, a text regularly read as a specific criticism of theatrical performance.[3] In the absence of their austere father, a bored group of young siblings and friends decide to stage a private play. When the father returns home unexpectedly, the family must face his not-unexpected displeasure. They should have known better; they did know better; they had taken advantage of his absence to do something inappropriate.

This "inappropriateness" might sound odd to us, as according to Lionel Trilling, "it is never made clear why it is so very wrong for young people in a dull country house to put on a play."[4] But the dangers of doing so quickly become obvious, and interestingly the play does not, as Madame de Genlis would fear, introduce inappropriate themes so much as give Austen's characters a chance to enact the desires they already harbor. Within the play, Austen's characters pair off in a manner that reflects their real-life affections, and their rehearsals become a chance to act on the flirtatious impulses that might otherwise be kept in check. Maria Bertram, playing the part of poverty-stricken Agatha, "act[s] well—too well" (137) in her scenes with Henry Crawford, subject of her romantic interests offstage and her long-lost, fondly reclaimed son Frederick on it. Mary Crawford, who interrupts them "at one of the times when they were trying *not* to embrace," mockingly calls them "indefatigable rehearsers . . . if *they* are not perfect, I *shall* be surprised" (140). But Mary herself is just such a performer. She and her love-interest Edmund, in the roles of lovers Amelia and Anhalt, rehearse with a "nature and feeling" that give the perceptive Fanny pain (141). Theatrical performance for Austen is blatantly, dangerously a realm for self-expression.[5] In place of antitheatrical assumptions that dismiss playacting as a manifestation of insincerity, spectators and readers now recognize performance as an enactment of personal feeling. And as the strategic space between actor and role is lost, the personal expressions of these actors—more than theatricality itself—become the subject of Austen's critique.

In contrast to, and in compensation for, these moments of staged and blatant expression, we have Fanny's fear of the stage, and her almost paralytic shyness. From her first appearance at Mansfield Park, Fanny is "timid and shy . . . shrinking from notice" (12). Critics have characterized her as "too nearly nothing" (141); she is "a negative presence": "she almost *is not*."[6] Such a girl naturally shuns the spotlight; she is content to be a spectator, at most, a prompter. But as David Marshall has compellingly argued, Fanny cannot escape a theatrical position altogether.[7] Her shyness at times draws the attention of others; her very resistance to acting at times forces her to perform. Or, to put this another way, her self-effacing conduct is not so much an absence of style, as a style itself.

Indeed, critics frequently use Fanny's self-effacing manner as a stylistic template for those other invisible figures, the narrator who spends most of the novel hiding behind free-indirect discourse, and the "supervising author who [will] not speak *in propria persona*."[8] But what kind of authorial performance does this formulation give us? What does it mean to make your mouthpiece, silent? Or, at best, a mouthpiece for others? For Marshall, it means that "the style of silence . . . is for Austen the true womanly style."[9] D.A. Miller takes this idea of effacement one step further; for him, Austen's "Style" (capital "S") manifests itself in the "stringency of its refusal to realize its author personally . . . her subject remain[s] the negation of her subjectivity."[10] This effacement applies even to her gender: thus for Miller, Austen's Style is neuter, impersonal.[11]

Notably, these critical interpretations of Austen conflate a literary and an existential sense of style. Austen's writing is understood in terms of her characters' states of being (or not-being); Austen's writing also serves as a key to her own "personal" style, or lack thereof. Style became an unstylish topic among literary critics for this very reason, as discussions of it seem inevitably to shade into discussions of authorial personality. And yet, it can be useful to recognize an interplay between style as way of being, and style as a literary form.

For once we acknowledge this interplay, we see that interpretations of Austen's literary style attribute to the author a theatrical strategy of expression quite at odds with that adopted by the Crawfords and Bertrams. Whether silent, impersonal, or neuter, Austen's literary style firmly establishes a space between the "womanly" author and the text she narrates. At the same time, her free-indirect discourse, a rhetorical technique that implies the speaker's attitude, makes her narrator—much like Fanny—a speaker who speaks only when spoken "through."[12] Fanny and narrator spend most of the novel as go-betweens and intermediaries: at once removed from discourse and, through this very removal, crucial conduits for it. Austen presents us with a style of regressive deferral (every mouthpiece leads to another mouthpiece) that explains, perhaps, why we slide so easily from discussions of character, to narrator, to discussions of Austen herself.

Austen's literary "Style" is therefore a mask, an act of effacement or disguise, unlike the other theatrical displays in this novel that embody sex through an enactment of sexual desire.[13] Yet the stylistic mask also functions as a conduit, in the etymological sense of persona, *per sonare*, "to sound through." As one colleague put it for me, in "these moments of free indirect discourse . . . the narrator borrows language and thought from her female characters [to] spea[k] both freely and indirectly"—a freedom reminiscent of those earlier characters in this study, who have the ability to articulate grievances without repercussion, as long as they stay within a theatrical frame. In this formulation, "examples of free indirect discourse would not be 'unspeakable sentences,' as described by linguists and narratologists, but moments of theater."[14]

Austen's treatment of theater in this novel then suggests both a stylistic and a generic shift—away from the flamboyance and theatricals of the Crawford-Bertrams, and to the mediated style of communication represented by Fanny and by the novel itself. On a generic level, theater in Austen's text is sequestered, upheld as different from the other literary amusements in which the young people engage. But as Austen by extension distances her literary project from the theatricals of the Bertrams, she becomes able once again to summon theatrical strategies for her own expressive ends. In contrast to the revelatory—and suppressed—rehearsals of the Crawford-Bertrams (in which all space between actor and role is lost), Austen's adamantly impersonal narrator reestablishes the space between author and text. And in doing so, she ("she"?) highlights the method by which this space is bridged: note the critical temptation to read characters like Fanny as "a . . . self-portrait of the absent author," however ambivalent.[15]

In this reading, the so-called "antitheatricality" of *Mansfield Park* would merely interrupt what Martin Puchner calls the "unmediated theatricality of the stage."[16] Puchner's phrase gestures toward the fact that we expect theatricality from the theater, but it can also illustrate the way in which the stage for Austen has become more about the conflation of actor and role than a mediated practice. Austen's critique of theater therefore restores to her novelistic narrative the mediated process of communication that defines an earlier type of theatricality, even as it depicts theatricality taking on a new narrative form—we might call it the "mediated theatricality of the novel." In this impersonal narrator, in this persona that is not a persona, are embodied the shifting theatrical attitudes of the nineteenth century. Whether it be relegated to the closet, or castigated in a novel, theater has not disappeared. It has just, appropriately and necessarily, disguised itself as something else.

But to end with Austen is to end with a question: what does it mean that by the nineteenth century the "true womanly style" of fiction involves the negation of femininity? The "absolute impersonality" of Austen's narrator seems a direct contradiction to the project of the previous chapters, which apply the acknowledged slippage between actor and role to the construction of fictional texts, such that these texts too become roles through which authors may channel thoughts and feelings.[17] While both Miller and Marshall attribute a theatrical strategy of self-expression to a woman writer, now this strategy manifests as a style of writing, or a characteristic of genre, that effaces gender: gender and style seem to have cancelled each other out.

Yet Austen's treatment of theater and her impersonal style can also represent an intensification of the expressive project this book has defined. If theatrical self-expression has become too evident to remain theatrical, to regain its strategic capabilities it must be disguised—in this case, and in true masquerade style, as its antithesis. I would suggest that Austen's impersonal style marks the culmination of a process in which theatricality was repositioned into new, narrative forms, and in which fiction, as the convention of this new narrative form, was increasingly seen in gendered terms. If, as Michael McKeon puts it, "the 'feminine' character of the novel form lies in its deceptive indirection,"[18] then the novel, with the advertisement of its own fictional status, has absorbed both the gender and the deceptive potential previously associated with the stage.

It has also, then, absorbed the stage's paradoxical potential for self-expression. To illustrate this claim, let us return for a moment to Marthe Robert's assessment of the novel as a consummate dissembler, dependent upon the theatrical "as if." The novel, according to Robert, "can only choose between two ways of deceiving . . . For either a story does not pretend to anything else . . . or it masquerades as reality, in which case it must naturally beware of betraying its intention to delude."[19] The novel is always a form of masquerade that varies only in the extent to which it obscures or highlights this fact. In the first case, the narrative acts *as if* it were not fictional, "and the book is then said to be realistic, naturalistic, or simply true to life"; in the second, the novel stresses its theatrical *as if*, "in which case it is called a work of fantasy, imagination or subjectivity, or perhaps classified under the general heading of symbolism."[20] Always involved in one disguise or the other, a novel can, nonetheless, tell the truth. To quote Robert again, "since the most innocent lies are the most obvious, a novel can only be convincingly truthful when it is utterly deceitful, with all the skill and earnestness required to ensure the success of its deception."[21] As with Fantomina's final confession, veracity comes, not from the absence of fiction, but from the acknowledgment of it.

We see the same process occurring in the anecdote from Samuel Johnson's *The Rambler* that introduced this book, except this time fiction is recognized as theatrical—and feminine. Let us return too, to Johnson's fable:

The Muses wove in the loom of Pallas, a loose and changeable robe, like that in which Falsehood captivated her admirers; with this they invested Truth, and named her Fiction. She now went out to conquer with more success; for when she demanded entrances of the Passions, they often mistook her for Falsehood, and delivered up their charge; but when she had once taken possession, she was soon disrobed by Reason, and shown out, in her original form, with native effulgence and resistless dignity.[22]

Concerned with how she may effectively gain entrance to resistant hearts, Truth costumes herself to look like Falsehood. The observing Passions welcome what they believe to be artifice (a fitting antitheatrical assumption), only to discover Truth in her place. Like Haywood, Johnson suggests that to be true, sometimes one must pretend. And Truth, for Johnson, is a woman.

Yet Fiction in Johnson's account represents more accurately *how* a feminine Truth conveys herself to her readers. What Johnson means by Fiction is therefore not quite what Austen or Marshall means by the term; to talk about the style *of* fiction indicates that fiction has become an object, a genre—a specific narrative form. For Johnson, Fiction remains equivalent to performance. Again, if we read carefully, we see that Fiction is a dress, and a method, and a mode of behavior; Truth may be woman, but Fiction is womanly style. This formulation recalls the earlier assessment, that women have long been "portrayed . . . as duplicitous, deceptive, costumed, showy." Fiction, defined most broadly as an act of feigning and illustrated here through fancy vestments, fits into this litany of theatrical and feminine traits.

Except, and here we enter into a Cretan liar paradox, if "womanly style" is defined by indirection or feigning, then, by definition, it should not seem womanly, at all. Austen's stylistic detachment would thus maintain, not change, the style of indirection characterized by Johnson as "womanly," and in the process restore theatricality to an ostensibly "antitheatrical" space (the novel). Similarly, if we agree with Miller's assessment of Austen's "neuter" style, then an author's fictions no longer express her own femininity or specifically feminine feelings—except to recognize Fiction itself as a feminine performance is to de-emphasize the need for it to serve as a conduit for feminine desires. Using the terminology of Robert, the "as if" has simply shifted. As the gendered convention of fiction becomes equated with genre itself, the impersonal style of Austen's novel exemplifies once again the typical, feminine masquerade strategy of one "wholly intent on concealing [her] tricks." [23]

*   *   *

"The impulse towards autobiography may be spent. She may be beginning to use writing as an art, not as a method of self-expression,"[24] states Virginia Woolf, in tracing developments in women's writing, in praising exactly the kind of turn that Austen, according to D.A. Miller, would represent. Woolf, like Miller, professes a dislike of writing that is too personal, too self-expressive, and like many contemporary critics, she labels the work of early modern women writers as inevitably, exclusively limited to this approach. Such "self-expressive" writing is not mediated or indirect: it screams out the author's grievances; it reeks of womanliness. Such writing, Woolf even suggests, is not art.

At a recent conference on women writers, I was struck again by how scholarship on women from earlier historical periods still suffers from this bias, as the gender of these writers encourages critics to read their texts as a form of autobiography, even though to do so threatens to discount a literary, creative dimension of the text. Yet as this reading of Austen illustrates, the shift Woolf praises—toward a more impersonal, less obviously "self-expressive" style at the turn of the century—would merely perpetuate a pattern this study has outlined throughout. The writers featured here deploy a consistently mediated form of expression, so that fiction and autobiography not only coexist in their work, but the coexistence is crucial to the existence of each: autobiographical assertions are at once enabled and contained by the overtly theatrical setting in which they are made. This book thus posits women's writing as an act of "art" and "self-expression" simultaneously. The play of fiction allows us to appreciate all acts of authorship as a conduit for authorial beliefs, without being chained to the author. The play of fiction means that we can find a woman in her fiction, and still read it *as* fiction, and as literature.

Notes

NOTES TO CHAPTER 1

1. All quotations from the Prologue to William Hatchett's *The Rival Father* (London: Mears and Corbett, 1730).
2. The exact status of the relationship, along with so much of Haywood's life, remains shrouded in mystery, but eighteenth-century sources speculated on a more-than-professional connection between the two. See the second edition of David Erskine Baker, *Biographia Dramatica; or, A Companion to the Playhouse*, ed. Isaac Reed, 2 vols. (London: Mess. Rivingtons et. al., 1782), 1: 208; see too Christina Blouch, "Eliza Haywood and the Romance of Obscurity," *Studies in English Literature* 31 (Summer 1991): 535–52, especially p. 549n28.
3. See Katherine Eisaman Maus, "'Playhouse Flesh and Blood': Sexual Ideology and the Restoration Actress," *English Literary History* 46 (1979): 599.
4. See Terry Castle, *Masquerade and Civilization: The Carnivalesque in Eighteenth-Century English Culture and Fiction* (Stanford: Stanford University Press, 1986), 84, 53. See too Dror Wahrman, *The Making of the Modern Self: Identity and Culture in Eighteenth-Century England* (New Haven, CT: Yale University Press, 2004), 158–59.
5. Wendy Doniger, *The Woman Who Pretended to Be Who She Was: Myths of Self-Imitation* (Oxford: Oxford University Press, 2005).
6. G. Gabrielle Starr, *Lyric Generations: Poetry and the Novel in the Long Eighteenth Century* (Baltimore: Johns Hopkins University Press, 2004), 2.
7. David Marshall, *The Figure of Theater: Shaftesbury, Defoe, Adam Smith, and George Eliot* (New York: Columbia University Press, 1986).
8. Kathryn Shevelow, *Women and Print Culture: The Construction of Femininity in the Early Periodical* (New York: Routledge, 1989), 20. For more on the destablization of generic categories in this century, see Michael McKeon, *The Origins of the English Novel: 1600–1740* (Baltimore: Johns Hopkins University Press, 1987), 25–64; Richard A. Barney, *Plots of Enlightenment: Education and the Novel in Eighteenth-Century England* (Stanford: Stanford University Press, 1999), 5–24.
9. See Nora Nachumi, "Acting Like a 'Lady': British Women Novelists and the Eighteenth-Century Stage," *Romanticism on the Net* 12 (November 1998): 1–6. Also see Nachumi's new book, *Acting Like a Lady: British Women Novelists and the Eighteenth-Century Theater* (New York: AMS Press, Inc., 2008).
10. See for example Laura Brown, *English Dramatic Form, 1660–1760: An Essay in Generic History* (New Haven, CT: Yale University Press, 1981). For a more formalist approach to cross-genre study (though in this case, between eighteenth-century novels and poetry) see Starr, *Lyric Generations*.

11. Martha Nussbaum, *Love's Knowledge: Essays on Philosophy and Literature* (Oxford: Oxford University Press, 1990), 9.
12. Letter from Mary Hoare to Elizabeth Inchbald, 22 February 1807, in *The Memoirs of Mrs. Inchbald: Volumes One and Two*, ed. James Boaden (London: Richard Bentley, 1833), 2: 361, emphasis hers.
13. See Catherine Gallagher, "The Rise of Fictionality," in *The Novel: Volume 1, History, Geography, and Culture*, ed. Franco Moretti (Princeton, NJ: Princeton University Press, 2006), 336–63.
14. See Catherine Gallagher, *Nobody's Story: The Vanishing Acts of Women Writers in the Marketplace, 1670–1820* (Berkeley: University of California Press, 1994); Lennard Davis, *Factual Fictions: The Origins of the English Novel* (New York: Columbia University Press, 1983).
15. See Ellen Donkin, *Getting into the Act: Women Playwrights in London 1776–1829* (New York: Routledge, 1995).
16. See Gallagher, *Nobody's Story*, 22–23; Jacqueline Pearson, *The Prostituted Muse: Images of Women and Women Dramatists 1642–1737* (New York: Harvester and Wheatsheaf, 1988); Donkin, *Getting into the Act*, 20; and Kristina Straub, *Sexual Suspects: Eighteenth-Century Players and Sexual Ideology* (Princeton, NJ: Princeton University Press, 1992), 102–3.
17. Susannah Centilivre, dedication to *The Platonick Lady* (1707), qtd. in Melinda Finberg, *Eighteenth-Century Woman Dramatists* (Oxford: Oxford University Press, 2001), xxi, emphasis hers; letter from Hester Thrale Piozzi to Sir James Fellowes, 28 March 1819, qtd. in Donkin, *Getting into The Act*, 165.
18. Qtd. in C. Kegan Paul, *William Godwin: His Friends and Contemporaries* (Boston: Roberts Brothers, 1876), 74–75.
19. Qtd. in James Boaden, *Memoirs of Mrs. Inchbald: Volumes One and Two* (London: Richard Bentley, 1833), 2: 210; Frances Burney, *The Wanderer*, ed. Margaret Anne Doody, Robert L. Mack, and Peter Sabor (Oxford: Oxford University Press, 1991), 95; Elizabeth Inchbald, Preface to *The Winter's Tale*, in *Remarks for The British Theatre (1806–1809)* (Delmar, NY: Scholars' Facsimiles and Reprints, 1990), 6.
20. Frances Burney, *The Journals and Letters of Fanny Burney*, ed. Joyce Hemlow et. al., 12 vols. (Oxford: Clarendon Press, 1972–1984), 4: 395.
21. Tracy C. Davis and Thomas Postlewait, eds., *Theatricality* (Cambridge: Cambridge University Press, 2003), 16–17.
22. See Maus, "'Playhouse Flesh and Blood,'" 603–9. See too Felicity Nussbaum: "there are also actress characters who resist unifying representation with reality in order to teach women that they need to perform to protect their private subjectivities," "'Real, Beautiful Women': Actresses and *The Rival Queens*," *Eighteenth-Century Life* 32 (Spring 2008): 141.
23. Frances Burney to her sister Esther, 17 December 1785, qtd. in Margaret Anne Doody, *Frances Burney: The Life in the Works* (New Brunswick, NJ: Rutgers University Press, 1988), 169. Letter cited more completely in Chapter 3.
24. See Lawrence J. Klein, "Gender, Conversation, and the Public Sphere in Early Eighteenth-Century England," in *Textuality and Sexuality: Reading Theories and Practices*, eds. Judith Still and Michael Worton (New York: St. Martin's Press, 1993), 100–15; Amanda Vickery, "Golden Age to Separate Spheres? A Review of the Categories and Chronology of English Women's History," *The Historical Journal* 36 (1993): 383–414; Paula McDowell, *The Women of Grub Street: Press Politics and Gender in the London Literary Marketplace 1678–1730* (Oxford: Oxford University Press, 1998); Betty A. Schellenberg, *The Professionalization of Women Writers in Eighteenth-Century Britain* (Cambridge: Cambridge University Press, 2005).

25. Gallagher, *Nobody's Story*.
26. For more on the topic of hypocrisy, see Jenny Davidson, *Hypocrisy and the Politics of Politeness: Manner and Morals from Locke to Austen* (Cambridge: Cambridge University Press, 2004). For associations between women and hypocrisy, see Mary Poovey, *The Proper Lady and the Woman Writer: Ideology as Style in the Works of Mary Wollstonecraft, Mary Shelley, and Jane Austen* (Chicago: University of Chicago Press, 1984), 21.
27. See poststructuralist studies of emotion, such as Rei Terada, *Feeling in Theory: Emotion After the "Death of the Subject"* (Cambridge, MA: Harvard University Press, 2001); for a more historical approach to this question, see Adela Pinch, *Strange Fits of Passion: Epistemologies of Emotion, Hume to Austen* (Stanford: Stanford University Press, 1996), 13.
28. Terada, *Feeling in Theory*, 28, emphasis hers.
29. Ibid., 40–41.
30. See Joseph Roach, *The Player's Passion: Studies in the Science of Acting* (Newark, DE: University of Delaware Press, 1985), 78–84. For more on the development of physiognomy, see Lucy Hartley, *Physiognomy and the Meaning of Expression in Nineteenth-Century Culture* (Cambridge: Cambridge University Press, 2001).
31. Denis Diderot, *The Paradox of Acting*, trans. Walter Herries Pollock, in *The Paradox of Acting; Masks or Faces?*, ed. Lee Strasberg (New York: Hill and Wang, 1957). The paradox, finally, is the idea of dual consciousness: the idea that an actor's felt emotion may exist alongside a detached consciousness, which shapes the emotion into a performance.
32. Henry Fielding, *Tom Jones* (1749; New York: Norton, 1995), 556.
33. Hypocrisy derives from the Greek word *ypocrisise*, meaning "the acting of a part on the stage, feigning, pretence." (The etymological spelling with an "h" became current in the sixteenth century.) See OED online, "hypocrisy." See too Davidson, *Hypocrisy*.
34. Lisa A. Freeman, *Character's Theater: Genre and Identity on the Eighteenth-Century English Stage* (Philadelphia: University of Pennsylvania Press, 2002), 35.
35. Henry Fielding, "An Essay on the Knowledge of the Characters of Men," in *The Complete Works of Henry Fielding, Esq.* (New York: Croscup Sterling, 1902), 284, 305.
36. Wahrman, *Making of the Modern Self*, 256–57. Significantly, the "history of emotional experience" (xvi) is one of the few categories of identity with which Wahrman's study does not engage.
37. See Wahrman, *Making of the Modern Self*; Deidre Shauna Lynch, *The Economy of Character: Novels, Market Culture, and the Business of Inner Meaning* (Chicago: University of Chicago Press, 1998), 3, 11; Freeman, *Character's Theater*, 27.
38. Freeman, *Character's Theater*, 27; see too Lynch, *Economy of Character*, 70–79. Still, Lynch's comment—that the gestural expressions of actors "confirmed that the motions of the human mind *were externally manifested . . . in uniform . . . ways*"—associates acting with some belief in interiority (71; emphasis mine).
39. See Diderot, *Paradox*; see Roach on Diderot, *The Player's Passion*, 116–59, especially pp. 133–34.
40. Henry Fielding, *Amelia*, ed. Martin C. Battestin (1752; Middletown, CT: Wesleyan University Press, 1983), 68. Quotation from Castle, *Masquerade and Civilization*, 180.
41. John Bender highlights the novel's "unique technical capacity to represent consciousness in the form of unspoken thoughts . . . and sensations," *Imagining*

the *Penitentiary* (Chicago: University of Chicago Press, 1987), 253. Leo Braudy describes the genre as creating "character apprehended from within" and producing a "rhetoric of essences rather than surfaces," "Penetration and Impenetrability in Clarissa," in *Modern Essays on Eighteenth-Century Literature*, ed. Leopold Damrosch, Jr. (New York: Oxford University Press, 1988): 274, 271. Nancy Armstrong argues that the eighteenth-century novel, influenced by the conduct book, created an image of the domestic woman who has "depths in the self" beneath the material surface of her body, *Desire and Domestic Fiction: A Political History of the Novel* (Oxford: Oxford University Press, 1987), 76. In contrast, Lynch and Warhman claim the early eighteenth-century novel as concerned only with the superficial dimensions of character. See Lynch, *Economy of Character,* 9 and passim; Wahrman, *Making of the Modern Self,* 182.

42. Again by contrast, see Wahrman, who argues for a clear division between the superficial, early eighteenth-century "self" and a late eighteenth-century self associated with psychological depth.

43. Ibid., 176, 189, 272.

44. See Gail Kern Paster, *Humoring the Body: Emotions and the Shakespearean Stage* (Chicago: University of Chicago Press, 2004); see too *Reading the Early Modern Passions: Essays in the Cultural History of Emotion*, eds. Gail Kern Paster, Katherine Rowe, and Mary Floyd-Wilson (Philadelphia: University of Pennsylvania Press, 2004), which asserts that "early modern psychology only partially shares the priority we place on inwardness, alongside very different conceptions of emotions as physical, environmental, and external phenomena" (15).

45. Freeman, *Character's Theater*, 31–32; Joseph Roach, "Darwin's Passion: The Language of Expression on Nature's Stage," *Discourse* 13 (1990–1991): 45–49; Joseph Roach, *The Player's Passion*, 145. For more on this process, see Chapter 4.

46. Wahrman, *Making of the Modern Self,* 276.

47. See too Steven Mullaney's observation that "emotion" became a term for feeling around 1660—the same time that "individual" took "on its modern meaning" ("Emotion and Its Discontents" [paper presented at MLA Division on English Renaissance Literature, Chicago, 1999]).

48. Pinch, *Strange Fits of Passion*, 16. She notes a few exceptions: Henry Home, Lord Kames, for example, "distinguishes between a passion, which is a feeling accompanied by a desire for action, and emotion, which is an 'internal motion or agitation of the mind' that 'passeth away without desire.'" But for most eighteenth-century writers, "the many names for emotion travel . . . freely" (16). She is quoting from Kames, *Elements of Criticism*, 7th ed., 2 vols. (Edinburgh: John Bell, 1788), 1: 41.

49. Sophia Lee, *The Chapter of Accidents* (London: T. Cadell, 1782), ii.

50. Frances Burney, *The Diary and Letters of Madame D'Arblay, 1778–1840*, ed. Charlotte Frances Barrett, 7 vols. (London: Henry Colburn Publisher, 1842–1846), 1: 158–59; Burney, *The Journals and Letters of Fanny Burney*, 4: 395.

51. Mary Hays, *The Memoirs of Emma Courtney* (1796; Orchard Park, NY: Broadview, 2000).

52. Jonas Barish, *The Antitheatrical Prejudice* (Berkeley: University of California Press, 1981), 3.

53. Qtd. in Boaden, *Memoirs*, 2: 155; emphasis hers.

54. See Gallagher, both *Nobody's Story* and "The Rise of Fictionality."

55. Samuel Johnson, *The Rambler*, eds. W.J. Bate and Albrecht B. Strauss, vols. 3–5 of *The Yale Edition of the Works of Samuel Johnson* (1751; New Haven, CT: Yale University Press, 1969), 4: 152.

56. Gallagher, *Nobody's Story*, 174.
57. Carolyn R. Miller, "Genre as Social Action," *The Quarterly Journal of Speech* 70 (May 1984), 151.
58. William Makepeace Thackeray, *Vanity Fair* (1853; New York: Penguin, 2001), 5–6.
59. Jean-Christophe Agnew, *Worlds Apart: The Market and the Theater in Anglo-American Thought, 1550–1750* (Cambridge: Cambridge University Press, 1986), 112.
60. Bonnie Costello, "Elizabeth Bishop's Impersonal Personal," *American Literary History* 15 (Summer 2003): 339.
61. Pinch, *Strange Fits of Passion*, 53–54.
62. Jill Campbell, "Fielding's Style," *ELH* 72 (2005): 411.
63. Ibid., 412.
64. Ibid., 423.
65. For this assessment of Behn, see Gallagher, "Who Was That Masked Woman? The Prostitute and the Playwright in the Works of Aphra Behn," *Nobody's Story*, 1–48; for this assessment of Austen, see D. A. Miller, *Jane Austen, or The Secret of Style* (Princeton, NJ: Princeton University Press, 2003).
66. Donkin, *Getting into the Act*, 19.
67. Ibid., 20.
68. See Emily Hodgson Anderson, "Novelty in Novels: A Look at What's New in Aphra Behn's *Oroonoko*," *Studies in the Novel* 39 (Spring 2007): 1–16, in particular p. 10.
69. Marthe Robert, *The Origins of the Novel* (Bloomington, IN: Indiana University Press, 1983), 35.
70. See Gallagher's essay, "The Rise of Fictionality," for the source of this phrase.
71. Miller, *Jane Austen*, 96n2.

NOTES TO CHAPTER 2

1. Sterling's poem introduces the first volume of Haywood's third edition of *Secret Histories, Novels, and Poems*, 4 vols. (London: A. Bettesworth, 1732).
2. OED online; "passion" (n), 6b.
3. Again Sterling's phrase, from "To Mrs. Eliza Haywood, on Her Writings."
4. Eliza Haywood, Dedication to "The Fatal Secret," *Secret Histories, Novels and Poems*, 2nd edition, vol. 3 (London: Dan Browne, 1725).
5. See Richard Steele, *Tatler* no. 19, *The Lucubrations of Isaac Bickerstaff, Esq.*, 6 vols. (London: C. Bathurst et al., 1786), 1: 208.
6. See Catherine Gallagher, *Nobody's Story: The Vanishing Acts of Women Writers in the Marketplace, 1670–1820* (Berkeley: University of California Press, 1994), 1–144.
7. Pope makes Haywood the prize in a pissing contest, and her lascivious appearance attests to her loose morals and lifestyle:
     See in the circle next, Eliza plac'd;
     Two babes of love close clinging to her waste [sic];
     Fair as before her 'Works' she stands confess'd
     In flowered brocade by bounteous Kirkall dress'd,
     Pearls on her neck, and roses in her hair,
     And her forebuttocks to the navel bare.
See Alexander Pope, *The Dunciad* (1728), ed. James Sutherland, 3rd ed., vol. 5, *The Poems of Alexander Pope*, ed. John Butt (London: Methuen, 1963) A. 2.149–54. Pope did remove the reference to her low-cut dress from later editions.

8. Reeve distinguishes Haywood from her contemporaries Aphra Behn and Delariviere Manley as one who had "the singular good fortune to recover a lost reputation, and the yet greater honour to atone for her errors"; Reeve reads Haywood's later writing as her "return to virtue" and her atonement for her earlier works. See Clara Reeve, *The Progress of Romance* (1785; New York: The Facsimile Text Society, 1930), 121–22.

9. Paula R. Backscheider, "Women Writers and the Chains of Identification," *Studies in the Novel* 19 (Fall 1987): 245, 255.

10. Conduct literature, which increased in volume and popularity in the eighteenth century, associated lady-like behavior with reserve, passivity, even silence; see Angeline Goreau, *The Whole Duty of a Woman: Female Writers in Seventeenth-Century England* (New York: The Dial Press, 1985) for relevant excerpts from these manuals. For example, *The English Gentlewoman* (1631) maintains, "bashful silence is an ornament to [the] sex" (qtd. in Goreau, *Whole Duty*, 38). If a woman must express herself, "'tis the duty of a young lady to talk with an air of diffidence, as if she proposed what she said, rather with a view to receive information herself, than to inform and instruct the company" (Charles Allen, *The Polite Lady: Or a Course of Female Education*, 2nd ed. [London: Newbery and Carnan, 1769], 205).

11. Eliza Haywood, *Fantomina: Or, Love in a Maze*, in *Popular Fiction by Women 1660–1730*, eds. Paula R. Backscheider and John J. Richetti (New York: Oxford, 1996), 234.

12. See Mary Poovey, *The Proper Lady and the Woman Writer: Ideology as Style in the Works of Mary Wollstonecraft, Mary Shelley, and Jane Austen* (Chicago: University of Chicago Press, 1984), 21. *The Ladies Library* (1722), for example, claims that "the Female Sex, whose Passions being naturally the more impetuous, ought to be the most strictly guarded, and kept under the severe discipline of reason" (qtd. in Poovey, *Proper Lady*, 21).

13. See Diderot, "De la Manière," "a being who is not totally engrossed in his action is . . . false and *mannered*," qtd. in Michael Fried, *Absorption and Theatricality: Painting and the Beholder in the Age of Diderot* (Berkeley: University of California Press, 1980), 99. See too David Marshall's work on Defoe, which explores how the planned performances of Moll and Roxana are associated with fraud and deception; Marshall, *The Figure of Theater: Shaftesbury, Defoe, Adam Smith, and George Eliot* (New York: Columbia University Press, 1986), 132–37.

14. This observation is in direct contradiction to Juliette Merritt's claim that "in all of Haywood's amatory fiction, desire, to be considered sincere, must be spontaneous, irresistible, ungovernable, and irrational" (Juliette Merritt, *Beyond Spectacle: Eliza Haywood's Female Spectators* [Toronto: University of Toronto Press, 2004], 28).

15. See too psychologist Stephen A. Mitchell's discussion of the relationship of desire to novelty, *Can Love Last? The Fate of Romance over Time* (New York: W.W. Norton, 2002), 27. He also writes, in contradiction to Haywood, that "spontaneity . . . is discovered not through action but through refraining from one's habitual action . . . desire and passion cannot be contrived" (199).

16. Joseph Roach, "Culture and Performance in the Circum-Atlantic World," in *Performativity and Performance*, eds. Andrew Parker and Eve Kosofsky Sedgwick (London: Routledge, 1995), 46.

17. See Homi K. Bhabha, *The Location of Culture* (New York: Routledge, 1994); Linda Hutcheon, *A Theory of Parody: The Teachings of Twentieth-Century Art Forms* (New York: Methuen, 1985); Elin Diamond, *Unmaking Mimesis: Essays on Feminism and Theater* (London: Routledge, 1997).

18. Eliza Haywood, *A Wife to be Lett*, in *Selected Fiction and Drama of Eliza Haywood*, ed. Paula R. Backscheider (Oxford: Oxford University Press, 1999), 3–4; emphasis hers. All subsequent citations will be given as page numbers from this edition.

19. As the speaker of these lines, Theophilus knew all about the self-expressive potential of the stage. Cast in this production as the rakish fop Toywell, Theophilus was playing to an audience who knew him for the foppish aspects of his personal life; for Theophilus, Toywell simply provided one more outlet for his personal idiosyncrasies. The part would also provide him with a suggestive model for future behavior. While his role is incidental to the main plot of Haywood's play, in which the mercenary Mr. Graspall agrees to let rakish Sir Harry Beaumont sleep with his wife for a mere 2,000 pounds, Theophilus would go on to prostitute his wife Susannah to his friend William Sloper in a similar manner—and in return for a generous allowance. See Kathryn Shevelow, *Charlotte* (New York: Henry Holt and Company, 2005), 271–72.

20. She acted her first role in Shadwell's 1715 production of *Timon of Athens*. See Marcia Heinemann, "Eliza Haywood's Career in the Theater," *Notes & Queries* 20 (1973): 9. As a playwright, Haywood would ultimately produce four plays: *The Fair Captive* (1722), adapted from a play by Captain Hurst; *A Wife to be Lett* (1723, an original composition); *Frederick, Duke of Brunswick-Lunenburgh* (1729, an original composition); and, *The Opera of Operas* (1733), a collaboration with William Hatchett. This final play is itself an adaptation of Fielding's *The Tragedy of Tragedies*.

21. Lawrence Klein, *Shaftesbury and the Culture of Politeness: Moral Discourse and Cultural Politics in Early Eighteenth-Century England* (Cambridge: Cambridge University Press, 1994), 11.

22. Lisa A. Freeman, *Character's Theater: Genre and Identity on the Eighteenth-Century English Stage* (Philadelphia: University of Pennsylvania Press, 2002), 3–4. For more detailed information on playhouse conditions, see J.L. Styan, *The English Stage: A History of Drama and Performance* (Cambridge: Cambridge University Press, 1996).

23. The gendered dimensions of this altercation are fascination; Charke quarreled with her father because of her cross-dressing, her persistent tendency to take her "breeches parts" offstage. See Shevelow, *Charlotte*, 199.

24. Shevelow, *Charlotte*, 199–209.

25. William Shakespeare, *Hamlet*, ed. A.R. Braunmuller (New York: Penguin, 2001), 3.2.22 .

26. For more on the financial circumstances of married women in the eighteenth century, see Susan Staves, *Married Women's Separate Property in England, 1660–1833* (Cambridge, MA: Harvard University Press, 1990).

27. The appearance of actresses on the restoration stage made these roles especially popular, in part because male dress accentuated the female figure and legs. Among the many examples of the "breeches part" in restoration drama, see the character of Hellena in Aphra Behn's comedy *The Rover* (1677).

28. Polly Stevens Fields, "Manly Vigor and Woman's Wit: Dialoguing Gender in the Plays of Eliza Haywood," in *Compendious Conversations: The Method of Dialogue in the Early Enlightenment*, ed. Kevin Cope (Frankfurt: Peter Lang, 1992), 263. As Elin Diamond puts it, "a female performer in breeches . . . points *both* to gender slippage and to gender constraint" (Diamond, *Unmaking Mimesis*, 73; emphasis hers).

29. Aphra Behn, *The Rover*, in *The Rover and Other Plays*, ed. Jane Spencer (Oxford: Oxford University Press, 1995), 4.2.197–382.

30. The playbills advertised that Mrs. Haywood assumed the role due to the illness of another actress, though no sources list what actress was originally

assigned to the part. See John Elwood, who suggests that the substitution was likely part of a plan to exploit Haywood's curiosity value ("A Critical Edition of *Miss Betsy Thoughtless*," [Ph.D. diss., Urbana, IL: University of Illinois-Urbana-Champaign, 1962], 5). The prologue to the play, which announces that "a dangerous Woman-Poet wrote the play" and that "she, who can talk so well, may yet act better," supports his suggestion that Haywood's role in the play was not a last minute substitution, but the result of a premeditated decision (Elwood, "Critical Edition," 167).

31. Heinemann, "Haywood's Career," 11.

32. Qtd. in George Frisbie Whicher, *The Life and Romances of Mrs. Eliza Haywood* (New York: Columbia University Press, 1915), 10. Haywood's claim is suspect for many reasons, one of which is that she never again gives any sign that she is significantly concerned with the opinion of her relations, if she even had any.

33. See Elwood, "Critical Edition," 7–10. The company gave their final performances, *The Historical Register* and *Eurydice Hiss'd*, on 23 May 1737. On 25 May two new plays were advertised for the 30th, but these plays were never performed. The Licensing Act did not take effect until 24 June; Robert Hume argues that Walpole did not wait for the Licensing Act, but persuaded theater manager John Potter to prevent any further performances. See Hume, *Henry Fielding and the London Theater* (Oxford: Clarendon Press, 1988), 242–44, for more details on this legislation and the last days of the Little Haymarket.

34. Dror Wahrman, *The Making of the Modern Self: Identity and Culture in Eighteenth-Century England* (New Haven, CT: Yale University Press, 2004), 51.

35. Henry Fielding, *Joseph Andrews, with Shamela and Related Writings*, ed. Homer Goldberg (1742; New York: Norton, 1987), 163–64.

36. Eliza Haywood, *The Female Spectator, Volumes 1 and 2*, eds. Kathryn R. King and Alexander Pettit, in *Selected Works of Eliza Haywood*, Part 2, 3 vols. (London: Pickering and Chatto, 2001), 2: 207. All subsequent citations will be from this edition.

37. For more on treatments of hypocrisy in the eighteenth century, see Jenny Davidson, *Hypocrisy and the Politics of Politeness: Manners and Morals from Locke to Austen* (Cambridge: Cambridge University Press, 2004). Fielding's coquettes, from Sapphira to Shamela to the "Fair Sex" in general, behave in a consistently hypocritical manner, and in Shamela's narrative this is indicated by the way emotional expression is consistently prefaced by the verb "pretend": "I pretended to be shy . . . I pretended to be Angry . . . I pretended to be Ashamed" (qtd. in Davidson, *Hypocrisy*, 134). By contrast, Davidson notes that Haywood's female-authored version of Shamela, her *Anti-Pamela*'s Syrena Tricksy, comes to a bad end not because of "the tendency to deceive but [because of] the tendency to be open" (135).

38. See Janet Todd: "a woman who engages in it [coquetry] can no longer be a free agent because her identity resides not in herself but in her reputation and that has been compromised." Janet Todd, *The Sign of Angellica: Women, Writing and Fiction, 1660–1800* (London: Virago Press, 1989), 280.

39. John J. Richetti, *The English Novel in History, 1700–1780* (New York: Routledge, 1999), 85.

40. Eliza Haywood, *Fantomina: Or, Love in a Maze*, in *Popular Fiction by Women 1660–1730*, eds. Paula R. Backscheider and John J. Richetti (New York: Oxford, 1996), 227. All subsequent citations will be from this edition.

41. Richetti, *English Novel*, 41.

42. Ibid., 41.

43. See too Margaret Case Croskery, "Masquing Desire: The Politics of Passion in Eliza Haywood's *Fantomina*," in *The Passionate Fictions of Eliza Haywood: Essays on Her Life and Work*, eds. Kirsten T. Saxton and Rebecca P. Bocchicchio (Lexington, KY: University Press of Kentucky, 2000), 86.
44. Eliza Haywood, *The History of Miss Betsy Thoughtless*, ed. Beth Fowkes Tobin (Oxford: Oxford University Press, 1997), 45–46. Subsequent citations will be to this edition.
45. Shevelow, *Charlotte*, 194.
46. Beth Fowkes Tobin, *The History of Miss Betsy Thoughtless*, ed. Beth Fowkes Tobin (Oxford: Oxford University Press, 1997), 570n45.
47. Peter Lewis, *Fielding's Burlesque Drama: Its Place in the Tradition* (Edingburgh: Edinburgh University Press, 1987), 203.
48. The phrase (Coleridge's) is anachronistic, though the sentiment is not. Starting in the Renaissance, "a conditional credibility, not faith, was the playwright's aim." See Jean-Christophe Agnew, *Worlds Apart: The Market and the Theater in Anglo-American Thought, 1550–1750* (Cambridge: Cambridge University Press, 1986), 111.
49. Marthe Robert, *The Origins of the Novel* (Bloomington, IN: Indiana University Press, 1983), 15.
50. See Jonas Barish *The Antitheatrical Prejudice* (Berkeley: University of California Press, 1981); Katherine Eisaman Maus, "'Playhouse Flesh and Blood': Sexual Ideology and the Restoration Actress," *ELH* 46 (1979): 604. For more on the effect of the Licensing Act on British drama, see Matthew J. Kinservik, *Disciplining Satire: The Censorship of Satiric Comedy on the Eighteenth-Century Stage* (Lewisburg, PA: Bucknell University Press, 2002); Felicia Hardison Londré, *The History of World Theater: From the English Restoration to the Present* (New York: Continuum 1999), 70–97; Vincent J. Liesenfeld, *The Licensing Act of 1737* (Madison: University of Wisconsin Press, 1984).
51. See Gallagher, *Nobody's Story*. See too Catherine Gallagher, "The Rise of Fictionality," in *The Novel: Volume 1, History, Geography, and Culture*, ed. Franco Moretti (Princeton, NJ: Princeton University Press, 2006), 336–63; Lennard Davis, *Factual Fictions: The Origins of the English Novel* (New York: Columbia University Press, 1983), 8.
52. Haywood's naming technique contradicts certain claims about "formal realism" that Ian Watt associates with the mid-century novel (specifically, the increased attention to particularity that is supposed to accompany character development); see Watt's discussion of proper names in *The Rise of the Novel* (1957; reprint, Berkeley: University of California Press, 1967), 19.
53. William Warner, "The Elevation of the Novel in England: Hegemony and Literary History," *ELH* 59 (1992): 583. See too his *Licensing Entertainment: The Elevation of Novel Reading in Britain, 1684–1750* (Berkeley: University of California Press, 1998).
54. Kathryn King, "*The Female Spectator* (1744–1746)," in *The Female Spectator, Volumes 1 and 2*, eds. Kathryn R. King and Alexander Pettit, *Selected Works of Eliza Haywood*, Part 2, 3 vols. (London: Pickering and Chatto, 2001), 2: 4.
55. As based on her initial observations that prostitutes sit "in a Corner of the Pit" (*Fantomina*, 227).
56. See Tassie Gwilliam, *Samuel Richardson's Fictions of Gender* (Stanford: Stanford University Press, 1993), 111–33, for a discussion of Trueworth's sexual behaviors and his status as a paragon.
57. Richard A. Barney, *Plots of Enlightenment: Education and the Novel in Eighteenth-Century England* (Stanford: Stanford University Press, 1999), 288.

58. Beth Fowkes Tobin, Introduction, in *The History of Miss Betsy Thoughtless*, ed. Beth Fowkes Tobin (Oxford: Oxford University Press, 1997), xxi, xxxiv.

59. Deborah Nestor, "Virtue Rarely Rewarded: Ideological Subversion and Narrative Form in Haywood's Later Fiction," *Studies in English Literature* 34 (1994): 588.

60. Qtd. in Watt, *Rise of the Novel*, 252; Watt, *Rise of the Novel*, 253.

61. I'm indebted to Catherine Ingrassia for the observation that in this periodical, Haywood "parrots herself as an embedded fictional story retells the same plot that she conveyed in *The Mercenary Lover*." See Catherine Ingrassia, *Authorship, Commerce, and Gender in Early Eighteenth-Century England: A Culture of Paper Credit* (Cambridge: Cambridge University Press, 1998), 125.

62. Eliza Haywood, *The Mercenary Lover, Selected Fiction and Drama of Eliza Haywood*, ed. Paula R. Backscheider (Oxford: Oxford University Press, 1999), 124–62.

63. Eliza Haywood, *The Parrot* (1746), in *The Selected Works of Eliza Haywood*, ed. Alexander Pettit, Part 2, 3 vols. (London: Pickering and Chatto, 2001), 1: 242–49. All other references to this work are cited parenthetically.

64. Ingrassia, *Authorship, Commerce, and Gender*, 124.

65. Ibid., 125.

66. See Steven Shapin's discussion of "truth" as not merely an abstract term for knowledge about things, but a concept inseparable from "trust" and moral evaluations about individuals. What we accept as "true" is dependent upon whom we accept to be telling the truth. Truth therefore has a relationship to narrative and to identity; how an individual communicates is historically linked to how an audience judges him or her as a truthful person and as a disseminator of knowledge. Shapin, *A Social History of Truth: Civility and Science in Seventeenth-Century England* (Chicago: University of Chicago Press, 1994).

67. Eliza Haywood, *The Female Spectator, Vols. 1 and 2*, eds. Kathryn R. King and Alexander Pettit, in *The Selected Works of Eliza Haywood*, Part 2, 3 vols. (London: Pickering and Chatto, 2001), 2: 17.

68. See Kathryn R. King, Introduction to *The Female Spectator*, in *The Female Spectator, Volumes 1 and 2*, eds. Kathryn R. King and Alexander Pettit, *Selected Works of Eliza Haywood*, Part 2, 3 vols. (London: Pickering and Chatto, 2001), 2:x. See also Kathryn Shevelow, *Women and Print Culture: The Construction of Femininity in the Early Periodical* (New York: Routledge, 1989), 71.

69. See Christine Blouch, "Eliza Haywood and the Romance of Obscurity," *Studies in English Literature* 31 (1991): 535–51. Blouch's very thorough attempt to verify the facts of Haywood's biography reveals more mystery than it uncovers; she admits that several of her revelations "make Haywood's abbreviated biography shorter—since much of it has been called into question or discounted" (535).

70. David Erskine Baker, *Biographia Dramatica; or, A Companion to the Playhouse*, ed. Isaac Reed, 2 vols. (London: Mess. Rivingtons et. al., 1782), 1: 216.

71. See, for example, David Marshall's reading of Defoe, *The Figure of Theater*, 77.

72. Not all writers, nor even all women writers, specifically disavowed imitative forms of authorship, and in contrast to my observations, Betty A. Schellenberg presents imitation as a celebrated authorial strategy in the mid-eighteenth century. Yet she specifically connects this practice to mediocre writers, and even when a more celebrated writer, such as Sarah Fielding, adopts the strategy, Fielding recognizes it as a "humble task." See Betty A. Schellenberg, *The Professionalization of Women Writers in Eighteenth-Century Britain* (Cambridge: Cambridge University Press, 2005), 127. This observation corresponds to Clifford Siskin's claim that there was a "hierarchical distinction

between those writers qualified for 'original composition' and those, 'in the next place,' qualified 'for imitation.'" See Siskin, who is quoting eighteenth-century writer Charles Jenner (1770), in *The Work of Writing: Literature and Social Change in Britain, 1700–1830* (Baltimore: Johns Hopkins University Press, 1998), 185. The growing movement among women, then, to refuse to imitate others symbolizes the paradox that characterizes so much of women's writing at this historical moment: a simultaneous investment in propriety, and a sense of authorial ambition.

73. Elizabeth Inchbald, "To The Artist," *The Artist* 14 (13 June 1807); reprinted in *Nature and Art*, ed. Shawn Lisa Maurer (Orchard Park, NY: Broadview, 2005), 166. Inchbald also says, in the same vein as Burney, "beware how you imitate Mrs. Radcliffe, or Maria Edgeworth: you cannot equal them; and those readers who most admire their works, will most despise yours" (161).

74. Siskin, *Work of Writing*, 184. See Siskin too on how the question of what a novel should imitate is bound up with the question of whom a novelist should imitate (178).

75. Robert, *Origins of the Novel*, 35.

76. Frances Burney, *Early Journals and Letters of Frances Burney*, ed. Lars. E. Troide, 4 vols. (Montreal: McGill-Queen's University Press, 1988), 3: 310.

77. Whicher, *Life and Romances*, 26.

78. Janet Todd, *Sensibility: An Introduction* (New York: Methuen, 1986), 4.

79. Ibid., 141.

80. Ibid., 4.

81. Ellen Donkin identifies a resurgence in theatrical activity, especially among women, from about 1765–1800; see Donkin, *Getting into the Act: Women Playwrights in London 1776–1829* (New York: Routledge, 1995), 19.

82. See Mary Wollstonecraft, *A Vindication of the Rights of Woman*, ed. Miriam Brody (1792; New York: Penguin, 1992), 129, 131, 180–85.

83. See Wollstonecraft quoting *Hamlet*: "It is this system of dissimulation, throughout this volume, that I despise. Women are always to *seem* to be this and that—yet virtue might apostrophize them, in the words of Hamlet—Seems! I know not seems! Have that within that passeth show!" (*Vindication of the Rights of Woman*, 202).

84. Gallagher, *Nobody's Story*, 145.

NOTES TO CHAPTER 3

1. Samuel Richardson, *Pamela; Or, Virtue Rewarded*, ed. Peter Sabor (1740; New York: Penguin, 1980), 242.

2. Frances Burney, *Evelina*, ed. Margaret Anne Doody (New York: Penguin Books, 1994), 203. All subsequent references to this edition will be made parenthetically in the text.

3. For more general discussions of violence in Burney's work, see Margaret Anne Doody, *Frances Burney: The Life in the Works* (New Brunswick, NJ: Rutgers University Press, 1988); Julia Epstein, *The Iron Pen: Frances Burney and the Politics of Women's Writing* (Madison: University of Wisconsin Press, 1989); Barbara Zonitch, *Familiar Violence: Gender and Social Upheaval in the Novels of Frances Burney* (Newark, DE: University of Delaware Press, 1997).

4. Frances Burney, *Memoirs of Doctor Burney by his Daughter, Madame D'Arblay*, 3 vols. (London: Edward Moxon, 1832), 2: 168.

5. Frances Burney, *The Journals and Letters of Fanny Burney*, eds. Joyce Hemlow et. al., 12 vols. (Oxford: Clarendon Press, 1972–1984), 11: 286. All future references will be abbreviated *J&L*.

6. Burney, *Memoirs*, 2: 168.
7. Frances Burney, *The Diary and Letters of Madame D'Arblay*, ed. Charlotte Frances Barrett, 7 vols. (London: Henry Colburn Publishers, 1842–1846), 1: xv–xvi. Subsequent citations will be abbreviated *D&L*.
8. "Miss Humphries & Captain Coussmaker were the only two of the Audience I had ever before seen," Frances Burney, *The Early Journals and Letters of Frances Burney*, ed. Lars. E. Troide, 4 vols. (Montreal: McGill-Queen's University Press, 1988), 2: 239. All subsequent references will be abbreviated *EJL*.
9. Ibid., 238–39.
10. Ibid., 243.
11. Ibid., 242.
12. Ibid., 242.
13. Ibid., 248; emphasis hers.
14. See Michael Fried, *Absorption and Theatricality: Painting and the Beholder in the Age of Diderot* (Berkeley: University of California Press, 1980), for a description of this same paradox. Burney's journal mentions how she meets one of the audience members two months later, and he "scarse [sic] ever spoke to me, but with a quotation from Tom Thumb" (*EJL*, 2: 262).
15. Denis Diderot, *The Paradox of Acting*, trans. Walter Herries Pollock, *The Paradox of Acting/Masks or Faces?* ed. Lee Strasberg (New York: Hill and Wang, 1957), 60.
16. See too Emily Allen, "Staging Identity: Frances Burney's Allegory of Genre," *Eighteenth-Century Studies* 31 (Summer 1998): 433–51, for connections between stage fright and its paradoxical production of subjectivity in Burney's work.
17. Ruth Bernard Yeazell, *Fictions of Modesty: Women and Courtship in the English Novel* (Chicago: University of Chicago Press, 1984), 133.
18. Frances Burney, "To Doctor Burney," *The Wanderer; Or, Female Difficulties*, eds. Margaret Anne Doody, Robert L. Mack, and Peter Sabor (Oxford: Oxford University Press, 1991), 8. Samuel Crisp uses similar terminology when he comments on the composition of her first novel: "You wrote it because you could not help it—it came" (*EJL*, 3: 352).
19. Qtd. in Sarah Kilpatrick, *Fanny Burney* (London: David & Charles, 1980), 184.
20. *EJL*, 3: 386–87.
21. Ibid., 116.
22. Ibid., 301–2.
23. Ibid., 302.
24. *OED* online; "spectacle" (n), 2a: "a person or thing exhibited to, or set before, the public gaze as an object . . . of curiosity or contempt."
25. *EJL*, 3: 310.
26. Ibid., 316–17.
27. Sophy is akin to the actor as cold and tranquil spectator in Diderot's *Paradox*; her mind may, as Joseph Roach paraphrases, "coldly direct [her] body through sequences of passion without mentally experiencing the same emotions" (Roach, *The Player's Passion: Studies in the Science of Acting* [Newark, DE: University of Delaware Press, 1985], 147).
28. *EJL*, 3: 318.
29. Ibid., 246; emphasis hers.
30. Ibid., 141, 215. Several readers also referred to the climactic reunion scene between Evelina and Sir John as "a scene for a Tragedy" (*EJL*, 3: 29).
31. The reaction surprised Burney, as Susanna Burney had earlier told her of her father's positive responses to the play during a family reading. See Doody, *Frances Burney*, 93.

32. Frances Burney, *The Witlings and The Woman-Hater*, eds. Peter Sabor and Geoffrey Sill (Orchard Park, NY: Broadview Press, 2002). All subsequent citations will be from this edition. See Barbara Darby, *Frances Burney, Dramatist: Gender, Performance, and the Late-Eighteenth-Century Stage* (Lexington, KY: University Press of Kentucky, 1997), 22–42, and Doody, *Frances Burney*, 66–98, for a full reading of the play.
33. She is silent for large parts of Act 2 and for the entire end of Act 5. See Darby, *Frances Burney, Dramatist*, 171.
34. Doody, *Frances Burney*, 72.
35. *EJL*, 3: 238.
36. Ibid., 238–39.
37. *D&L*, 1: 308.
38. For more on the general struggles of the eighteenth-century female playwright and the specifics of Burney's frustrated career as a playwright, see Ellen Donkin, *Getting into the Act: Women Playwrights in London 1776–1829* (New York: Routledge, 1995), 1–40, 132–58.
39. The recent interest in Burney's dramas has prompted a debate about how successful this play might have been, had it reached the stage in its own time. Critics such as Elizabeth Yost Mulliken and Marjorie Lee Morrison seem to think Crisp and Charles Burney saved Frances from a bad mistake; Margaret Doody applauds the play's intelligence and maintains that it could entertain even today's audiences. See Elizabeth Yost Mulliken, "The Influence of the Drama on Frances Burney's Novels," (Ph.D. diss., Madison: University of Wisconsin, 1969); Marjorie Lee Morrison, "Fanny Burney and the Theater," (Ph.D. diss., Austin: University of Texas, 1957); Doody, *Frances Burney*, 91.
40. Frances Burney, *Cecilia*, eds. Peter Sabor and Margaret Anne Doody (Oxford: Oxford University Press, 1988). Subsequent parenthetical citations will be from this edition. Due to a caveat in her uncle's will, this Cecilia will inherit her money only if her future husband agrees to give up his surname and take hers. The name-proud Mrs. Delvile objects strongly to this term.
41. Anne Raine Ellis, Preface, *Cecilia*, ed. Anne Raine Ellis, 2 vols. (London: George Bell and Sons, 1882), 1: v.
42. The quotation is from Burney herself and is reproduced in *Cecilia*, ed. Anne Raine Ellis, 2 vols. (London: George Bell and Sons, 1882), 2: 223–24n1. Ellis includes numerous annotations that provide important contemporary responses to the novel.
43. Kristina Straub, *Divided Fictions: Fanny Burney and Feminine Strategy* (Lexington, KY: University Press of Kentucky, 1987), 177.
44. See too the reference later in this chapter to Camilla's death-bed letter and Elinor's Joddrel's suicide attempts (note 87).
45. Doody, *Frances Burney*, 129.
46. Ibid.,168.
47. Qtd. in Doody, *Frances Burney*, 168. Lord Hervey, a courtier in King George II's and Queen Caroline's attendance, described his experience at court in a very similar manner, as both artificial and restrained. To his friend Henry Fox he writes, "the ease and freedom of your tête à têtes are relaxations which I assure you very sincerely my mind often wishes for, to unweary itself after the fatigue of being in masquerade for weeks together [at court]" (Hervey, "to Henry Fox, 2–17–29/30," in *Lord Hervey and His Friends, 1726–38*, ed. the Earl of Ilchester [London: Murray, 1950], 48).
48. Frances Burney to her sister Esther, 17 December 1785, *D&L*, 2: 407–08; also qtd. in Doody, *Frances Burney*, 168–69.
49. *D&L*, 5: 7.

50. Joyce Hemlow, *The History of Fanny Burney* (Oxford: Clarendon Press, 1958), 215.
51. Doody, *Frances Burney*, 193.
52. Quotation from Hemlow, *History of Fanny Burney*, 220. See Michael E. Adelstein, *Fanny Burney*, (New York: Twayne, 1968), 87; Judy Simons, *Fanny Burney* (Totowa, NJ: Barnes & Noble, 1987), 133. Morrison also has a chapter on Burney's tragedies in her unpublished dissertation, "Fanny Burney and the Theater," 99–172. See too Doody, *Frances Burney*, 150–98; Darby, *Frances Burney, Dramatist*, 43–107.
53. Hemlow, *History of Fanny Burney*, 202.
54. *D&L*, 4: 271; emphasis mine.
55. Ibid., 5: 149.
56. Ibid., 214.
57. She revised *Edwy and Elgiva* for production in 1794; in 1797, after the publication of *Camilla*, she returned to *Hubert de Vere* with hopes to make it into a closet drama. Around 1814, she returned to her unfinished tragedy *Elberta* (though she never completed it), and in 1836, when she was in her mid-eighties, she timed readings of *The Siege of Pevensey* and *Hubert de Vere*. See Peter Sabor, Introduction, in *The Complete Plays of Frances Burney*, eds. Peter Sabor, Geoffrey M. Sill, and Stewart J. Cooke, 2 vols. (London: Pickering and Chatto, 1995), 1: xvii.
58. On 28 May 1790, Burney met her father at a performance of the *Messiah*, the first extended and semi-private contact she had had with him in four years. Here her father admits that he has "long . . . been uneasy . . . if you wish to resign—my house, my purse, my arms, shall be open to receive you back" (qtd. in Hemlow, *History of Fanny Burney*, 213).
59. Darby, *Frances Burney, Dramatist*, 191; emphasis hers.
60. Qtd. in Sabor, Introduction to *Edwy and Elgiva*, in *Complete Plays of Frances Burney*, 2: 7. Depictions of female suffering range among her other plays. Elberta raves wildly onstage, but she recovers more control at the end. Adela, the heroine of *The Siege of Pevensey*, suffers more silently. Like Cecilia Stanley's, her distress is indicated by speechlessness and not collapse, and this play, like *The Witlings*, has a happy ending, so that some of Burney's readers questioned the appellation of "tragedy." Cerulia, the heroine of *Hubert De Vere*, does suffer bodily and visibly, making a shocking final appearance as a madwoman to claim "gone is my hold on life: faint, faded, drooping, / I shake—I fall!—" (5.65–66). Next to *Edwy and Elgiva*, this seems to have been Burney's favorite play: in fact, she originally submitted *Hubert De Vere* to Kemble, only to withdraw it later in favor of *Edwy and Elgiva*. And after the debacle of her first production, she returned to *Hubert De Vere* with plans to revise it into a closet drama.
61. These sources include Tobias Smollett, *A Complete History of England*; David Hume, *The History of England*; Robert Henry, *The History of Great Britain*. See Darby, *Frances Burney, Dramatist*, 63.
62. This anecdote is taken from Thomas Campbell's *Life of Mrs. Siddons* and is quoted by Sabor, *Edwy and Elgiva*, in *Complete Plays of Frances Burney*, 2: 77n1.
63. Donkin, *Getting into the Act*, 153.
64. *J&L*, 3: 99; emphasis hers.
65. See Darby, *Frances Burney, Dramatist*, 54. See too Peter Sabor, "'Altered, improved, copied, abridged': Alexandre d'Arblay's Revisions to Burney's *Edwy and Elgiva*," *Lumen* 14 (1995): 127–37.
66. See Dogberry's rant in *Much Ado about Nothing*: "Dost thou not suspect my place? Dost thou not suspect my years? O, that he were here to write me

down an ass! But masters, remember that I am an ass; though it be not written down, yet forget not that I am an ass . . . O, that I had been writ down an ass!" (4.2.74–86). Burney's bit of doggerel highlights her theatrical knowledge and even suggests that her self-condemnation may, like Dogberry's, be ironic.

67. Richard Owen Cambridge, minor man of letters and friend of the Burneys.
68. Elizabeth Montague, sister of Sarah Scott and "Queen of the Blues" (the bluestocking movement).
69. *J&L*, 3: 109–11.
70. Frances Burney, *Camilla*, eds. Edward A. Bloom and Lillian D. Bloom (London: Oxford University Press, 1972). All subsequent parenthetical citations are from this edition. Mrs. Arlbery suggests that Camilla coquette with the rich Sir Sedley Clarendel, so that when she does finally reveal her preference for the less-wealthy Mandlebert, it will be clear that she does not love Edgar merely for his money (484).
71. See too Claudia Johnson, *Equivocal Beings: Politics, Gender, and Sentimentality in the 1790s—Wollstonecraft, Radcliffe, Burney, Austen*, (Chicago: University of Chicago Press, 1995), 143. Johnson, in contrast to this reading, characterizes Camilla's demise as "unwilled" (159).
72. Richardson, *Pamela*, 212.
73. Johnson, *Equivocal Beings*, 17.
74. G.J. Barker-Benfield emphasizes that in eighteenth-century literature feigned illness often shaded into real. He cites Ann Radcliffe's Emily, who, facing an interview with Montoni, found "her agitation increased so much that she almost resolved to excuse herself under what could scarcely be called a pretence of illness"; her psychological "suffering . . . the pressure of her anxiety" subsequently harms Emily's physical health. See Barker-Benfield, *The Culture of Sensibility: Sex and Society in Eighteenth-Century Britain* (Chicago: University of Chicago Press, 1992), 35.
75. Again, Camilla's plea recalls Pamela's, who upon reflection condemns suicide as irreverent, selfish, and rash, labeling herself "presumptuous Pamela" (Richardson, *Pamela*, 213).
76. *J&L*, 4: 395.
77. Frances Burney, *The Witlings and The Woman-Hater*, eds. Peter Sabor and Geoffrey Sill (Orchard Park, NY: Broadview Press, 2002). All subsequent citations will be from this edition. The play cannot be precisely dated, but Burney jotted notes for the play on scraps of letters sent to her in 1801. Though she apparently sketched a cast list for it, her departure for France in 1802 to join her husband forestalled any attempts to submit it for production. When she returned to England in 1812, she had no further contact with theater managers. See Sabor, Introduction to *The Woman-Hater*, in *Complete Plays of Frances Burney*, 1: 192; Sabor and Sill, Introduction, in *The Witlings and The Woman-Hater*, 19.
78. *EJL*, 3: 238.
79. Frances Burney, "To Doctor Burney," 4.
80. Frances Burney, *The Wanderer; Or, Female Difficulties*, eds. Margaret Anne Doody, Robert L. Mack, and Peter Sabor (Oxford: Oxford University Press, 1991). Subsequent parenthetical citations will be made to this edition.
81. Catharine Craft-Fairchild, *Masquerade and Gender: Disguise and Female Identity in Eighteenth-Century Fictions by Women* (University Park, PA: Pennsylvania State University Press, 1993), 143.
82. *EJL*, 2: 242.
83. Frances Burney, Draft Introduction to *Cecilia*, *Cecilia*, Appendix 1, eds. Peter Sabor and Margaret Anne Doody (Oxford: Oxford University Press, 1988), 945.

84. *D&L*, 5: 214.
85. *J&L*, 4: 395.
86. Elinor's outspokenness is reminiscent of Joyce's "conversational bluntness," though this same tendency is in Joyce a manifestation of class status, and in Elinor a manifestation of her revolutionary beliefs.
87. Claudia Johnson reads Camilla's "suicide" note in a similar manner. When she thinks she is dying, Camilla writes to Edgar and "heads the note . . . with the portentous words, 'not to be delivered till I am dead' . . . she realizes that only annihilation can make credible and pardon her obtrusion into speech, absolve her from the bother her subjectivity has caused" (Johnson, *Equivocal Beings*, 143).
88. Doody, *Frances Burney*, 341; Craft-Fairchild, *Masquerade*, 148. These moments really do become quite funny. During Elinor's third suicide attempt, she points a pistol to her temple, but Harleigh grabs her arm so that the gun discharges into the air. Nevertheless, the sound of the pistol going off "so close to her ear, and let off by her own hand, operated upon her deranged imagination with a belief that her purpose was fulfilled"; she sinks to the ground, positive that this time she is dying (580).
89. In contrast, contemporary readers Anna Letitia Barbauld and Mary Waddington both praised the novel, and rather significantly, most recent critical attention to the book has been from female scholars: Patricia Meyer Spacks, Kristina Straub, Julia Epstein, Margaret Anne Doody, and Catherine Craft-Fairchild, among others.
90. *The British Critic* (April 1814) criticized the book as "tedious and tiresome," the adventures as "dull and uninteresting" (qtd. in Craft-Fairchild, *Masquerade*, 123); Hazlitt called the story "teasing and tedious," and Burney's sentiments "insipid." William Hazlitt, "Review of *The Wanderer*," *Edinburgh Review* 24 (February 1815): 337.
91. The first quotation is in *EJL*, 3: 29. The second anecdote is cited in *Cecilia*, ed. Anne Raine Ellis, 2: 219n1: "I shall never forget," said Mrs. Delany, "your Grace's earnestness when we came to the part where Mrs. Delvile bursts a blood vessel. Down dropped the book, and just with the same energy as if your Grace had heard some real and important news, you called out, 'I'm glad of it, with all my heart!'"
92. David Marshall, *The Surprising Effects of Sympathy: Marivaux, Diderot, Rousseau, and Mary Shelley* (Chicago: University of Chicago Press, 1988), 19.
93. John Wilson Croker, "Review of *The Wanderer; Or, Female Difficulties*, by Madame D'Arblay," *Quarterly Review* 11 (April 1814): 125; quoted by Craft-Fairchild, *Masquerade*, 124.
94. Croker, "Review," 124; qtd. in Craft-Fairchild, *Masquerade*, 123.
95. Barker-Benfield, *Culture of Sensibility*, xviii.
96. Johnson, *Equivocal Beings*, 14.
97. Adela Pinch, *Strange Fits of Passion: Epistemologies of Emotion, Hume to Austen* (Stanford: Stanford University Press, 1996), 55.
98. Ibid., 53–54.
99. Eliza Haywood, Dedication to "The Fatal Secret," in *Secret Histories, Novels and Poems*, 2nd edition, vol. 3 (London: Dan Browne, 1725). Paula Backscheider notes that women writers often "set themselves up as experts in love . . . they established themselves as authorities in a field men were willing to grant them." Backscheider, "Women Writers and the Chains of Identification," *Studies in the Novel* 19 (Fall 1987): 254.
100. The quotation is from Pinch, *Strange Fits of Passion*, 71; emphasis hers.
101. The circulating, transpersonal nature of emotion in the eighteenth century is one of the key claims of Pinch's book.

NOTES TO CHAPTER 4

1. James Boaden, *Memoirs of Mrs. Inchbald: Volumes One and Two* (London: Richard Bentley, 1833), 1: 189.
2. P. Sumbel, *Memoirs of the Life of Mrs. Sumbel, Late Wells*, 3 vols. (London: C. Chapple, 1811), 2: 201.
3. Ellen Donkin, *Getting into the Act: Women Playwrights in London 1776–1829* (New York: Routledge, 1995), 26–27; for the more general situation of the female playwright, see Donkin, *Getting into The Act*, 1–40.
4. Thomas Crochunis, "Authorial Performances in the Criticism and Theory of Romantic Women Playwrights," in *Women in British Romantic Theatre: Drama, Performance, and Society, 1790–1840*, ed. Catherine Burroughs (Cambridge: Cambridge University Press, 2000), 230; Donkin, *Getting into The Act*, 27.
5. Inchbald, "by utilizing her inside position as an actress . . . was able to create professional access *for herself*" (Donkin, *Getting into The Act*, 114; emphasis hers).
6. Donkin, *Getting Into the Act*, 139.
7. Crochunis, "Authorial Performances," 230. See too Donkin, *Getting into the Act*, 11–12; Misty G. Anderson, *Female Playwrights and Eighteenth-Century Comedy: Negotiating Marriage on the London Stage* (New York: Palgrave, 2002), 24.
8. Note Sir Joshua Reynolds's comment to the young Burney: "'you have already had all the applause and fame you can have given you in the closet; but the acclamation of a theater will be new to you'" (Frances Burney, *The Diary and Letters of Madame D'Arblay*, ed. Charlotte Frances Barrett, 7 vols. [London: Henry Colburn Publishers, 1842], 1: 158–59).
9. Elizabeth Inchbald, "To the Artist," *The Artist* 14 (13 June 1807); essay reproduced in Elizabeth Inchbald, *Nature and Art*, ed. Shawn Lisa Maurer (New York: Broadview, 2005), 161–66. This quotation appears on p. 165.
10. Hannah Cowley, "An Address," *A School for Greybeards* (Dublin: William Porter, 1787), v; emphasis hers.
11. For statements on this supposed dichotomy in eighteenth-century theories of selfhood, see Dror Wahrman, *The Making of the Modern Self: Identity and Culture in Eighteenth-Century England* (New Haven, CT: Yale University Press, 2004), xi–xviii; Deidre Shauna Lynch, *The Economy of Character: Novels, Market Culture, and the Business of Inner Meaning* (Chicago: University of Chicago Press, 1998), 7–8, 44.
12. Terry Castle, *Masquerade and Civilization: The Carnivalesque in Eighteenth-Century English Culture and Fiction* (Stanford: Stanford University Press, 1986), 292.
13. Jane Spencer, Introduction to *A Simple Story*, by Elizabeth Inchbald, ed. J.M.S. Tompkins (Oxford: Oxford University Press, 1988), xv.
14. Qtd. in James Boaden, *Memoirs of Mrs. Inchbald: Volumes One and Two* (London: Richard Bentley, 1833), 2: 153.
15. Nora Nachumi, "'Those Simple Signs': The Performance of Emotion in Elizabeth Inchbald's *A Simple Story*," *Eighteenth-Century Fiction* 11 (April 1999): 317.
16. Elizabeth Inchbald, *A Simple Story*, ed. J.M.S. Tompkins (Oxford: Oxford University Press, 1988), 73. Subsequent citations will be to this edition.
17. See Gary Kelly, *The English Jacobin Novel, 1780–1805*, (Oxford: Clarendon Press, 1976), 79, 86; Elinor Ty, *Unsex'd Revolutionaries: Five Women Novelists of the 1790s* (Toronto: University of Toronto Press, 1993), 91; Candace Ward, "Inordinate Desire: Schooling the Senses in Elizabeth Inchbald's *A*

　　　Simple Story," *Studies in the Novel* 31 (1999): 6; Nachumi, "'Those Simple
　　　Signs,'" 317–38. The critics all assert versions of Nachumi's point that "bod-
　　　ies express emotions more authentically and more persuasively than words
　　　alone" (318).

18. Adela Pinch, *Strange Fits of Passion: Epistemologies of Emotion, Hume to
　　　Austen* (Stanford: Stanford University Press, 1996), 3.

19. Spencer, Introduction, xvi.

20. Jo Alyson Parker, "Complicating *A Simple Story:* Inchbald's Two Versions
　　　of Female Power," *Eighteenth-Century Studies* 30 (1997): 256. Many crit-
　　　ics assume, on the say-so of Inchbald's contemporary biographer James
　　　Boaden, that a novel manuscript started in 1779 was Part One of *A Simple
　　　Story,* and that the second part of her novel was written later and grafted
　　　onto the first. I would side with Michael Boardman and Patricia Sigl,
　　　though, who both regard this fact as unproven, especially as the second
　　　half of the novel develops temperaments in ways suggested by the first
　　　half. Sandford's evolving role from critic to confidant, Miss Milner's fore-
　　　shadowed downfall, and, most importantly, the change in Elmwood from
　　　expressive and pious to "implacable" (195) are all changes that are initi-
　　　ated in the beginning of the novel and carried through to the second part
　　　of the narrative. Much of Inchbald's other work, such as her play *Wives
　　　as They Were, Maids as They Are,* and her second novel, *Nature and Art,*
　　　also includes a temporal or generational divide. See Michael Boardman,
　　　"Inchbald's *A Simple Story:* An Anti-Ideological Reading," *The Eighteenth
　　　Century: Theory and Interpretation* 37 (1996): 284n17, and Patricia Sigl,
　　　"The Literary Achievement of Elizabeth Inchbald [1753–1821]," (Ph.D.
　　　diss., Swansea: University of Wales, 1980).

21. While Candace Ward claims that Lady Elmwood uses this letter "to thrust
　　　herself 'bodily' before [Elmwood's] mind's eye," this is nonetheless a body
　　　that expresses no emotion whatsoever. See Ward, "Inordinate Desire," 12.

22. Gerard A. Barker, *Grandison's Heirs: The Paragon's Progress in the Late
　　　Eighteenth-Century Novel* (Newark, DE: University of Delaware Press,
　　　1985), 90.

23. Parker, "Complicating *A Simple Story,*" 263.

24. Ibid., 263.

25. Matilda's swoon mirrors Evelina's speechless and effective prostration
　　　before Sir John, yet has a vastly different effect than the swoons in Burney's
　　　novels—a result perhaps of the very different conjugal relationships that
　　　each daughter recalls. Both heroines bear a moving physical resemblance to
　　　their dead mothers, but Evelina reminds Sir John of his disrespect toward
　　　Carolyn, while Matilda reminds Lord Elmwood of all her mother's crimes
　　　against himself.

26. Catharine Craft-Fairchild, *Masquerade and Gender: Disguise and Female
　　　Identity in Eighteenth-Century Fictions by Women* (University Park, PA:
　　　Pennsylvania State University Press, 1993), 120.

27. Lisa A. Freeman, *Character's Theater: Genre and Identity on the Eighteenth-Cen-
　　　tury English Stage* (Philadelphia: University of Pennsylvania Press, 2002), 31.

28. Qtd. by Joseph Roach, *The Player's Passion: Studies in the Science of Acting*
　　　(Newark, DE: University of Delaware Press, 1985), 86–87.

29. Ibid., 87.

30. For more on this process, see Joseph Roach, "Darwin's Passion: The Language
　　　of Expression on Nature's Stage," *Discourse* 13 (1990–1991): 40–58, and *The
　　　Player's Passion;* also Dene Barnett, *The Art of Gesture: The Practices and
　　　Principles of 18th-Century Acting,* (Heidelberg: Universitatsverlag, 1987).

31. James Burgh, *The Art of Speaking,* 7th edition (London: T. Longman, 1792),
　　　14; Barnett, *The Art of Gesture,* 47.

32. Qtd. in Barnett, *The Art of Gesture*, 47.
33. Alan T. McKenzie, *Certain, Lively Episodes: The Articulation of Passion in Eighteenth-Century Prose* (Athens, GA: University of Georgia Press, 1990), 6.
34. See, for example, Gilbert Austin, *Chironomia or, A Treatise on Rhetorical Delivery* (1806; Carbondale: Southern Illinois University Press, 1966); Henry Siddons, *Practical Illustrations of Rhetorical Gesture and Action*, (1822; New York: Benjamin Blom, 1968).
35. Sandra Richards, *The Rise of the English Actress* (New York: St. Martin's Press, 1993), 86–87.
36. Burgh, *The Art of Speaking*, 12–13.
37. For this anecdote see Roach, *The Player's Passion*, 145. The popularity of pictorial progresses in the eighteenth century also seems related to this belief, as William Hogarth's famous sequences and Joseph Highmore's version of *Pamela* both convey stories independent of text.
38. Burgh, *The Art of Speaking*, 14.
39. Roach, "Darwin's Passion," 48; emphasis mine.
40. As Lisa Freeman has so rightly pointed out, the "naturalism" of these innovative eighteenth-century performers needs to be considered within an eighteenth-century context; these acting styles would likely appear highly stylized to modern audiences. See Freeman, *Character's Theater*, 34.
41. Lindal Buchanan, "Sarah Siddons and Her Place in Rhetorical History," *Rhetorica* 25 (2007): 421.
42. Roach, *The Player's Passion*, 111.
43. See Gary Kelly, *Jacobin Novel*, 84–92; Spencer, Introduction, vii; Nachumi, "'Those Simple Signs,'" 318.
44. Freeman, *Character's Theater*, 15–16; Ruth Bernard Yeazell, *Fictions of Modesty: Women and Courtship in the English Novel* (Chicago: University of Chicago Press, 1984), 77.
45. Qtd. in Boaden, *Memoirs*, 2: 354.
46. Inchbald, "To the Artist," 166.
47. Ibid., 165.
48. Elizabeth Inchbald, Preface to *Wives As They Were, Maids As They Are*, in *Remarks for The British Theatre* (Delmar, NY: Scholars' Facsimiles and Reprints, 1990), 5. This facsimile reproduction contains all of Inchbald's prefaces arranged alphabetically according to play, with the original pagination. The citation provides the relevant play title and page number in that preface.
49. The play is reproduced in Boaden, *Memoirs*, 2: 295–352. Subsequent citations will refer to the pagination in Boaden.
50. Citations from Elizabeth Inchbald, *Wives as They Were, Maids as They Are*, in *The Plays of Elizabeth Inchbald*, ed. Paula R. Backscheider, vol. 2 (New York: Garland Publishing, Inc., 1980).
51. Daniel O'Quinn, "Scissors and Needles: Inchbald's *Wives as They Were, Maids as They Are* and the Governance of Sexual Exchange," *Theatre Journal* 51 (1999): 123.
52. Beth Kowaleski-Wallace, "Reading the Surfaces of Colley Cibber's *The Careless Husband*," *Studies in English Literature* 40 (2000): 475.
53. In another connection to Inchbald's earlier novel, Sir William names two of the four cardinal virtues of the Christian tradition (prudence, justice, fortitude, and temperance) also espoused by Elmwood (*A Simple Story*, 3).
54. Betsy Bolton, *Women, Nationalism, and the Romantic Stage: Theatre and Politics in Britain, 1780–1800* (Cambridge: Cambridge University Press, 2001), 224–25.
55. Misty Anderson and O'Quinn, previously cited, both assume Bronzely does not actually rape or seduce Lady Priory, and Annibel Jenkins's reading of the play in her biography of Inchbald concludes that "Lady Priory has defended

herself." See Jenkins, *I'll Tell You What: The Life of Elizabeth Inchbald* (Lexington: University Press of Kentucky, 2003), 415. Eighteenth-century audiences likewise saw Lady Priory as a figure of obedience and chastity; the contemporary review in the *Telegraph* dubs her "the *primitive wife* . . . proof to all seduction" (qtd. in Sigl, "Literary Achivement," 457). Yet the scene between Bronzely and Lady Priory actually ends with Bronzely in an agonizing state of indecision:

> I'll take you home directly . . . But, upon my life . . . I cannot do it . . . what are we to say when we go back?—No matter what, so you will but think kindly of me. . . . I am going to London immediately. Quick! Quick . . . for fear I should change my mind . . . I feel my good designs stealing away already—now they are flying rapidly. [*Taking Lady Priory's hand*]—please to look another way—I shall certainly recant if I see you . . . [*Exit, leading her off.*]
> BRONZELY [*Without*] Tell the post-boy he need not wait—I have changed my mind—I sha'n't go to London tonight. (79–80)

Bronzely's last line suggests that his lust is getting the best of him, and even if they do make it to the chaise, Lady Priory is not necessarily safe—many an eighteenth-century heroine has lost or nearly lost her virtue while in transit. My point is not to argue definitively for Lady Priory's rape; her composure when she returns to her husband suggests that perhaps she does retain her virtue. I merely want to point out that the emotional turmoil that grips Bronzely, and the general skepticism with which we are taught to judge appearances, mean we should at least speculate as to what happens offstage.

56. Kowaleski-Wallace, "Reading the Surfaces," 486.
57. Bolton, *Women, Nationalism*, 226.
58. Marthe Robert, *The Origins of the Novel* (Bloomington, IN: Indiana University Press, 1983), 10.
59. Crochunis, "Authorial Performances," 224. See too p.248n6.
60. Boaden, *Memoirs*, 1: 140.
61. Spencer, Introduction, vii; Anderson, *Female Playwrights*, 197.
62. Boaden, *Memoirs*, 2: 190; Donkin, *Getting into the Act*, 116.
63. See Marvin Carlson, "Elizabeth Inchbald: A Woman Critic in her Theatrical Culture," in *Women in British Romantic Theatre: Drama, Performance, and Society, 1790–1840* ed. Catherine Burroughs (Cambridge: Cambridge University Press, 2000), 213.
64. Elizabeth Inchbald, Preface to *Wives as They Were*, 3.
65. Crochunis, "Authorial Performances," 242.
66. Boaden states that Inchbald plays the character "Selima," but Donkin notes that no such character exists in the manuscript or in the printed version, and that the playbills in *London Stage* list Inchbald as playing "Irene" from the opening night (in 1784) until her final appearance on stage in 1789. Donkin notes that the manuscript of the play does list a character "Selim," a eunuch, which may have generated Boaden's error (Donkin, *Getting into the Act*, 209n15).
67. Boaden, *Memoirs*, 1: 189.
68. Ibid., 189.
69. All accounts of this incident follow Boaden's lead. Donkin repeats Boaden's version of the incident, then states that "the audience quickly discovered that the stuttering actress was also the 'anonymous' playwright" (Donkin, *Getting into the Act*, 119). Annibel Jenkins also cites Boaden, concluding that "[Inchbald's] stammer [was] an obvious identification" (Jenkins, *I'll Tell You What*, 159). Paula Backscheider follows suit, asserting that Inchbald tried to disguise her authorship, but that her "agitated stammer nearly gave her away" (Backscheider, Introduction, *Plays of Elizabeth Inchbald*, xii). Yet none of these scholars question why the stammer would identify Inchbald

as both actress *and* author of the piece. In conversation, Lisa Freeman suggested that Inchbald, as a playwright, would have had knowledge of the entire script, whereas Inchbald, as merely an actress, would have been in possession of just her part. Her knowledge, therefore, of the coming cue marks her as the playwright. The suggestion is provocative, though of course with enough rehearsal an actress would recognize a cue even without possession of the entire script.

70. Donkin, *Getting into the Act*, 119.
71. Boaden, *Memoirs*, 1: 5.
72. Ibid., 7.
73. Elizabeth Inchbald, *Such Things Are*, in *Selected Comedies: Elizabeth Inchbald*, ed. Roger Manvell (Latham, MD: University Press of America, 1987), 17.
74. See too Crochunis, "Authorial Performances," 242.
75. David Richter, *Falling into Theory: Conflicting Views on Reading Literature* (Boston: Bedford/St. Martin's, 2000), 251.
76. Wahrman, *Making of the Modern Self*, 51.
77. Originally cited in the *Sylph* 5 (6 October 1795): 35. Passage quoted in Catherine Gallagher, *Nobody's Story: The Vanishing Acts of Women Writers in the Marketplace, 1670–1820* (Berkeley: University of California Press, 1994), 277. See Gallagher for a further discussion of how this "identifying propensity" was understood to distract women from their domestic duties (257–88).
78. Alan Richardson, *Literature, Education, and Romanticism: Reading as Social Practice, 1780–1832* (Cambridge: Cambridge University Press, 1994), 3.
79. J.M.S. Tompkins, ed., *A Simple Story*, by Elizabeth Inchbald (Oxford: Oxford University Press, 1988), 345n338.
80. Boaden, *Memoirs*, 1: 346.
81. In a response reminiscent of reactions to *A Simple Story*, Shawn Lisa Maurer notes how "most readers . . . have been troubled by the apparent split between the two halves of [this] novel" (Introduction, in *Nature and Art*, by Elizabeth Inchbald, ed. Shawn Lisa Maurer [Orchard Park, NY: Broadview Press, 2005], 21). This time, the troubling split is stylistic more than temporal (though *Nature and Art* also spans two generations). According to William McKee, "when [Inchbald] is half way through the fate of the heroine so absorbs her interest that she largely forgets her sociological intent, and, instead of making the novel a treatise upon the disasters resulting from a false system of education, she makes it a tragedy of an outcast in the London streets." William McKee, *Elizabeth Inchbald, Novelist* (Washington, D.C.: Catholic University of America, 1935), 67.
82. Maurer, Introduction, 13.
83. Elizabeth Inchbald, *Nature and Art*, ed. Shawn Lisa Maurer (Orchard Park, NY: Broadview Press, 2005), 137–38. Subsequent references will be to this edition.
84. See Nancy Johnson, *The English Jacobin Novel on Rights, Property, and the Law: Critiquing the Contract* (New York: Palgrave, 2004), 85.
85. Mary Wollstonecraft, *A Vindication of the Rights of Men*, eds. Janet Todd and Marilyn Butler, vol. 5, in *The Works of Mary Wollstonecraft* (New York: New York University Press, 1989), 8.
86. See Donna T. Andrew and Randall McGowen, *The Perreaus and Mrs. Rudd: Forgery and Betrayal in Eighteenth-Century London* (Berkeley: University of California Press, 2001), 36. This legal practice seems indebted to the tradition in oratory, as described earlier by James Burgh, in which it is not the words spoken, but the manner in which they are spoken, that determines "what we mean" (Burgh, *The Art of Speaking*, 12–13).

87. Andrew and McGowen, *The Perreaus*, 37. See too p. 290n49, for a description of Garrick's reaction.
88. For more on this connection, see Judith Pascoe's chapter, "The Courtroom Theater of the 1794 Treason Trials," *Romantic Theatricality: Gender, Poetry, and Spectatorship* (Ithaca, NY: Cornell University Press, 1997), 33–67.

NOTES TO CHAPTER 5

1. Maria Edgeworth, "Notes Containing Conversations and Anecdotes of Children," *Practical Education*, ed. Susan Manly, in *The Novels and Selected Works of Maria Edgeworth*, 12 vols. (London: Pickering and Chatto, 2003), 11: 426. All subsequent citations to *Practical Education* will be taken from this edition.
2. A year later, when the family performed her play *Whim for Whim*, Edgeworth informs her cousin Sophie Ruxton that her father "is making a charming theatre in the room over his study: it will be twice as large as old Poz's little theatre in the dining room." See *A Memoir of Maria Edgeworth, edited by her children*, 3 vols. (London: Joseph Masters and Son, 1867), 1: 93.
3. *Professional Education*, written between 1807 and 1809, moves from the methodological approach of the earlier work to utilitarian questions concerning how to discern the appropriate profession for a child, and how to prepare him for it. Citations from this work are taken from *Essays on Professional Education* (London: J. Johnson and Co., 1812).
4. *The Life of Mr. James Quin, Comedian* (London: S. Bladon, 1766), 85–86.
5. Citations are from the second edition of the English translation, Madame de Genlis, *Adelaide and Theodore, or Letters on Education*, 2nd edition (London: C. Bathurst, 1784), 1: 146–47. Subsequent references are cited parenthetically in the text.
6. See Maria Edgeworth to Fanny Robinson, 15 August 1783, HM 28589, Huntington Library, San Marino, CA: "As for the Book you are so kind to enquire about Alas it was only an humble, and I am sorry to add an unsuccessful translation of Madame de Genlis Letters—I had just finished the third Volume, when a rival translation appeared in all its Glory—One volume however is printed & my father thinks of compressing the two others into one & publishing it in Dublin." The translation was never published, to the happiness of family friend Thomas Day, who disapproved of female authorship. Part of this letter is quoted in Marilyn Butler, *Maria Edgeworth: A Literary Biography* (Oxford: Clarendon Press, 1972), 148.
7. For the 1798 preface, see "Preface," *Practical Education*, ed. Susan Manly, in *The Novels and Selected Works of Maria Edgeworth*, 12 vols. (London: Pickering and Chatto, 2003), 11: 7; for the revisions made to the second edition, see the textual variants 7e on p. 495.
8. Butler, *Maria Edgeworth*, 64.
9. See Alan Richardson, *Literature, Education, and Romanticism: Reading as Social Practice, 1780–1832* (Cambridge: Cambridge University Press, 1994), 59. Locke, for example, discouraged the tutor from attempting to teach his pupil "all that was knowable"; instead, he should "put him in the right way of knowing and improving himself, when he has a mind to it." John Locke, *The Educational Writings of John Locke: A Critical Edition with Introduction and Notes*, ed. James L. Axtell (Cambridge: Cambridge University Press, 1968), 307. Rousseau, likewise, described Emile's mind as "universal not by its learning but by its faculty to acquire learning." Jean-Jacques Rousseau, *Emile or Education*, trans. Allan Bloom (New York: Basic Books, 1979), 207.

10. *Professional Education*, 297.
11. See *Memoirs of Richard Lovell Edgeworth, esq., begun by himself and concluded by his Daughter, Maria Edgeworth*, 2 vols. (London: R. Hunter, 1820), 2: 181–82.
12. Susan Manly, Introduction to *Practical Education*, ed. Susan Manly, in *The Novels and Selected Works of Maria Edgeworth*, 12 vols. (London: Pickering and Chatto, 2003), 11: xii.
13. Their title, too, contradicts Rousseau's dismissal of "practical suggestions"; in Edgeworth's philosophy, children should be made aware of the useful applications of what they learn. See Catherine Toal, "Control Experiment: Maria Edgeworth's Critique of Rousseau's Educational Theory," in *An Uncomfortable Authority: Maria Edgeworth and Her Contexts*, eds. Heidi Kaufman and Chris Fauske (Newark, DE: University of Delaware Press, 2004), 212–31.
14. Manly, Introduction, ix.
15. Ibid., vii.
16. Elizabeth Kowaleski-Wallace depicts Edgeworth as a "daddy's girl," enmeshed in a powerful form of patriarchal control. See Kowaleski-Wallace, *Their Fathers' Daughters: Hannah More, Maria Edgeworth, and Patriarchal Complicity* (Oxford: Oxford University Press, 1991), 97. Marilyn Butler and, more recently, Caroline Gonda, suggest instead that Edgeworth purposefully presented herself as an uncritical, unquestioning literary disciple to her father. Butler, *Maria Edgeworth*, 287; Caroline Gonda, *Reading Daughters' Fictions, 1709–1834: Novels and Society from Manley to Edgeworth* (Cambridge: Cambridge University Press, 1996), 237.
17. See for example the preface to *Moral Tales*, in which Edgeworth claims that the subsequent stories are "written to illustrate the opinions" delivered more dogmatically in the jointly authored books on educational practice. Maria Edgeworth, Preface to *Moral Tales*, *Moral Tales* (Philadelphia: Duffield Ashmead, 1867), iii. Quotation is from Catharine Gallagher, *Nobody's Story: The Vanishing Acts of Women Writers in the Marketplace, 1670–1820* (Berkeley: University of California Press, 1994), 270.
18. *Practical Education*, 402.
19. See Butler, *Maria Edgeworth*, 164, 152.
20. Qtd. in *A Memoir of Maria Edgeworth*, 1: 95.
21. *Practical Education*, 307.
22. Susan Greenfield, "'Abroad and at Home': Sexual Ambiguity, Miscegenation, and Colonial Boundaries in Edgeworth's *Belinda*," *PMLA* 112 (1997): 219, 224; Andrew McCann, "Conjugal Love and the Enlightenment Subject: The Colonial Context of Non-identity in Maria Edgeworth's *Belinda*," *Novel: A Forum on Fiction* 30 (1996 Fall): 61.
23. Jenny Uglow, *The Lunar Men: Five Friends Whose Curiosity Changed the World*, (London: Faber and Faber, 2002), xviii.
24. Membership in the society—which met from 1765 until 1813—included Erasmus Darwin, James Watt, Matthew Boulton, Joseph Priestly, Thomas Day, and Richard Edgeworth. Their meetings were timed by the moon for a very practical reason: it gave them enough light to travel home.
25. Richardson, *Literature, Education, and Romanticism*, 61.
26. Qtd. in Butler, *Maria Edgeworth*, 65. See, too, Edgeworth's preface to *The Parent's Assistant*: "In all sciences the grand difficulty has been to ascertain facts—a difficulty which, in the science of education, peculiar circumstances conspire to increase. Here the objects of every experiment are so interesting, that we cannot hold our minds indifferent to the result . . . an attempt to keep . . . a register has actually been made . . . every circumstance and conversation that has been preserved is faithfully and accurately related. These notes

have been of great advantage to the writer of the following stories." *The Parent's Assistant*, ed. Elizabeth Eger and Clíona ÓGallchoir, in *The Novels and Selected Works of Maria Edgeworth*, 12 vols. (London: Pickering and Chatto, 2003), 10: 2.

27. See also Barbara Benedict, who explores this etymological congruence in "Identity and Quest: Experimental Experience and the Eighteenth-Century Novel," *The Eighteenth-Century Novel* (New York: AMS Press, Inc., 2004) 4: 1–38.

28. *Practical Education*, 5.

29. See *OED* online; "experiment" (v), 1.

30. Uglow, *Lunar Men*, 188.

31. Day finally decided Sabrina was not for him, though the girl never appears to have fallen in love (not surprisingly) and was not hurt by this decision. In fact, she married happily, and eventually became the housekeeper to Frances Burney's brother Charles (Uglow, *Lunar Men*, 188).

32. See Butler, *Maria Edgeworth*, 73, 146.

33. Qtd. in Butler, *Maria Edgeworth*, 74.

34. Terry Castle, *The Female Thermometer: Eighteenth-Century Culture and the Invention of the Uncanny* (Oxford: Oxford University Press, 1995), 23, 22. See for example Hogarth's *Credulity, Superstition, and Enthusiasm*, the image of which forms the cover for Castle's book.

35. The tale was finally published in *The Juvenile Library* (London: T. Hurst, 1801), 2: 378–84, a periodical for adolescents. Edgeworth was by this time a well-known author, and Marilyn Butler suggests that the editor of the *Juvenile Library* sought to capitalize on her name by including the tale in his periodical (Butler, *Maria Edgeworth*, 146).

36. Maria Edgeworth, "The Mental Thermometer," MS. Eng. Misc. ca. 1896, Bodleian Library, Oxford, UK.

37. *Practical Education*, 306. And in a passage that illustrates how an interest in education does not subsume an interest in the individual, Edgeworth goes on to specify that "[the teacher] must not only have acquired a knowledge of the process by which his own ideas and habits were formed, but he must have extensive experience of the varieties of the human mind . . . he must not imagine, that there is but one method of teaching, which will suit all persons alike" (306).

38. Gallagher, *Nobody's Story*, 282–83.

39. Antonio Damasio, *Descartes' Error: Emotion, Reason, and the Human Brain* (New York: Penguin Books, 1994), xi.

40. Ibid., xv.

41. Maria Edgeworth, *Letters for Literary Ladies*, ed. Claire Connolly (London: Everyman, 1993), 39. All subsequent references to this edition are cited parenthetically in the text.

42. Maria Edgeworth, *Whim for Whim*, ed. Marilyn Butler, in *The Novels and Selected Works of Maria Edgeworth*, 12 vols. (London: Pickering and Chatto, 2003), 12: 372.

43. *Parent's Assistant*, 118.

44. Edgeworth's original sketch of *Belinda* contains the quoted description, to support the claim that "the contrast between the apparent prosperity and real misery of Lady Delacour must be strongly marked." See Maria Edgeworth, "Original Sketch of Belinda," *Belinda*, ed. Kathryn J. Kirkpatrick (Oxford: Oxford University Press, 1994), 480.

45. Qtd. in Butler, *Maria Edgeworth*, 151.

46. Butler, *Maria Edgeworth*, 164.

47. *A Memoir of Maria Edgeworth*, 1: 93.

48. Maria Edgeworth, "Whim for Whim," MS. Eng. Misc. d. 648, Bodleian Library, Oxford, UK.
49. Maria Edgeworth, *Whim for Whim*, ed. Marilyn Butler, in *The Novels and Selected Works of Maria Edgeworth*, 12 vols. (London: Pickering and Chatto, 2003), 12: 299–394. Future references will cite act, scene, and page number parenthetically in the text.
50. The Illuminati were a society founded in 1776 by the German professor Adam Weishaupt; they displayed an interest in progressive Enlightenment ideals and a distaste for civil and ecclesiastical authority. Edgeworth learned about the society from John Robison's book *Proofs of a Conspiracy* (1798) (in a letter to Sophy Ruxton, Edgeworth writes, "to explain illuminatism, I refer you to Robinson's [sic] book called 'Proofs of a Conspiracy.' It was from this book . . . that we took the idea of Count Babelhausen" [*Memoir of Maria Edgeworth*, 1: 94]). Edgeworth's interest in Illuminatism contains an eerie echo of her early fables, as Weishaupt claimed "the general object" of Illuminatism to be "the happiness of the human race" (*Proofs of a Conspiracy* [Dublin: W. Watson and Son, 1798], 114). Robison, in his turn, argues that Weishaupt depicted religion, governments, and private property as obstacles to human happiness so that he could further his true purpose: to destroy all religions, overthrow all governments, and abolish all private property (Robison, *Proofs*, 100–271). Edgeworth certainly modeled her Babelhausen on Robison's negative portrait of Weishaupt, as the Count spouts the doctrines of Illuminatism for his own mercenary motives.
51. While the tongue-test may seem to us a somewhat primitive experiment, educated eighteenth-century scientists were, in Jenny Uglow's words, "inveterate tester[s] and taster[s]," sniffing and sampling their way to clarity (or death, depending on the toxicity of their evidence). Uglow describes how one scientist discovered, and then sniffed, a new, greenish gas (chlorine)—an experiment that probably killed him (*Lunar Men*, 235).
52. See Marilyn Butler on Edgeworth's tendency to create the character of the "good-hearted black boy," *Jane Austen and the War of Ideas* (Oxford: Clarendon Press 1975), 137. See too Anne K. Mellor, *Romanticism and Gender* (New York: Routledge, 1993), 78–80. Yet Quaco is even more than what Mellor dubs "the voice of innocent virtue" (80); he is possessed of a rational mind, capable of conducting experiments and making deductions from his observations. Quaco is thus an important pre-text for *Belinda's* Juba.
53. *Professional Education*, 297.
54. Julia V. Douthwaite, *The Wild Girl, Natural Man, and the Monster: Dangerous Experiments in the Age of Enlightenment* (Chicago: University of Chicago Press, 2002), 158.
55. Here again Edgeworth shows her indebtedness to Madame de Genlis's *Adèle et Théodore*, as these children are also involved in scenarios staged without their knowledge. Leslie H. Walker terms these scenes "tests" that comprise the Baronness' "course on experimental virtue." See Walker, "Producing Feminine Virtue: Strategies of Terror in Writings by Madame de Genlis," *Tulsa Studies of Women's Literature* 23 (2004): 221.
56. Butler, *Maria Edgeworth*, 279.
57. Ibid., 151.
58. Ibid., 151.
59. Maria Edgeworth to Fanny Robinson, 6 December 1783, HM 28591, Huntington Library, San Marino, CA.
60. Butler, *Maria Edgeworth*, 165.
61. Ibid., 165.

62. Sheridan claimed that he did not have enough actors to play the Irish parts, and that the London audience might not sympathize with the Irish characters (Butler, *Maria Edgeworth*, 277).

63. "While he reads, he should be warned not to take any thing for granted; not to believe, that, because he is perusing an author of high authority, he must therefore resign his understanding implicitly" *(Professional Education*, 297).

64. *Practical Education*, 215.

65. For broader accounts of anti-novel discourse, see Jacqueline Pearson, *Women Reading in Britain, 1750–1835: A Dangerous Recreation* (Cambridge: Cambridge University Press, 1999) and John Tinnon Taylor, *Early Opposition to the English Novel: The Popular Reaction from 1760 to 1830* (New York: King's Crown Press, 1943).

66. *Practical Education*, 172–173.

67. *Practical Education*, 192; Maria Edgeworth, *Letters for Literary Ladies*, ed. Claire Connolly (London: Everyman, 1993), 45–46.

68. Maria Edgeworth, "Advertisement," *Belinda*, ed. Kathryn J. Kirkpatrick (Oxford: Oxford University Press, 1994), 3. All subsequent citations are taken from this edition and included parenthetically in the text. Austen's critique appears in *Northanger Abbey*, as "the impolitic custom so common with novel writers, of degrading by their own contemptuous censure the very performances, to the number of which they are themselves adding." Jane Austen, *Northanger Abbey*, ed. Marilyn Butler (New York: Penguin, 1995), 36.

69. Gallagher, *Nobody's Story*, 275.

70. As Caroline Gonda says, "for a young lady making her entrance into the world, she has too little to learn, learns it too quickly and thereafter is too level-headed and prudent for most readers' tastes" (*Reading Daughters' Fictions*, 211).

71. Kirkpatrick is one of the few critics to tackle the question, "if Lady Percival is Edgeworth's ideal domestic woman, why does the reformed Lady Delacour preside at the end of the novel, and why is it *her* choice of suitor whom the heroine marries?" Kathryn J. Kirkpatrick, "The Limits of Liberal Feminism in Maria Edgeworth's *Belinda*," in *Jane Austen and Mary Shelley and Their Sisters*, ed. Laura Dabundo (New York: University Press of America, 2000), 77.

72. Qtd in Richard A. Barney, *Plots of Enlightenment: Education and the Novel in Eighteenth-Century England* (Stanford: Stanford University Press, 1999), 65. John Locke, *Some Thoughts Concerning Education*, in *The Educational Writings of John Locke*, ed. James L. Axtell (Cambridge: Cambridge University Press, 1968), 109–325; sec. 125.

73. Barney, *Plots of Enlightenment*, 64.

74. Frances Ferguson, "Reading Morals: Locke and Rousseau on Education and Inequality," *Representations* 6 (Spring 1984): 82. For example, Locke recounts a Tom-Sawyer-like anecdote of a difficult child who is persuaded to learn to read when he is set up, unbeknownst to him, to overhear a conversation amongst his elders about the select privileges and great benefits of reading lessons (Locke, *Education*, sec. 148).

75. Barney, *Plots of Enlightenment*, 86; emphasis his.

76. See Alan Richardson "Romantic Voodoo: Obeah and British Culture, 1797–1807," *Studies in Romanticism* 32 (1993): 19–20.

77. The fact that Belinda has the children show Juba the function of phosphorous, instead of doing it herself, recalls the moment in *Whim for Whim* when Chrysse and Helle reveal to Caroline who wears the Aspasia costume (5.4.377–78). Edgeworth's decision in *Belinda* to position the children as educators recalls

her play, and the prior example shows that she quite seriously grants children an insight and pedagogical ability sometimes missing in their mentors.

78. Maria Edgeworth, *Leonora*, 2 vols. (London: J. Johnson, 1806). All subsequent references to this edition are cited parenthetically in the text.

79. Barney, *Plots of Enlightenment*, 86.

80. McCann, "Conjugal Love and the Enlightenment Subject," 70.

81. Heather MacFadyen, "Lady Delacour's Library: Maria Edgeworth's *Belinda* and Fashionable Reading," *Nineteenth-Century Literature* 48 (March 1994): 428.

82. Gallagher, *Nobody's Story*, 275.

83. Ibid., 276.

84. Greenfield, "'Abroad and at Home,'" 224.

85. Ibid., 224.

86. Ibid., 224.

87. Mitzi Meyers, "My Art Belongs to Daddy? Thomas Day, Maria Edgeworth, and the Pre-Texts of *Belinda*: Women Writers and Patriarchal Authority," in *Revising Women: Eighteenth-Century "Women's Fiction" and Social Engagement*, ed. Paula R. Backscheider (Baltimore: Johns Hopkins University Press, 2000), 145.

88. As the title of Moody's work indicates, these critics often situate nineteenth-century drama in the context of "illegitimate theatre"; see Jane Moody, *Illegitimate Theatre in London, 1770–1840* (Cambridge: Cambridge University Press, 2000). See too Catherine B. Burroughs, *Closet Stages: Joanna Baillie and the Theater Theory of British Romantic Women Writers* (Philadelphia: University of Pennsylvania Press, 1997) and Julie A. Carlson, *In the Theatre of Romanticism: Coleridge, Nationalism, Women* (Cambridge: Cambridge University Press, 1994).

89. Richard Lovell Edgeworth to Rowland Hunter, 15 January 1816, MS. Eng. lett. ca. 1722, Bodleian Library, Oxford, UK; emphasis his.

90. Preface, *Comic Dramas in Three Acts* (London: R. Hunter, 1817), vii.

91. James Boaden, *Memoirs of Mrs. Inchbald: Volumes One and Two* (London: Richard Bentley, 1833), 2: 209–10.

92. See Catherine Burroughs, "The Persistence of Closet Drama: Theory, History, Form," in *The Performing Century: Nineteenth-Century Theatre's History*, eds. Peter Holland and Tracy C. Davis (New York: Palgrave, 2007), 215–35. Burroughs (like Richard Edgeworth) specifically defines closet drama as "a play written solely to be read" (215); she also discusses closet drama as "primarily a tool for learning . . . [and] reflection" (219).

93. The term "academic dramas" is from Marta Straznicky, "Closet Drama," in *A Companion to Renaissance Drama*, ed. Arthur F. Kinney (Oxford: Blackwell Publishing, 2002), 426; the quoted phrase is from the introductory address to Hannah More's closet drama *The Search after Happiness* (Bristol: S. Farley, 1773). For examples of these "lesson[s] in the guise of play[s]," see (among others) C. Short, *Dramas for the use of young ladies* (Birmingham: Swinney and Walker, 1792); Elizabeth Pinchard *Dramatic Dialogues, for the use of young persons* (London: E. Newberry, 1792); Charlotte Smith, *Rural Walks . . . Intended for the use of young persons* (London: T. Cadell, 1795). See too Burroughs, "Persistence of Closet Drama," 225–30.

94. Qtd. in Butler, *Maria Edgeworth*, 279.

95. See Edgeworth's correspondence with Fanny Robinson, HM 28586–28592 Huntington Library, San Marino, CA. I quote her references to Frances Burney in totality to emphasize the obsessive nature of her inquiries: "I think you did not say you had seen Miss Burney yourself, I wish you had for I wish very much to know what kind of woman she is" (3rd letter, undated, 1783);

again, "You are acquainted with Miss Burney pray tell me all you know of her—and more . . ."; and again, "If I should meet Miss Burney . . . I should be completely happy—if you can find any means of procuring me the honor of her correspondence you will do me a particular favor . . . Don't forget Miss Burney" (15 August 1783); and again, "I have delayed sending my letter in hopes of hearing from you my dear Fanny [Robinson] . . . tonight however is post night & I hope to hear from you, and, (for I can't help flattering myself) from Miss Burney" (20 October 1783); and finally, disappointingly, "this instant have I rec'd your most entertaining letter (I hate the word *Epistle* though it's a favorite of your's) and though I think I seldom if ever was more anxious about anything in my life, you contrived to make me forget my disappointment about Miss Burney entirely" (2 November 1783).

96. Qtd. in Boaden, *Memoirs of Mrs. Inchbald*, 2: 191.
97. Ibid., 177.
98. Qtd. in Butler, *Maria Edgeworth*, 402n4.

NOTES TO THE EPILOGUE

1. Tracy C. Davis and Thomas Postlewait, eds., *Theatricality* (Cambridge: Cambridge University Press, 2003), 16–17.
2. Jane Austen, *Mansfield Park*, ed. Kathryn Sutherland (New York: Penguin, 1996), 278. All subsequent references to this edition will be made parenthetically in the text.
3. See in particular Lionel Trilling, "The Sentiment of Being and the Sentiments of Art," *Sincerity and Authenticity* (Cambridge, MA: Harvard University Press, 1973), 68, and Jonas Barish, *The Antitheatrical Prejudice* (Berkeley: University of California Press, 1981), 299–307. For more nuanced readings of antitheatricality in *Mansfield Park*, see Jenny Davidson, *Hypocrisy and the Politics of Politeness: Manners and Morals from Locke to Austen* (Cambridge: Cambridge University Press, 2004), 146–69; Joseph Litvak, *Caught in the Act: Theatricality in the Nineteenth-Century English Novel* (Berkeley: University of California Press, 1992), 1–26.
4. Lionel Trilling, *The Opposing Self: Nine Essays in Criticism* (New York: Viking, 1955), 218.
5. See David Marshall, "True Acting and the Language of Real Feeling: *Mansfield Park*," *The Frame of Art: Fictions of Aesthetic Experience, 1750–1815* (Baltimore: Johns Hopkins University Press, 2005), 72–90.
6. Leo Bersani, *A Future for Astyanax: Character and Desire in Literature* (New York: Columbia University Press, 1984), 76–77; see too Marshall, "True Acting," 88; Trilling, *The Opposing Self*, 225–28.
7. Marshall, "True Acting," 86–87.
8. Ibid., 89.
9. Ibid., 89.
10. D.A. Miller, *Jane Austen, or The Secret of Style* (Princeton, NJ: Princeton University Press, 2003), 56.
11. Ibid., 32–38. Also, see Miller's comment that "throughout this essay I have capitalized Style when it suggests absolute impersonality; where it appertains to an obvious personal project, I have kept it in lowercase" (Ibid., 96n2).
12. As Miller puts it, free indirect style "plainly offers *a third term* between character and narration . . . free indirect style gives a virtuoso performance . . . of the narration's persistence in detachment from character, no matter how intimate the one becomes with the other" (*Jane Austen*, 59; emphasis his).

13. See too Marshall, who finally wonders "rather, if the style or *persona* of silence must mask the true womanly style" (Marshall, "True Acting," 89).
14. Brad Pasanek, "Emily Hodgson Anderson's '*Mansfield Park* and the "Womanly Style" of Fiction': Review and Summary," *UCLA Center for the Study of Women Newsletter* (March 2007). Internet: http://www.csw.ucla.edu/Newsletter/Mar07/pasanek.html
15. Marshall, "True Acting," 89.
16. Martin Puchner, *Stage Fright: Modernism, Anti-Theatricality, and Drama* (Baltimore: Johns Hopkins University Press, 2002), 22.
17. The quoted phrase is Miller's, *Jane Austen*, 96.
18. Michael McKeon, "Prose Fiction: Great Britain," *Theory of the Novel: A Historical Approach*, ed. Michael McKeon (Baltimore: Johns Hopkins University Press, 2000), 601.
19. Marthe Robert, *The Origins of the Novel* (Bloomington: Indiana University Press, 1983), 15.
20. Ibid., 35.
21. Ibid., 15–16.
22. The quotation is from *The Rambler* no. 96 (16 February 1751). This citation is taken from Samuel Johnson, *The Rambler*, ed. W.J. Bate and Albrecht B. Strauss, vols. 3–5 of *The Yale Edition of the Works of Samuel Johnson* (New Haven, CT: Yale University Press, 1969) 4: 152.
23. Robert, *Origins of the Novel*, 35.